IMAGES
of America

CENTRAL CITY

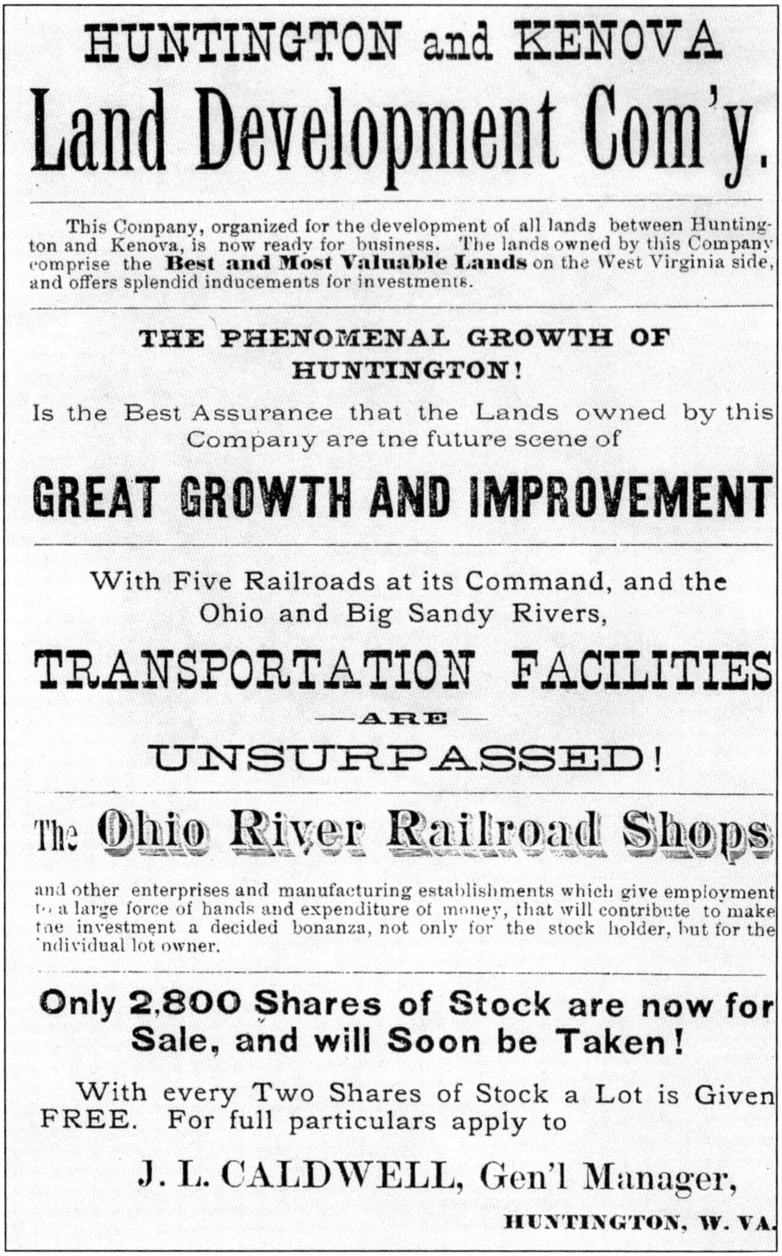

HUNTINGTON and KENOVA

Land Development Com'y.

This Company, organized for the development of all lands between Huntington and Kenova, is now ready for business. The lands owned by this Company comprise the **Best and Most Valuable Lands** on the West Virginia side, and offers splendid inducements for investments.

THE PHENOMENAL GROWTH OF HUNTINGTON!

Is the Best Assurance that the Lands owned by this Company are the future scene of

GREAT GROWTH AND IMPROVEMENT

With Five Railroads at its Command, and the Ohio and Big Sandy Rivers,

TRANSPORTATION FACILITIES

—ARE—

UNSURPASSED!

The Ohio River Railroad Shops

and other enterprises and manufacturing establishments which give employment to a large force of hands and expenditure of money, that will contribute to make the investment a decided bonanza, not only for the stock holder, but for the individual lot owner.

Only 2,800 Shares of Stock are now for Sale, and will Soon be Taken!

With every Two Shares of Stock a Lot is Given FREE. For full particulars apply to

J. L. CALDWELL, Gen'l Manager,

HUNTINGTON, W. VA.

This advertisement appeared in the local newspapers from 1892 to 1895.

On the Cover: In 1904, J. Rankin Boone opened a general store at 1311 Adams Avenue. The Cavendish brothers, Leonard and George, who were brothers-in-law to J. Rankin Boone, bought the store and contents. Through the years, they dealt with such widely assorted merchandise as groceries, produce, hay, grain, feed, hardware, chinaware, wallpaper, carpets, linoleum, notions, and scores of miscellaneous items. Later they specialized in china and wallpaper. The store closed its doors on February 28, 1963, after 52 years. The cover picture was taken in 1911. The people from left to right are Flora ?, C. Leonard Cavendish, George Cavendish, and a salesman.

IMAGES
of America

CENTRAL CITY

Lola Roush Miller

ARCADIA
PUBLISHING

ISBN 978-0-7385-4242-3

Published by Arcadia Publishing
Charleston, South Carolina

Printed in the United States of America

Library of Congress Catalog Card Number: 2005936198

For all general information contact Arcadia Publishing at:
Telephone 843-853-2070
Fax 843-853-0044
E-mail sales@arcadiapublishing.com
For customer service and orders:
Toll-Free 1-888-313-2665

Visit us on the Internet at www.arcadiapublishing.com

Contents

ACKNOWLEDGMENTS

Undertaking a project like this, which deals with history that has taken place before most of the living were born, can be frustrating and rewarding. I would be remiss if I did not mention a few specific people who were always encouraging and helpful. My most important mentor was Winifred Arthur, affectionately known as Winnie. I truly believe that if Winnie had not put together the first Central City glass exhibit and organized the first Central City Reunion, Old Central City would not be acknowledged today.

The first historians and businessmen include Winnie Arthur, Sally O. Cyrus, Ken Bolen, Jim Hardiman, David Hardiman, Jim Wiseman, Loretta Baker, Nancy Heiner, Barbara Cumpton, Barbara George, and the author. This nucleus, joined later by others, began the activities and publicity that brought people to the current Central City. The A. Michael Perry family and the Heiner family have been very helpful in supporting the efforts of the Old Central City Association.

Judy Rule, director of the Cabell County Public Library, has given permission for the use of most of the materials gathered for this book and housed in the Cabell County and West Huntington Public Libraries. Some pictures and interesting tidbits were found in *Cabell County Annals and Families* by George S. Wallace (1935) and *A Centennial History of Huntington, West Virginia, 1871–1971* by Doris Miller. Other materials have been gained from the Marshall University Special Collections, KYOWVA Genealogical Society (a name chosen for the tri-state area—Kentucky, Ohio, and West Virginia), Earl Bush, Fred Duncan, Leonard Samworth, Jimmie Taylor, Larry Lucas, Don Daniel McMillian, and individual families too numerous to mention. I will say to all of those who are not named—your help and suggestions were appreciated and not forgotten.

My four children, their mates, plus my seven grandchildren were important in my decision to write this collection because I want them to realize that the past can be important to the future. We all need to remember the struggles and successes of those who went before us.

The main thing I want the reader to realize is that I tried to keep the subject matter on the very early history and have obviously not touched on dozens of interesting businesses and moments in the life of Central City/West Huntington. Any mistakes or discrepancies are totally unintentional, and I ask for your indulgence and tolerance. This has been purely a labor of love with an interest in preserving Central City.

Sincerely,
Lola Roush Miller

INTRODUCTION

In 1890, several businessmen had a dream of an industrial town to complement the railroad and residential town of Huntington. The town was formed over the area of several large farms just west of the Huntington city limits. The first official map, drawn by civil engineer George McKendree, named Central City, included Third Street West on the east to Twenty-third Street West on the west. The Ohio River bordered to the north and the hills to the south.

Five main industrial plants were the hubs of Central City. The businessmen who formed the city worked hard to entice these factories to come to a brand-new town, which was a gamble. These companies were offered whole city blocks on which to build and expand. These five industries were the D. E. Abbott Company, Hartzell Handle Factory, the Huntington Tumbler Plant, Fesenmeier Brewery, and the Central City Bung Company. They came, along with several small businesses, and a town was born.

It was a booming little burg. People bought building plots and built homes to be near the new thriving businesses. Grocery stores sprung up on almost every block. With incorporation in 1893, the need for government brought the formation of a city council, election of a mayor, and appointments of policemen and firemen. The official town opened its own post office as well as a jail. Then in 1909, Huntington annexed Central City with its 5,000 residents. One hundred years later, very few in Huntington know about Central City. Somehow the little town that had been so prominent at the turn of the century was truly swallowed up by Huntington and forgotten, only to become known as West Huntington.

In 1988, Winifred Arthur, known to her friends as Winnie, came to the West Huntington Public Library and asked if her homemakers club could put an exhibit of Central City glass in the library. This was a historical project they were sponsoring. Being the branch librarian, I agreed, but the answer to the question I asked was to change my life, professionally and personally, "Where is Central City?" I was told I was standing in it. I could not believe that I had lived in Huntington for 25 years and worked on Fourteenth Street West for 7 years and had never heard of Central City.

When the City of Huntington started the renovation of this area of town later in 1988, the historians decided it was time to let the world know how important the little lost city had been to the growth and prominence of Huntington at the turn of the century. The renovating took place in five phases on Fourteenth Street West, which was the main street of Central City. These improvements included new streets and curbs, new lighting, a park with a gazebo, and a farmer's market. As each phase was completed, a new enthusiasm and interest in getting to know more about Central City took place.

An Old Central City Historical Committee was formed headed by Winnie Arthur and me. This committee, including Sally O. Cyrus and the Westland Homemakers Club, invited descendants of the original Central City families for a Central City reunion. This reunion took place in the spring of 1989. The response was amazing. More than 100 people attended an informal gathering at Central Christian Church. Many brought pictures and artifacts, but the most amazing thing was the sharing of stories about the families, the businesses, and the happenings of the area.

With a few newspaper articles and word of mouth, people began bringing pictures, memorabilia, and materials to the West Huntington Public Library. As the librarian and because of a great curiosity about Central City, I launched on a quest for as much information as I could find on this interesting but hidden history of the area.

During all of this activity, the merchants of West Huntington embarked on their own venture. During the late 1980s, several antique stores began opening on Fourteenth Street and adjacent streets. Having an open house in local stores became the goal of Christmas 1991. With the help of the City of Huntington and the area schools, a wonderful thing happened—Christmas in Old Central City.

This beginning launched a revitalization of the whole area. A great variety of businesses have made their home in Central City, and the area has now earned the title of "Antique Capital of West Virginia." The history committee and merchants banned together in 1991 and formed the Old Central City Association, whose main focus is to preserve and promote Old Central City.

After nearly 18 years, I feel like I have only found the tip of the iceberg about the history of this intriguing little town. I know there is so much untapped history still out there. A line had to be drawn as to what to include. This has been a real challenge because there are loyal businesses that were not included because of the time span. I would not want to exclude the Fitzpatricks and Mrs. Helen Napier, of Abbott's Frame Company, who have been on Fourteenth Street West for a long time. Other names include W. W. Payne, Zihlman's, Billman's, Gissel's, and the stockyards, just to name a very few. These among many many more were so important to the area.

I do not want to overstate the situation, but if I don't tell this story as I know it, Central City may be lost again.

One

Before Central City

The story of Central City parallels the settlement of the Ohio River Valley and the westward movement of the United States. According to Doris Miller's *Centennial History of Huntington, 1871–1971*, there is no historical record of any permanent Indian settlements on the site of the present city of Huntington. However artifacts found there and in close surrounding areas tell us that there were a lot of activities from hunting parties and family groups that freely roamed the river valleys of the Ohio, Guyandotte, and Big Sandy.

These same river valleys became the reward for soldiers who served under Washington at the Battle of Great Meadows in 1754. On December 15, 1772, Governor Dinwiddie, as agent for King George III, granted 28,627 acres along the Ohio, lower Guyandotte, and Big Sandy Rivers to John Savage and 59 others. These tracts of land became known as the Savage Grant. Although the monetary value was 49¢ an acre, this land, with an ample water supply, was very valuable for its accessibility for transportation. None of the soldiers who received the grant ever lived on his land, but all the tracts were eventually claimed by descendants or assignees of the 60 men.

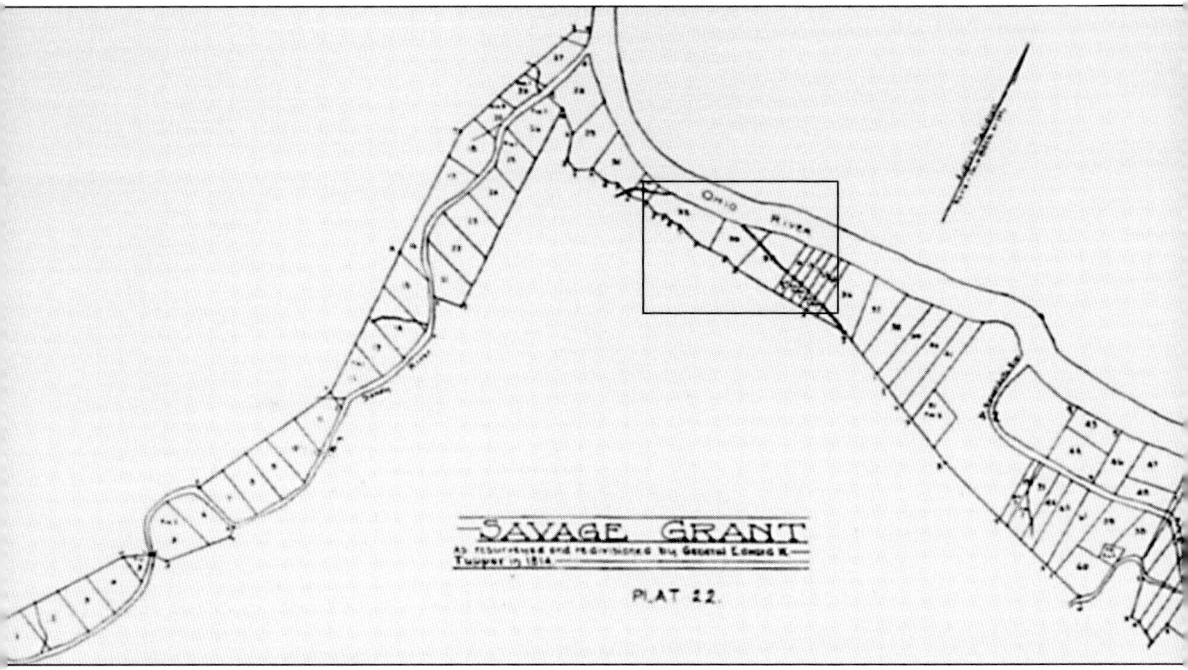

Two towns were established within the Savage Grant before Central City. Guyandotte was incorporated in 1810 and Huntington in 1871. The land, west of Huntington to the now Wayne County border, was all farmland owned by six families. These farms were contained within plots numbers 32–35 of the Savage Grant. They were large because they included the land from the Ohio River on the north to the hills to the south.

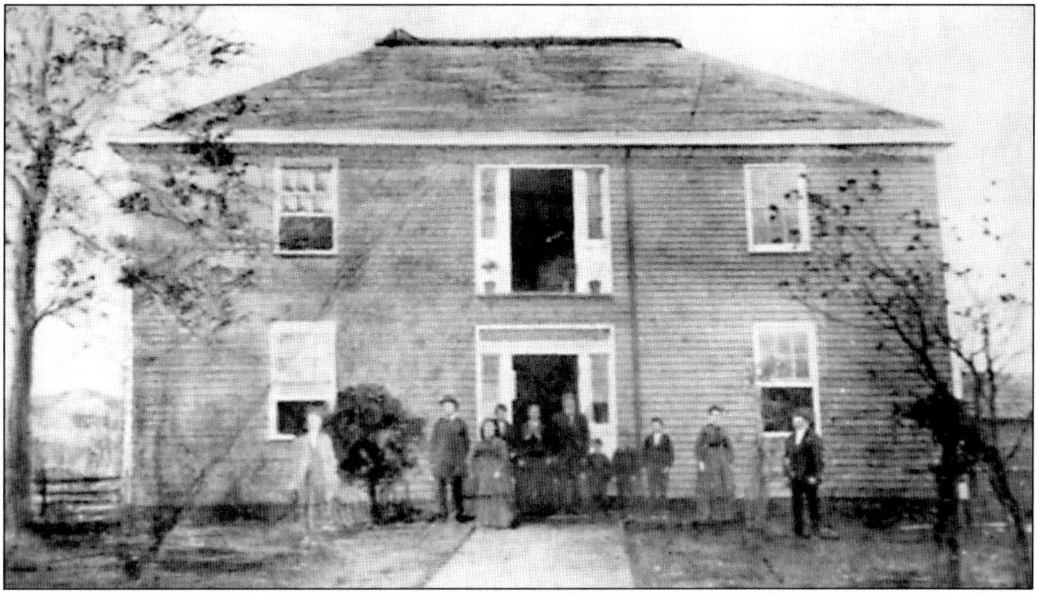

Samuel Woodrow Johnston owned the first farm that ran from the First Street west boundary of Huntington to Fifth Street West (using modern street names). According to deed records, the land was purchased in 1849. The cornerstone of the house bears the date 1854. Third Street West was known as Johnston Lane. The Lambert Collection at West Virginia University states that Samuel was one of the earliest settlers of the region. He participated in the Civil War and was affectionately known as Colonel in his later years.

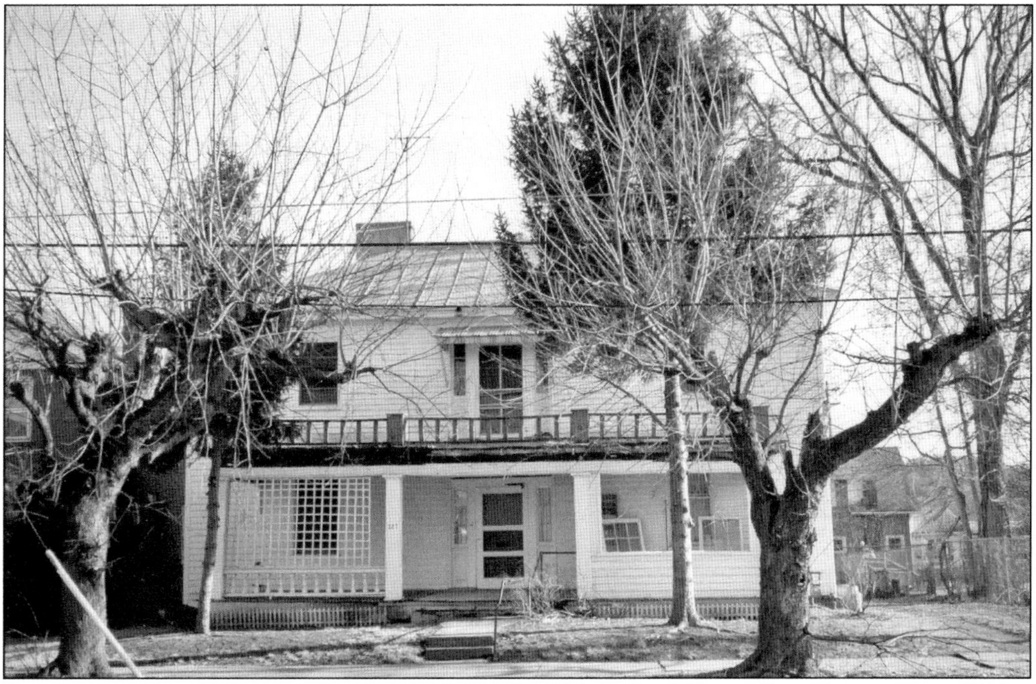

The Johnstons were known for their Southern hospitality, especially toward travelers and circuit riders, and the produce they grew and shipped downriver to other markets, including Cincinnati. The shipping point was the foot of Johnston Lane, known as Johnston's Landing.

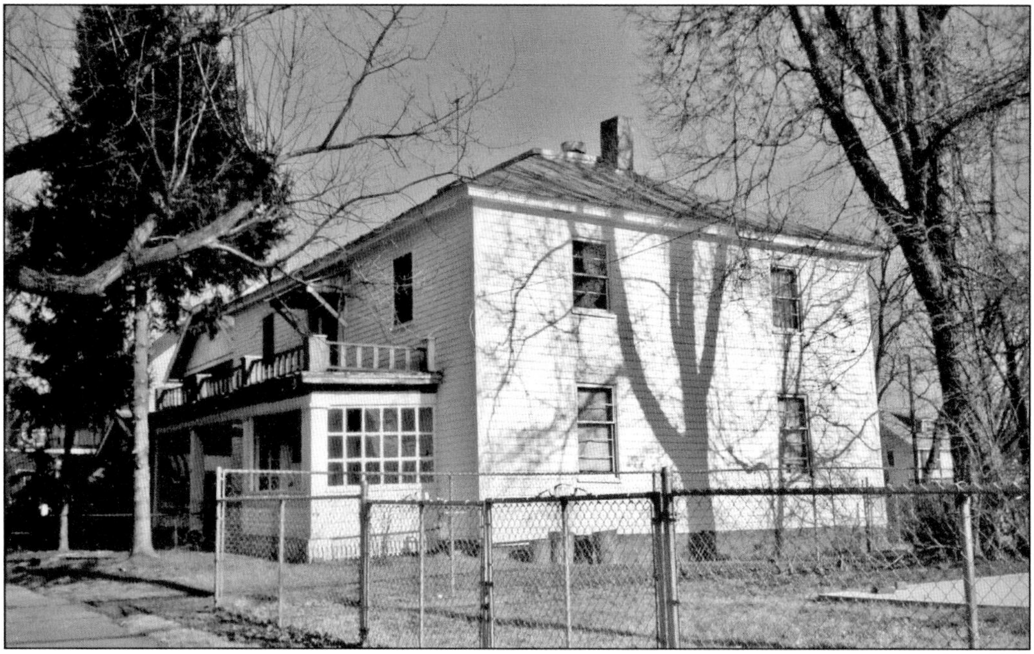

The original Johnston house still stands on the southeast corner Seventh Avenue and Third Street West. Many renovations have taken place, but the main house remains the same. Samuel Johnston had 15 children with two wives. Samuel died in 1883 and is buried in Spring Hill Cemetery. There are several Johnston descendants in the area.

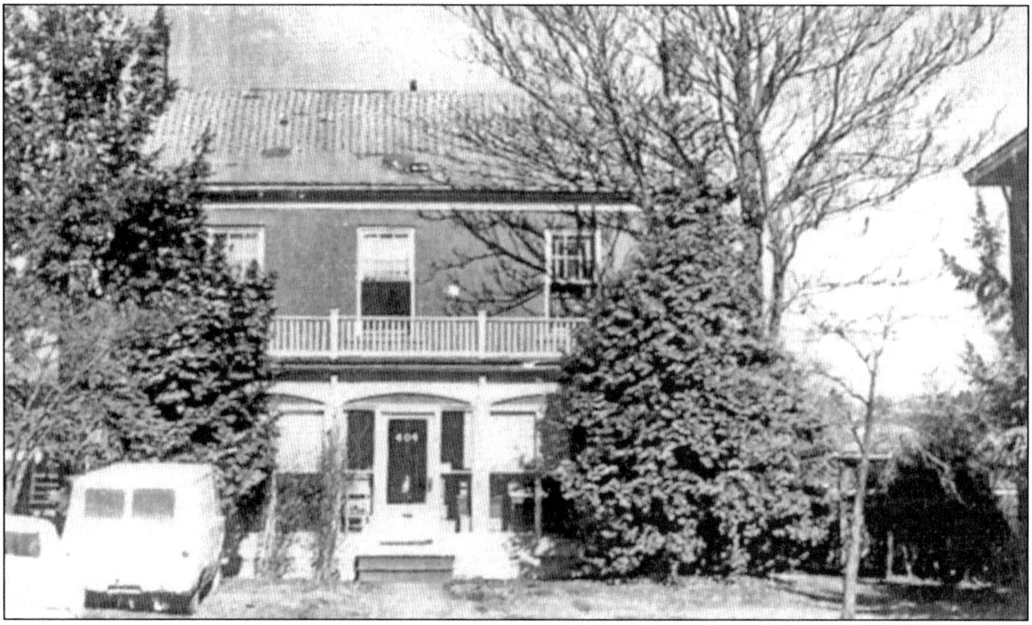

According to courthouse records, Samuel Johnston deeded four acres to his son, Napoleon Bonaparte, "with love and affection" in 1871, about the time of St. Cloud subdivision development. A house is not mentioned, but sometime soon after, a house was built at 404 Washington Avenue (above). The house is still there, although the brick has been painted white and renovations have changed the appearance.

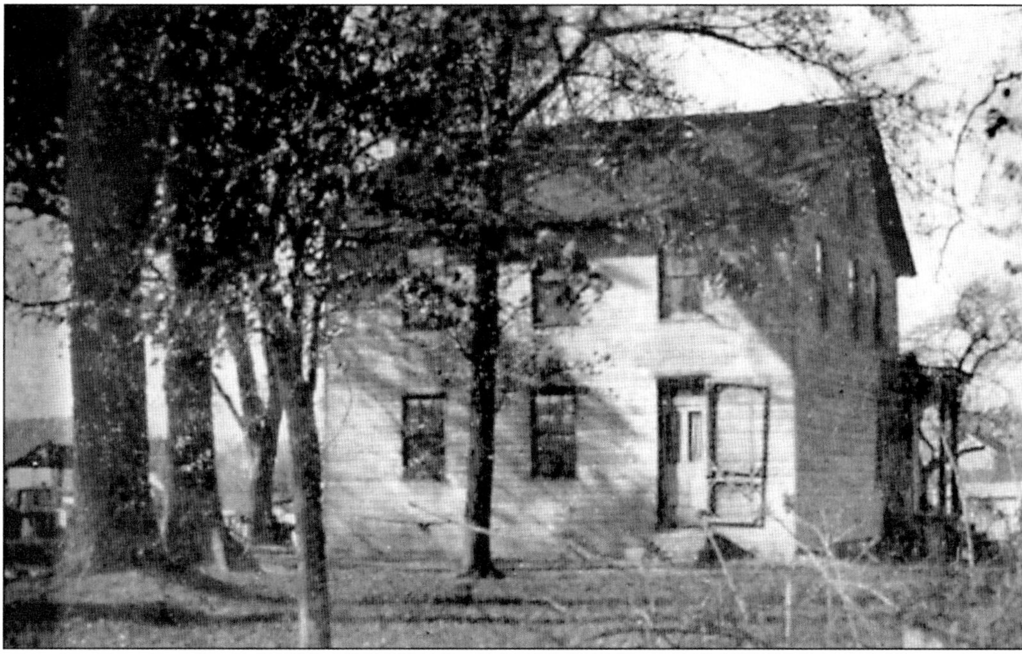

The second farm was also a Johnston farm. It was owned by James Johnston (unrelated to Samuel). The borders of this farm were from the Samuel Johnston farm on the east to Ninth Street West. James had come from Ireland in 1818 and traveled to this area by flatboat. James and Martha had four children, one of which was born on the trip down the Ohio. This house is said to have been built around 1840 and was the main family home. As can be noted in this picture, the house had fallen in to disrepair by the 1930s but has been renovated in later years.

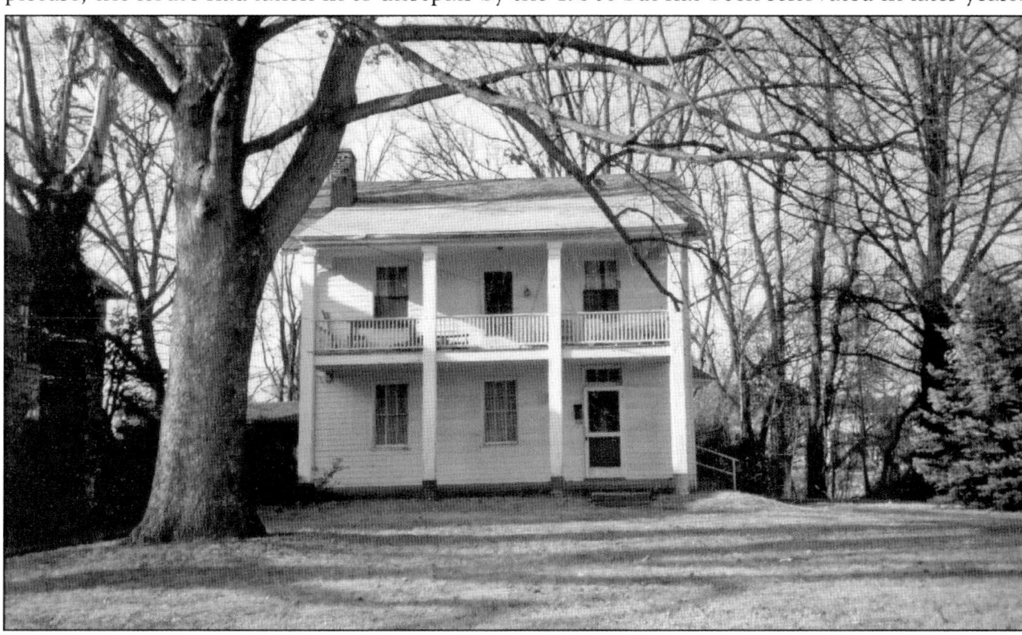

This is the James Johnston home today. James bought this farm around 1821. James was very well respected and is said to have had a large and impressive funeral. He is buried just across the Ohio River in Burlington, Ohio, where his brothers lived.

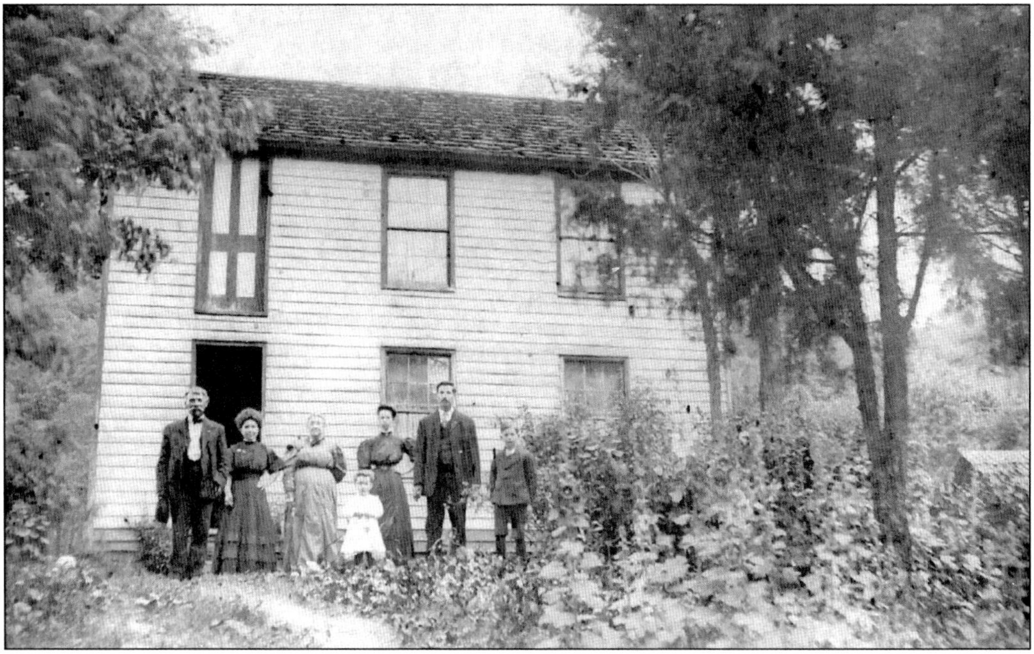

James built three homes on the farm. This house is thought to be one of the earlier ones. Alexander Pine had the next tract of land west of the James Johnston farm to Twelfth Street West. Albert Pine, perhaps the father or brother of Alexander, operated a gristmill on Four Pole Creek at Twelfth Street West. Permission for this mill was given in 1846.

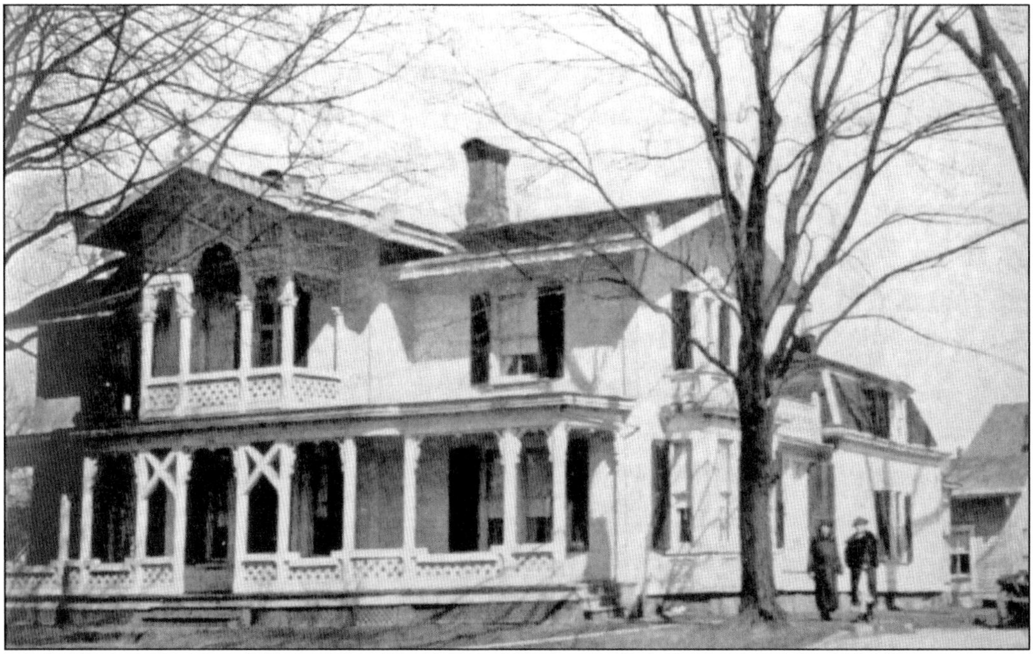

It was on Park Street (now Ninth Street West) that H. Chester Parsons built his home in 1870. Parsons moved his family here from Vermont to become a director of the C&O Railroad as appointed by Collis P. Huntington, the owner of the railroad. It is said that Parsons rode the first train that came into Huntington.

Parsons was also a lawyer for the railroad. He had an electric power station built to operate some small projects he wanted to start. A subdivision was designed that included the Parsons home. The subdivision was named St. Cloud after a town in New England. It extended from what is now Washington Avenue to the C&O Railroad track and from Seventh Street West to Eleventh Street West.

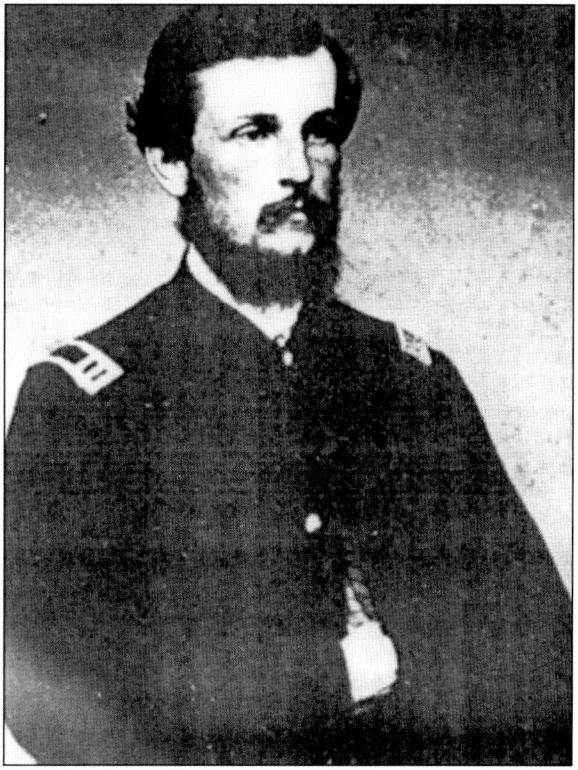

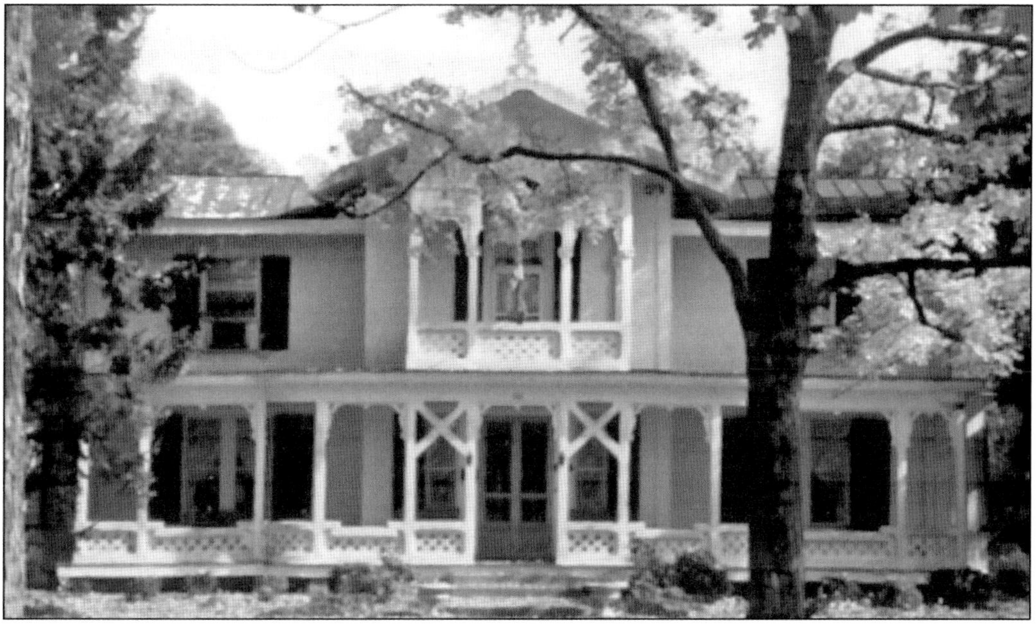

St. Cloud did have several small businesses brought in by Parsons, including a broom factory, a gristmill, a planing mill, and a shingle and heading mill among others. However, his projects evidently did not succeed beyond a few years. The subdivision became a part of Central City in 1893, and the street names were changed at that time. The house still stands at 729 Ninth Street West.

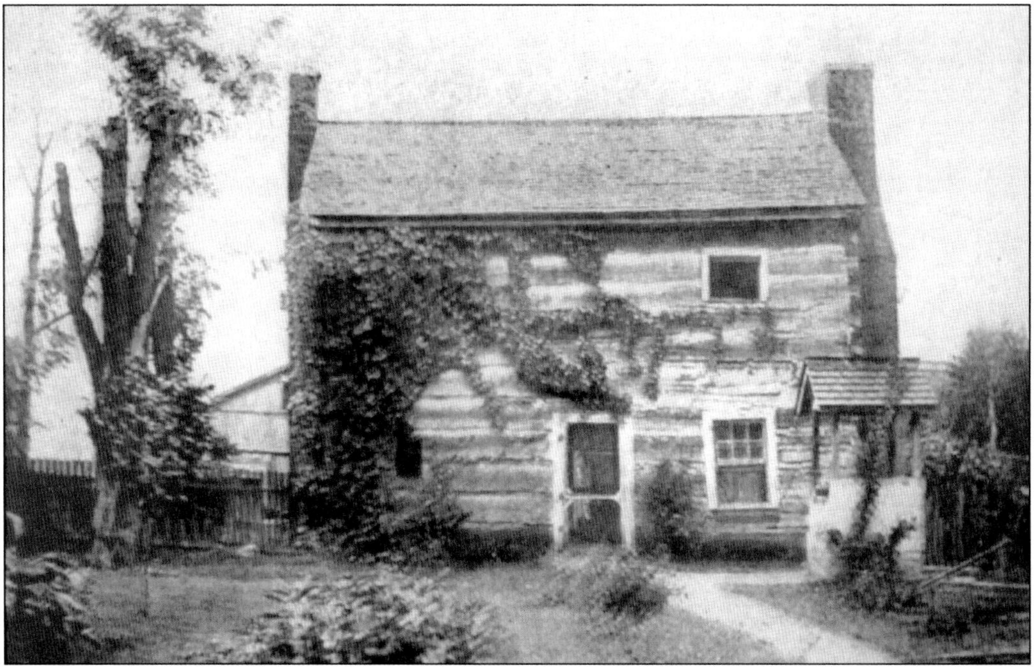

The Martin Hull farm ran from Twelfth Street West to Fifteenth Street West. Fourteenth Street West was known as Hull Lane. There is a Hull cemetery in the nearby area. The riverfront was Hull Landing.

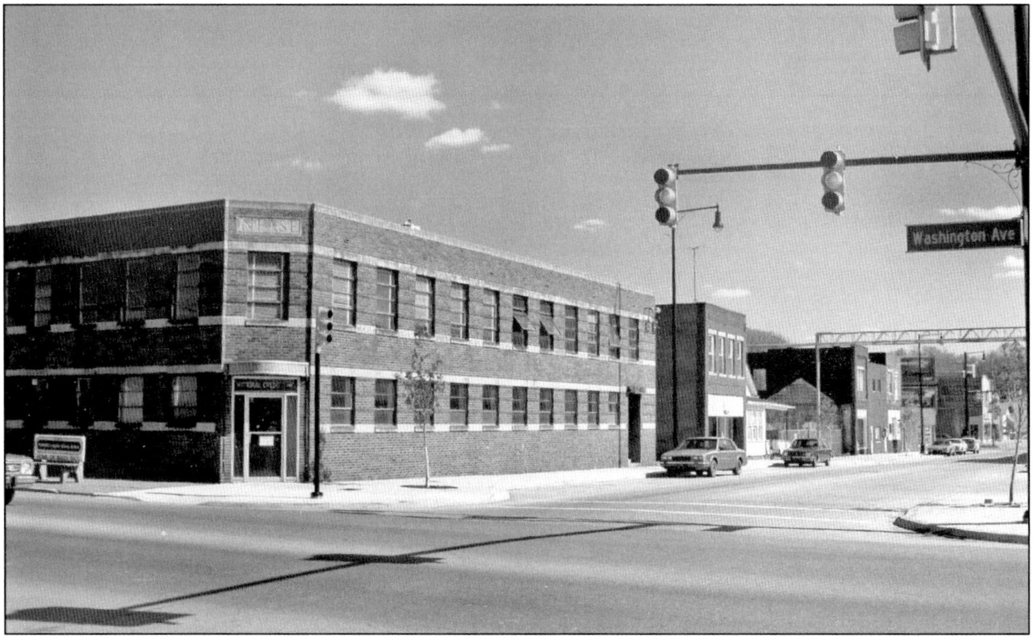

The house stood approximately where the Heiner's Bakery's newest addition stands on Washington Avenue today. This picture, taken in 1989, shows the buildings that were removed for that new addition on Washington Avenue and Fourteenth Street West. The land west of Hull farm was owned by David Frampton and William Williams and came to the Cabell/Wayne County line.

The farmland from Samuel Johnston to William Williams was purchased by several businessmen who formed the Huntington and Kenova Land Company and began selling lots for the new town of Central City. They built this house for an office on the northeast corner of Fifteenth Street West and Washington Avenue.

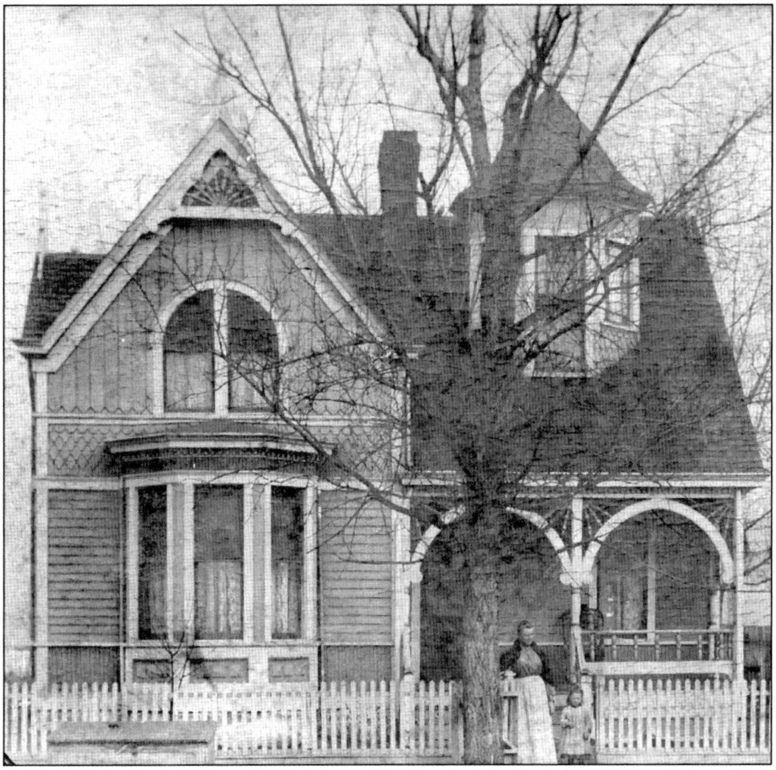

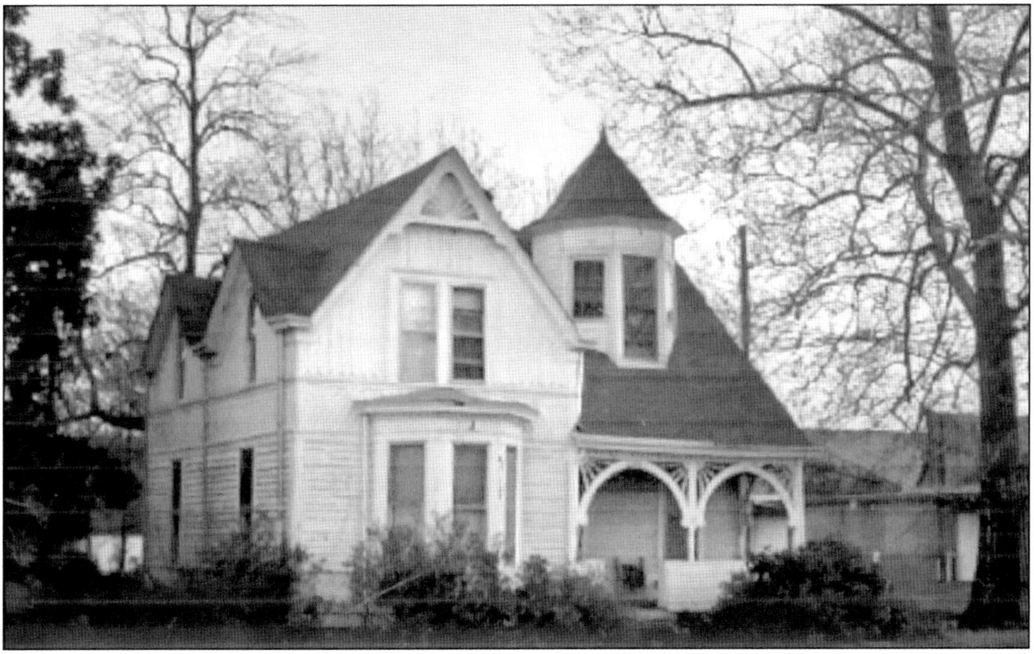

The men who had the dream for Central City were J. L. Caldwell, G. F. Miller, George McKendree, S. S. Vinson, and Z. T. Vinson. According to the *West Virginia Heritage Encyclopedia,* the name Central City was chosen because the town was midway between Guyandotte, West Virginia, and Catlettsburg, Kentucky. These were two major towns along the Ohio River in the late 1800s.

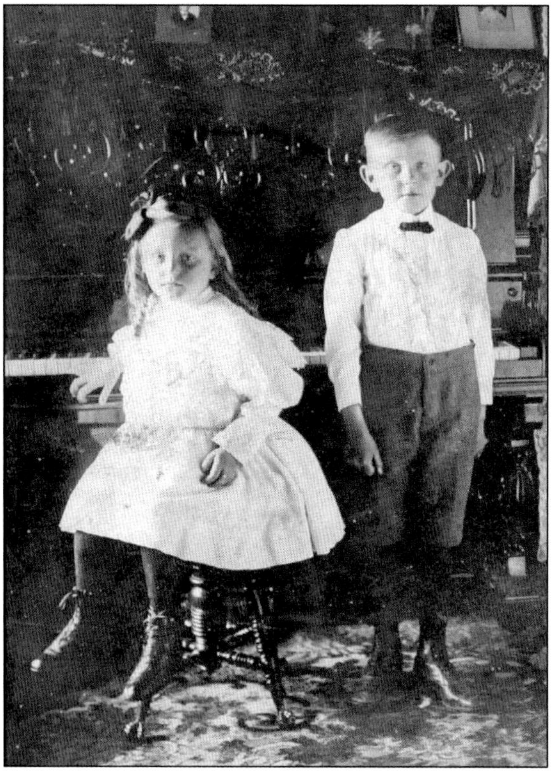

After the major sales were over, the director of the Huntington and Kenova Land Company sold the house/office to the Mestel family, who maintained ownership until 2003. The picture at left was taken in the parlor of Gertrude and Fred Mestel. Fred Sr. was a foreman in the D. E. Abbott Picture Frame Factory.

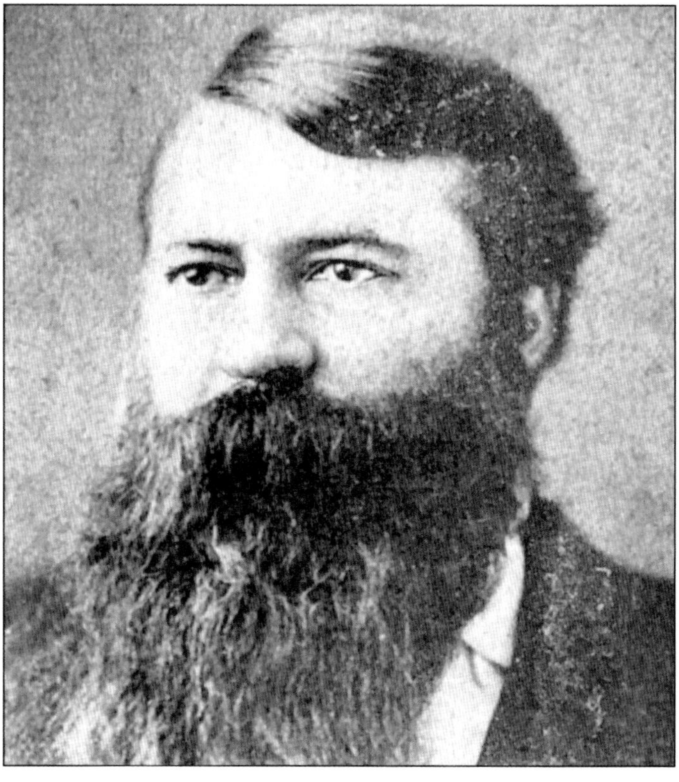

Engineer George McKendree laid out the map of Central City. The avenues ran east and west and were named for the presidents of the United States in order of their terms, with the exception of the second Adams. These street names began after the river street named Virginia. From that point, they were named Washington to Harrison. The cross thoroughfares were numbered and ran from Third Street West to Twenty-third Street West.

Two

A New Industrial Town

The newly organized Huntington and Kenova Land Company saw its plans come to fruition on July 31, 1893, when Central City was granted incorporation. The company realized that the railroad town of Huntington, with its majority of residential areas, needed the complement of an industrial town. This became the theme of Central City. The town offered whole city blocks to several businesses that needed large areas for expansion. Within months, five major industries had committed to coming to the new area.

The men who led Central City into the new century already had prominence in Huntington. Realizing the potential of the new town, several bought land in Central City and built homes. Floyd and Martin V. Chapman, also influential, owned a couple of newspapers. Two were published for Central City. Martin was also the first mayor. Z. Taylor Vinson, who was well known in the neighboring community of Kellogg, was a big investor in the Huntington and Big Sandy Railroad. J. L. Caldwell was president of the First National Bank of Huntington.

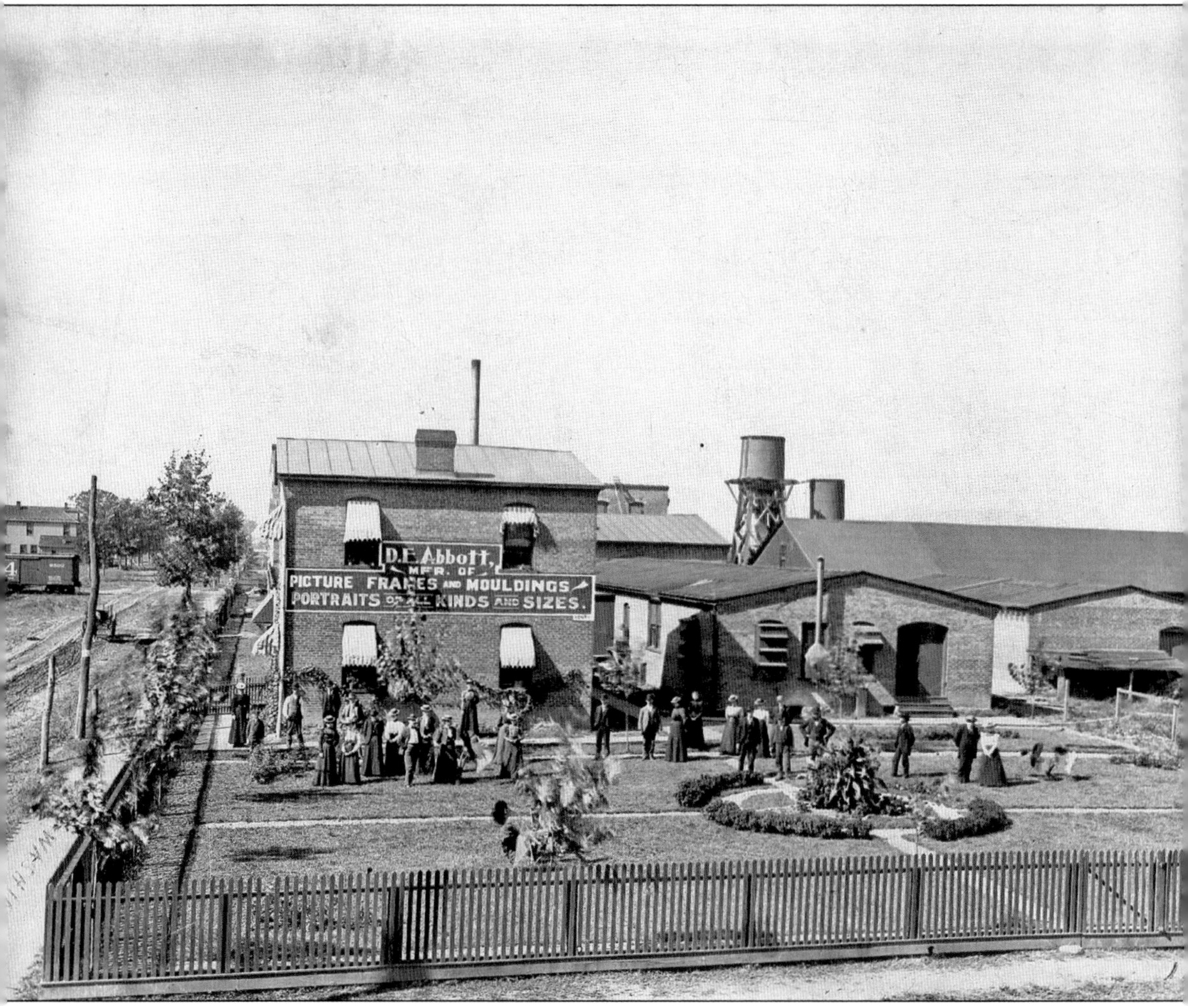

With the promise of the land company for certain development, the Addison Thompson and Associates built a plant between Fourteenth and Fifteenth Streets West and Washington and Virginia Avenues. For a few years, the plant manufactured blown and pressed tableware and novelties in crystal and colors. The plant employed about 150 people. However, in 1898, D. E. Abbott bought the building, changed it into a company that manufactured picture frames, and employed artists who enlarged pictures and painted portraits. The picture above was taken in 1899.

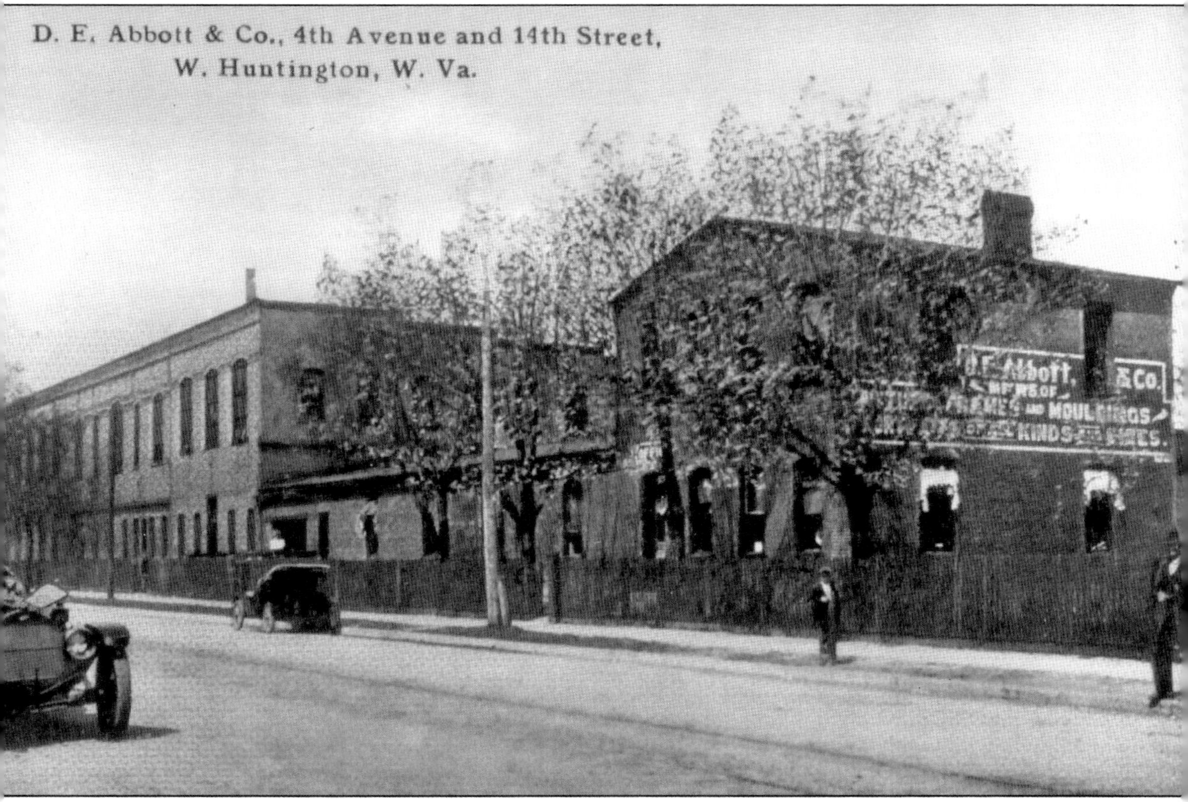

The D. E. Abbott Company shipped picture frames by railroad car and riverboat to all parts of the eastern United States. They also had a great market in Europe, especially for the fancy gilded frames shipped to Germany and Austria. This plant became one of the largest of its kind in the southeastern United States. In 1919, Abbott sold the manufacturing company and equipment to the Cravens-Green Company.

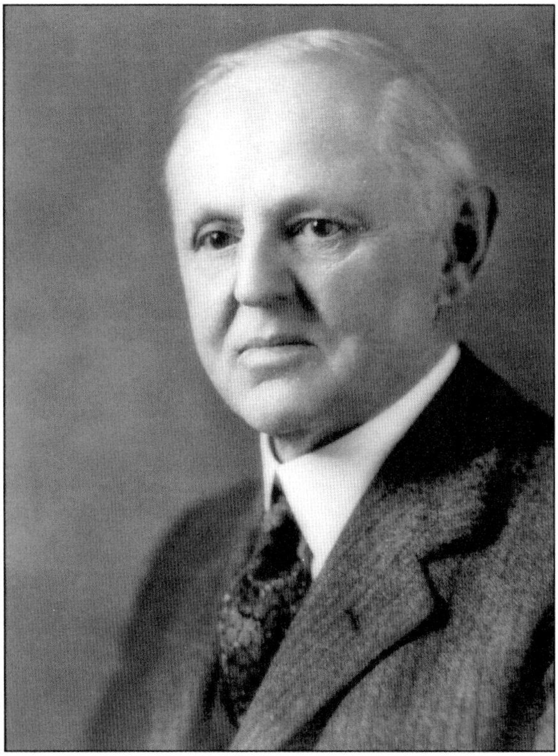

Darwin Eugene Abbott was born in Canada in 1856. His family moved to Vermont, and it was there the family met the H. Chester Parsons family. Darwin came to Central City from Vermont by driving a team of horses that pulled a wagon full of the Parsonses' household belongings. He remained in Huntington, attended Marshall Academy, and became a notable photographer in the area. After he took over the Addison plant in Central City, he married and eventually bought the Parsons family home, where he lived until his death on July 10, 1942, after complications attributed to a fall from his front porch a few days earlier.

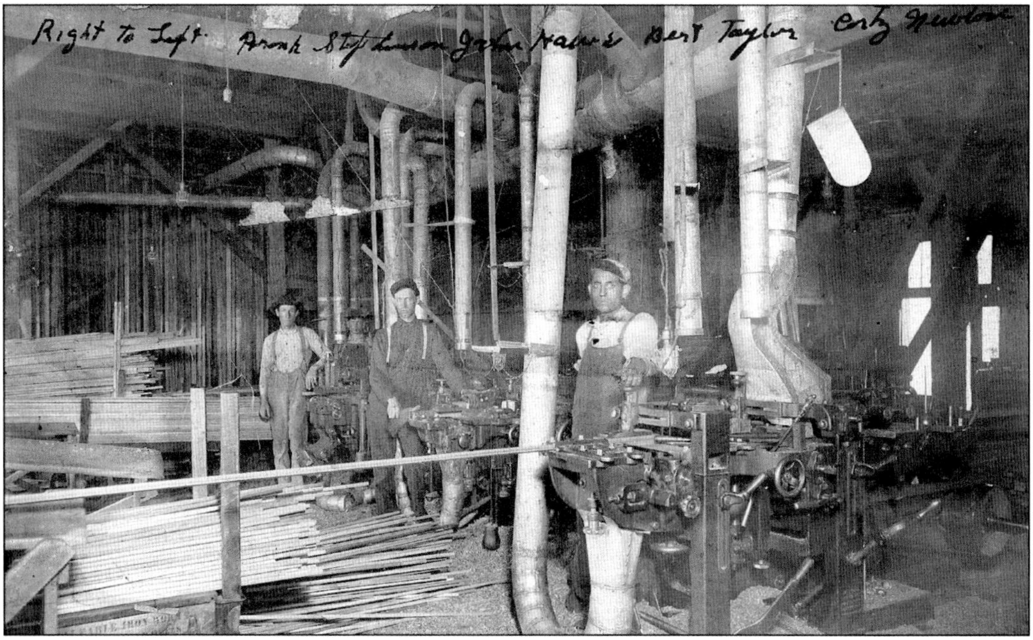

When Abbott sold his factory to Cravens-Green in 1919, he continued his original business on a smaller scale in the original building, which is still standing. The faithful workers that he retained continued to make frames. It is said that the quality of the frames was superior. It is possible, because of the breadth of sales overseas, that some Abbott frames hang in the galleries and museums of Europe.

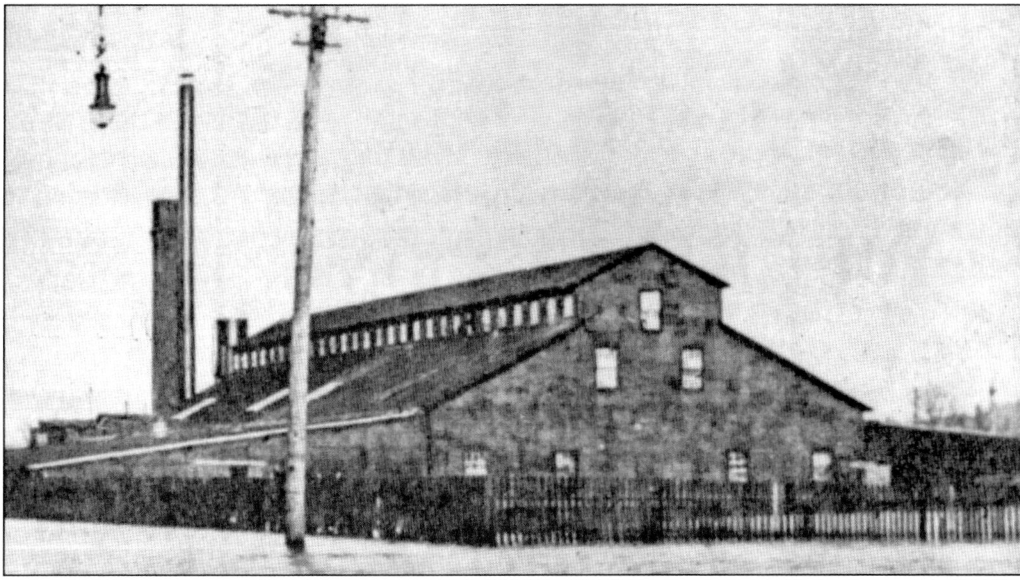

On the south side of Washington Avenue between Fourteenth and Fifteenth Streets West was the Hartzell Handle Factory. The original plant was located in Guyandotte as the Hartzell, Caldwell, and Marr Handle Factory. In 1887, it burned. The Hartzell brothers, Enos and Irvin, opened a plant in Central City. The industry manufactured hickory handles for axes, hammers, hatchets, spades, and other tools. The supply of hickory timber was very accessible by rail and river from the mountains of West Virginia. However, the supply of hickory dwindled, and the plant was eventually dismantled and the land sold. Enos Hartzell lived to be 102 and is buried in Spring Hill Cemetery.

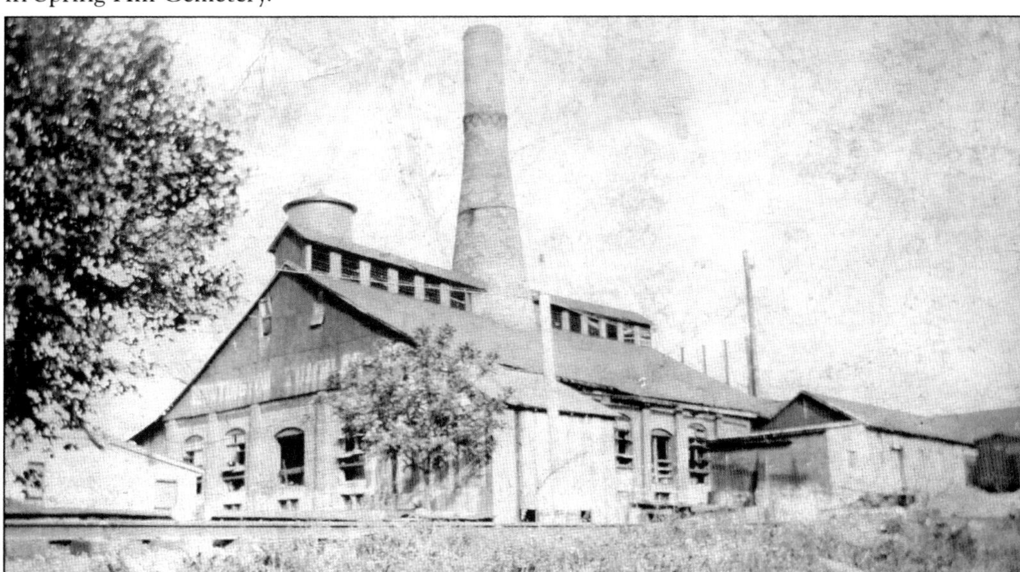

The Huntington Tumbler Plant began as the West Virginia Flint Bottle Company in 1891 on Fifteenth Street between Madison and Jefferson Avenues. It manufactured fruit jars and bottles. After a couple of owners, it was sold to Anton Zihlman in 1900. Zihlman had learned the glass industry in Germany and had come to Central City by way of Bellaire, Ohio, and Cumberland, Maryland.

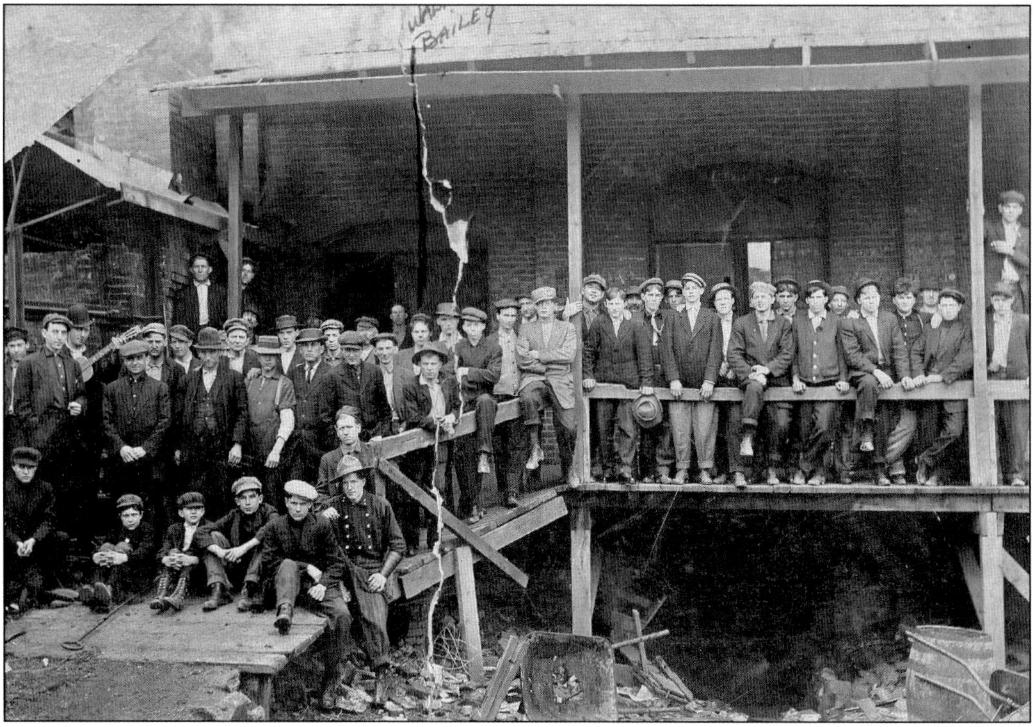

The Huntington Tumbler Plant employed 150 people at one time. Many members of the same family worked together. *The Huntington Advertiser* of August 20, 1895, says that several glass blowers and molders had arrived from Martin Ferry and Wheeling to work at the glass factory. A newspaper from 1896 states that the glass factory had a capital stock of $100,000.

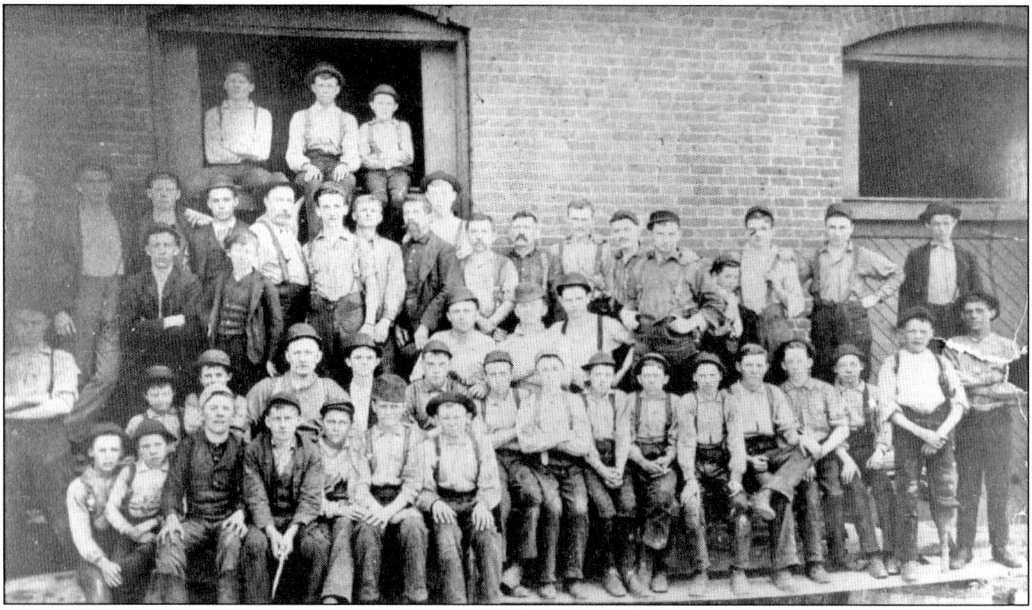

This is another group of employees in the early 1900s. It seems the company took regular or yearly pictures of the workers. The plant's fires were kept burning with large quantities of coal from the Pearl Mining Company at Dingess, West Virginia, on the Norfolk and Western Railroad.

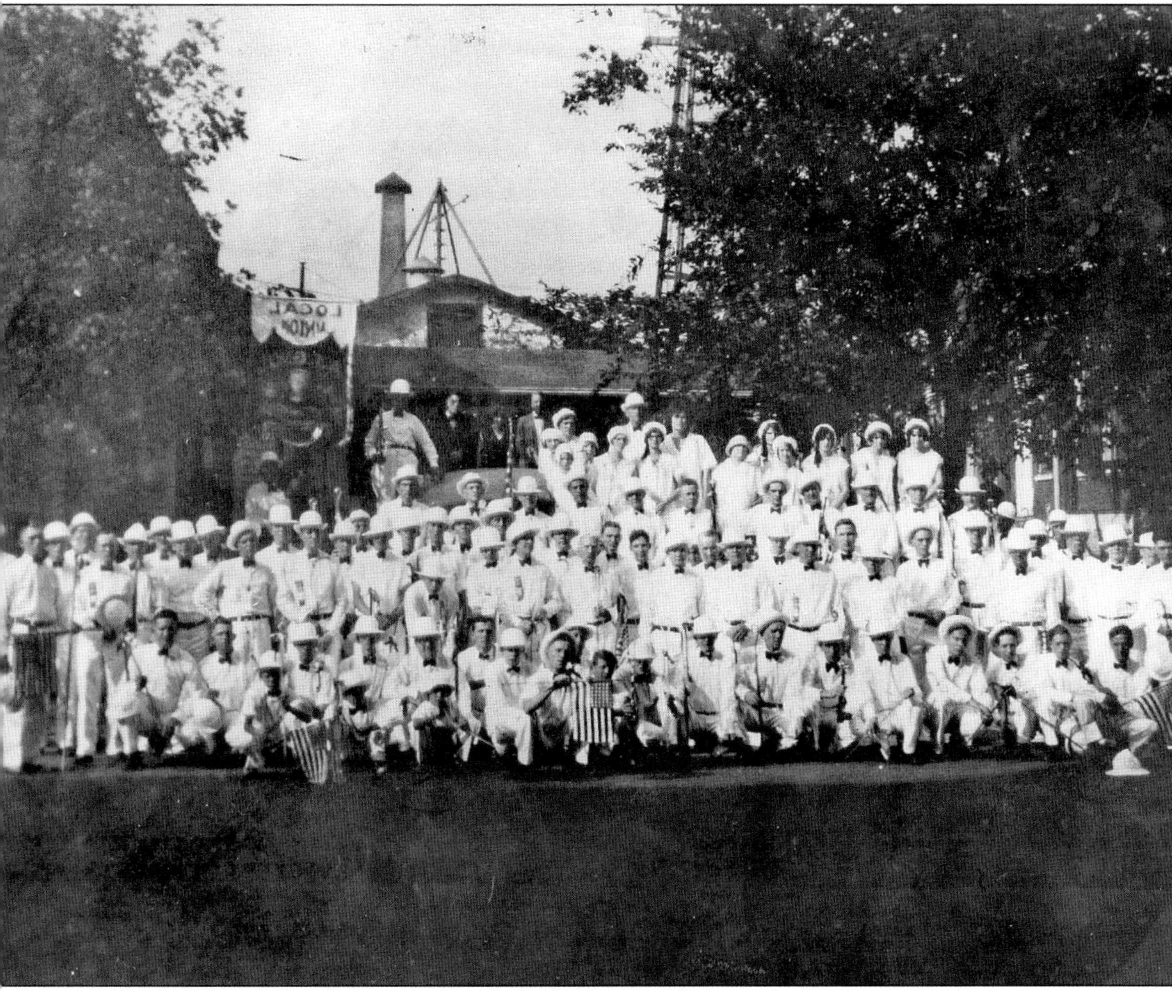

Parades were a serious means of recreation for hardworking people. As we will see in future pictures, factory workers loved dressing well and marching in Labor Day and Memorial Day parades. In the picture above, the employees of the Huntington Tumbler Plant are all decked out in their finery and carrying glass canes. These canes were made at the end of the day from glass scraps, and only workers were entitled to own them. There are several in collections in Huntington.

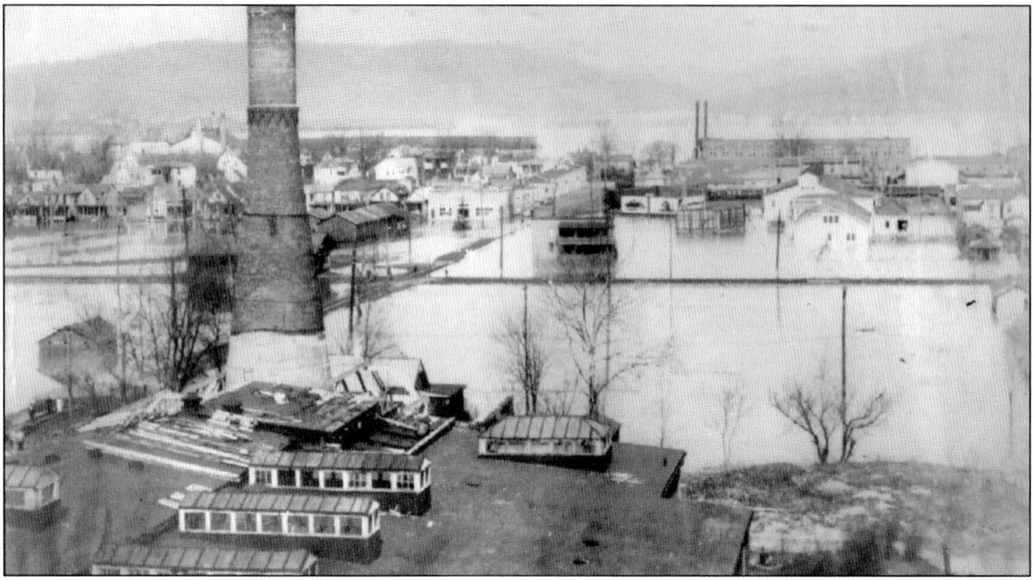

This picture was taken from the top of the Fesenmeier Brewery during the 1913 flood. The tumbler plant is in the foreground. The D. E. Abbott and Hartzell Handle Factory are seen at the top. The Ohio River is along the top just below the hills.

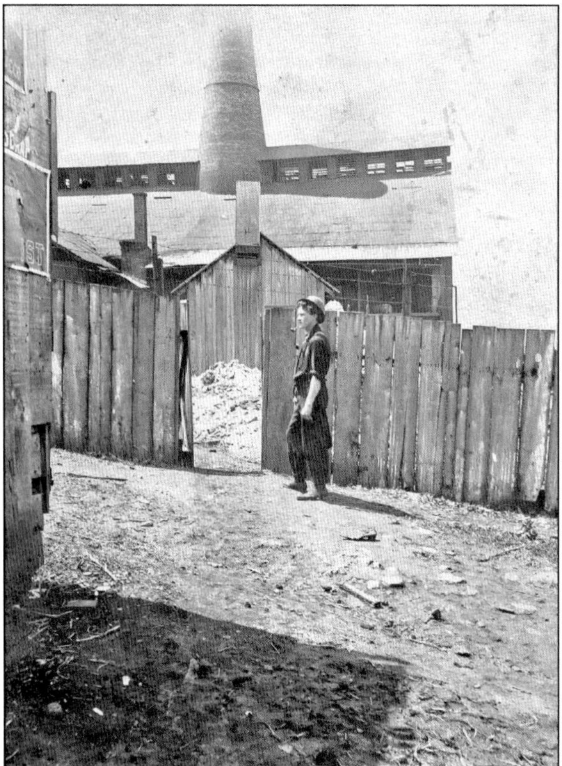

Axel Muller was a pioneer in glass blowing and designing in 1907. According to a relative, Anita Muller, he began blowing glass at the age of 9 in Sweden. He came to work at Huntington Tumbler at the age of 21. He was a notable craftsman. His picture appeared in *National Geographic* in 1940 in an article on the rapid growth of the glass industry in West Virginia.

Another craftsman was Lucian Wetherall. This picture shows him putting a design on a tumbler. The quality of the glassware was very upscale, although it was common in the households of the workers and Central City residents. It has been said that many newlyweds began their married lives with Huntington Tumbler products.

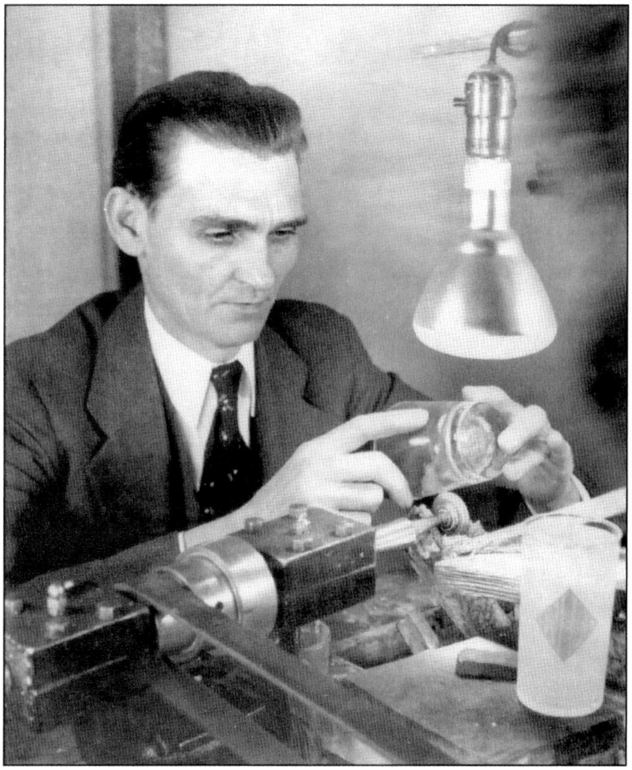

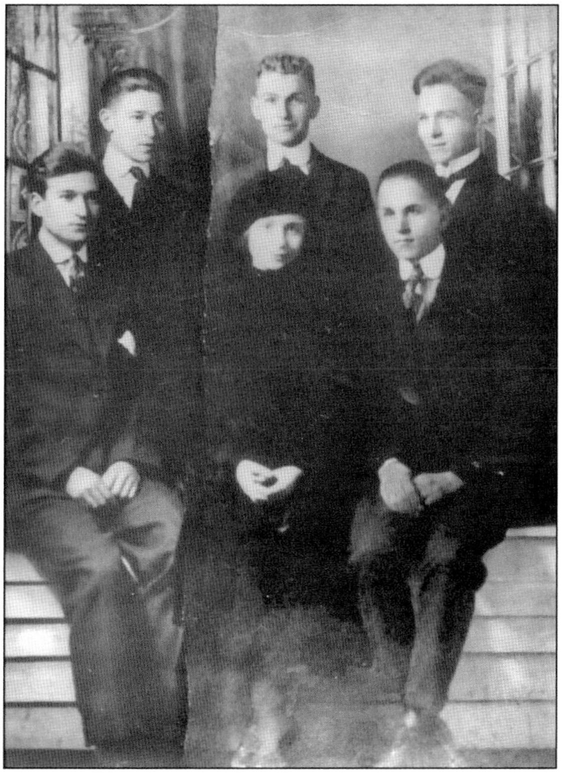

The Wetherall family was very prominent in Central City. The family originally owned a mill that stood where the Keith-Albee Theatre is now in downtown Huntington. They came to Central City and built a home at 1342 Jefferson Avenue. The Wetherall sons all worked in the Central City businesses. From left to right are (first row) Leonard, Helena, and Sidney; (second row) Alton, Lucian (the glass craftsman), and Eldon.

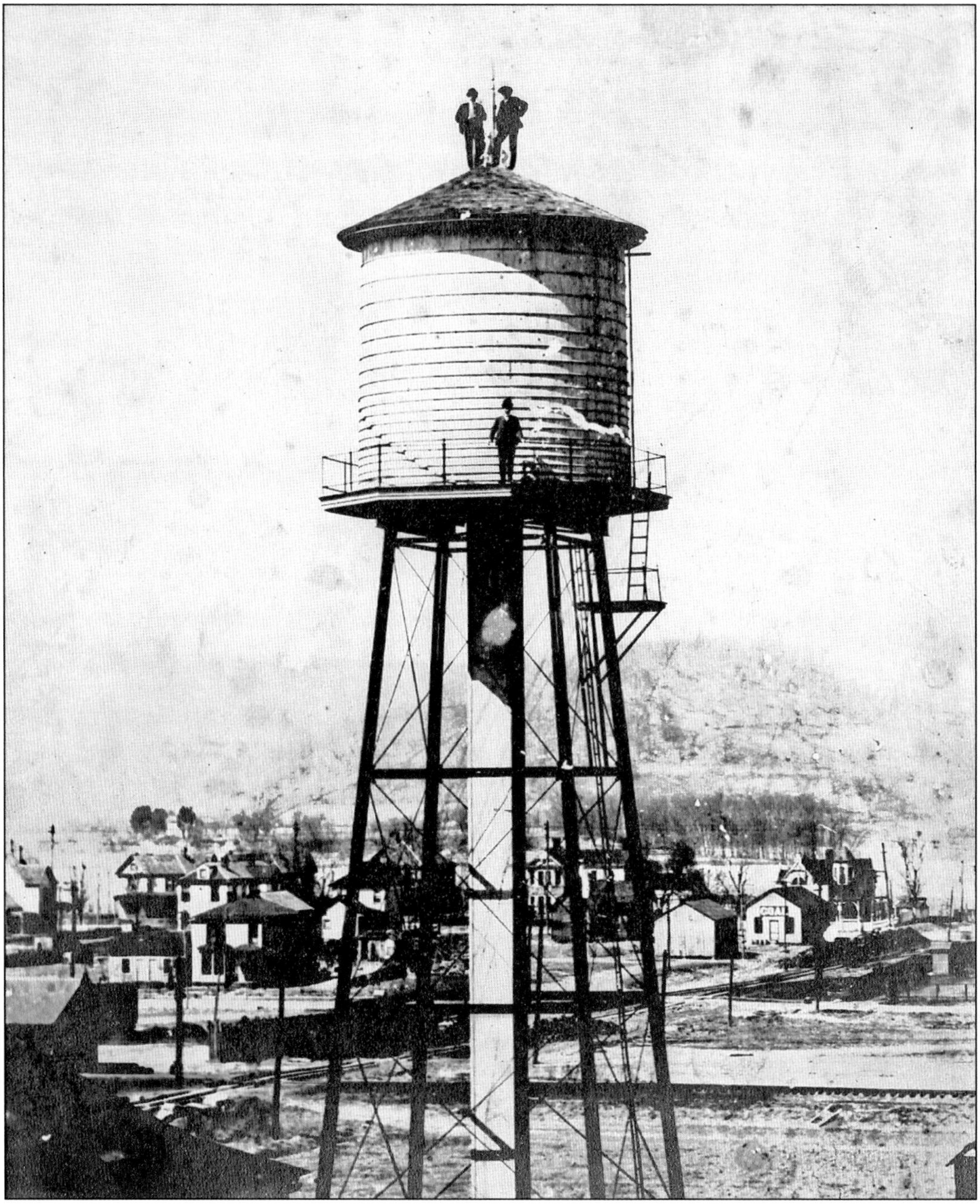

Most factories had their own water tower. The Huntington Tumbler Plant was no exception. Note the brave climbers on top. This tower was a landmark for the area because it could be seen from a distance. Although there were several in Central City, this water tower stood taller and on higher ground than most.

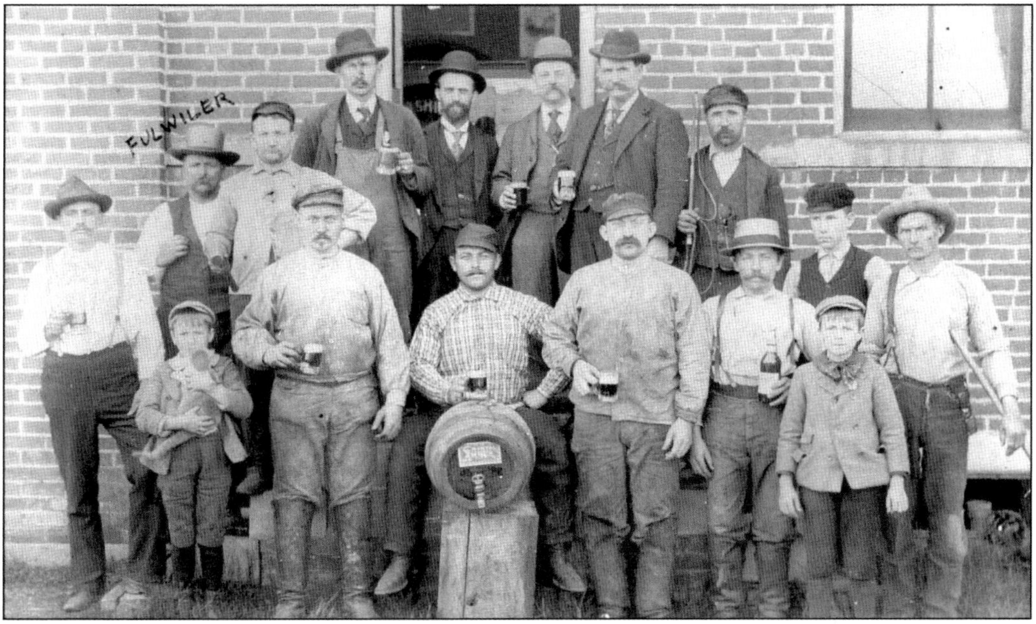

Michael Fesenmeier has a similar story to Anton Zihlman of the Huntington Tumbler Plant. He was born in Germany and learned his trade there. Then he arrived in America at Cumberland, Maryland. The brewery in Central City had been started in 1891 under the name of Huntington Brewing Company and was sold in 1896 to the American Brewing Company. The workers above were a part of the 1896 business. Fesenmeier took over the struggling business in 1899 and renamed it the West Virginia Brewery.

The first product introduced by Fesenmeier was West Virginia Special Export. This product became known in a widespread area. A 1903 newspaper advertisement states, "When mercury is up—there is nothing that will invigorate and refresh you like a glass of sparkling and delicious West Virginia Beer. For the business man, the working man, the housewife who attends to her own work and the nursing mother, it is a boon that is appreciated for it gives strength and refreshment."

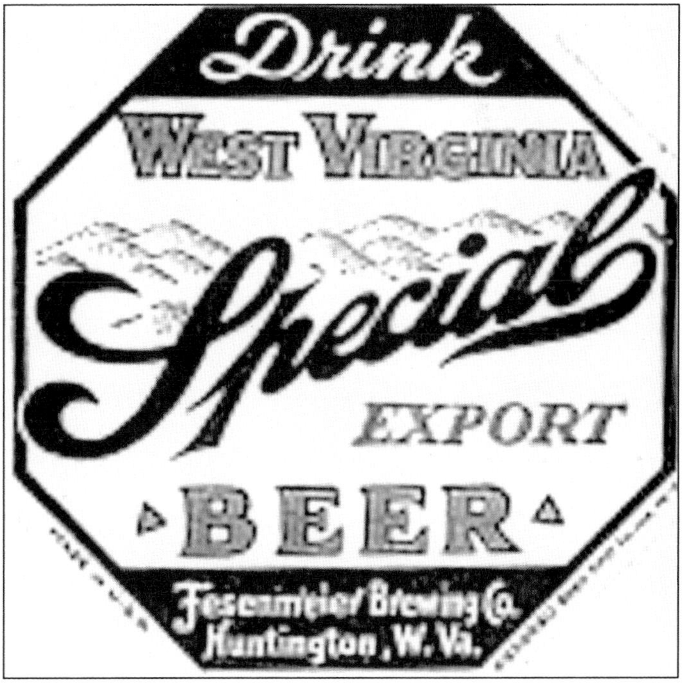

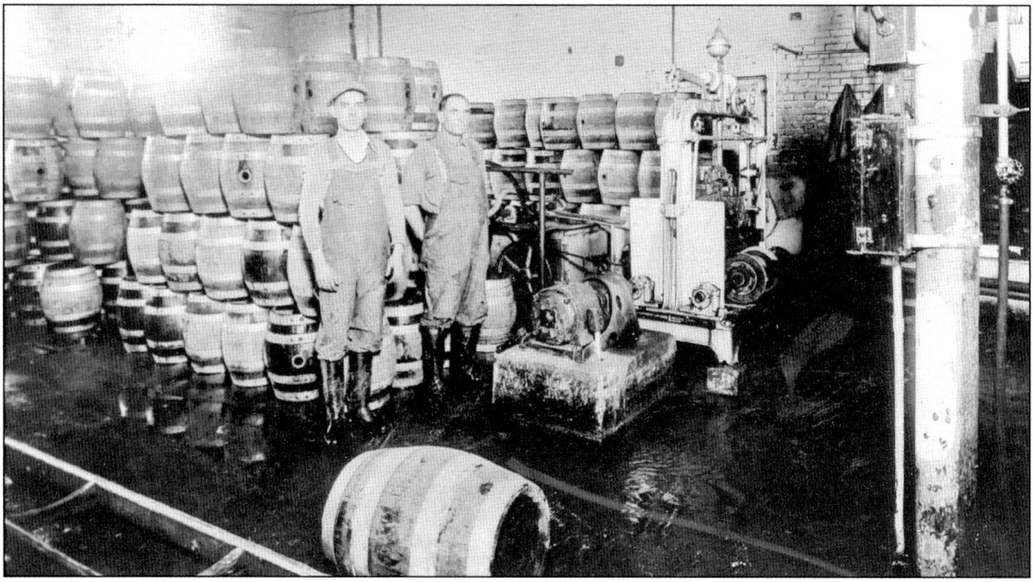

Kegs were the main containers for the early brewery. Delivery was one of the greatest obstacles of the early plant. Unpaved streets and swamps in the low-lying parts of the city made it impossible for team traffic to get from Central City to Huntington. It was necessary to keep extra horses stationed at various places to pull the wagons through the mud or ship the short distance by rail. Warehouses were located in downtown Huntington, but the demand sometimes exceeded the shipping facilities.

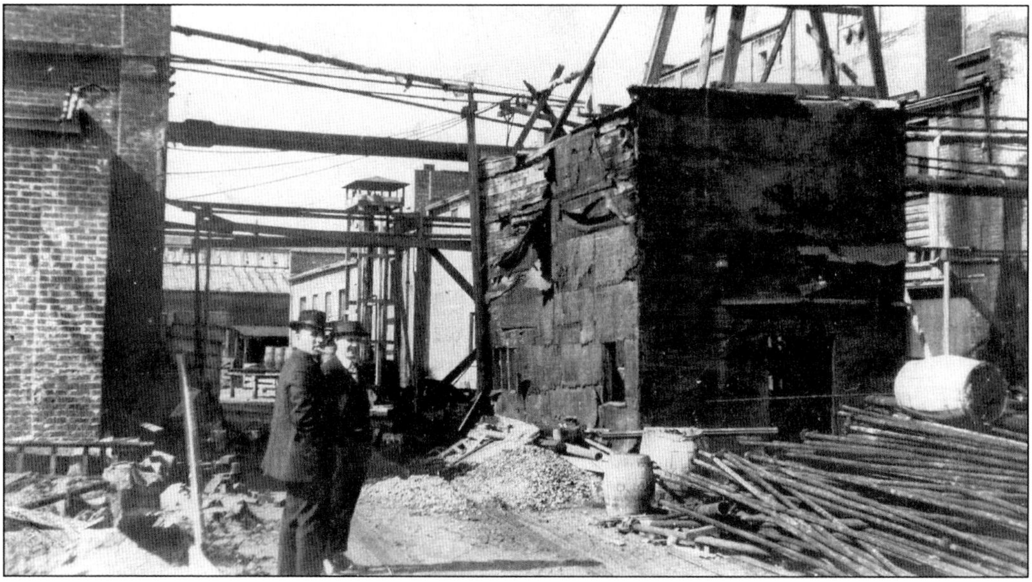

In 1906, the brewery had a massive catastrophic fire. According to *The Huntington Advertiser* on June 9, 1906, "the high central portion was destroyed this morning" and the fire originated in the mill room. The ice plant on the east and storage on the west were saved. The company would be enabled to resume business in full within 30 days. New machinery had already been ordered. Due to low water pressure, the Central City Fire Department could do little to check the progress of the flames. The Huntington hose cart and the hook and ladder responded and soon controlled the flames.

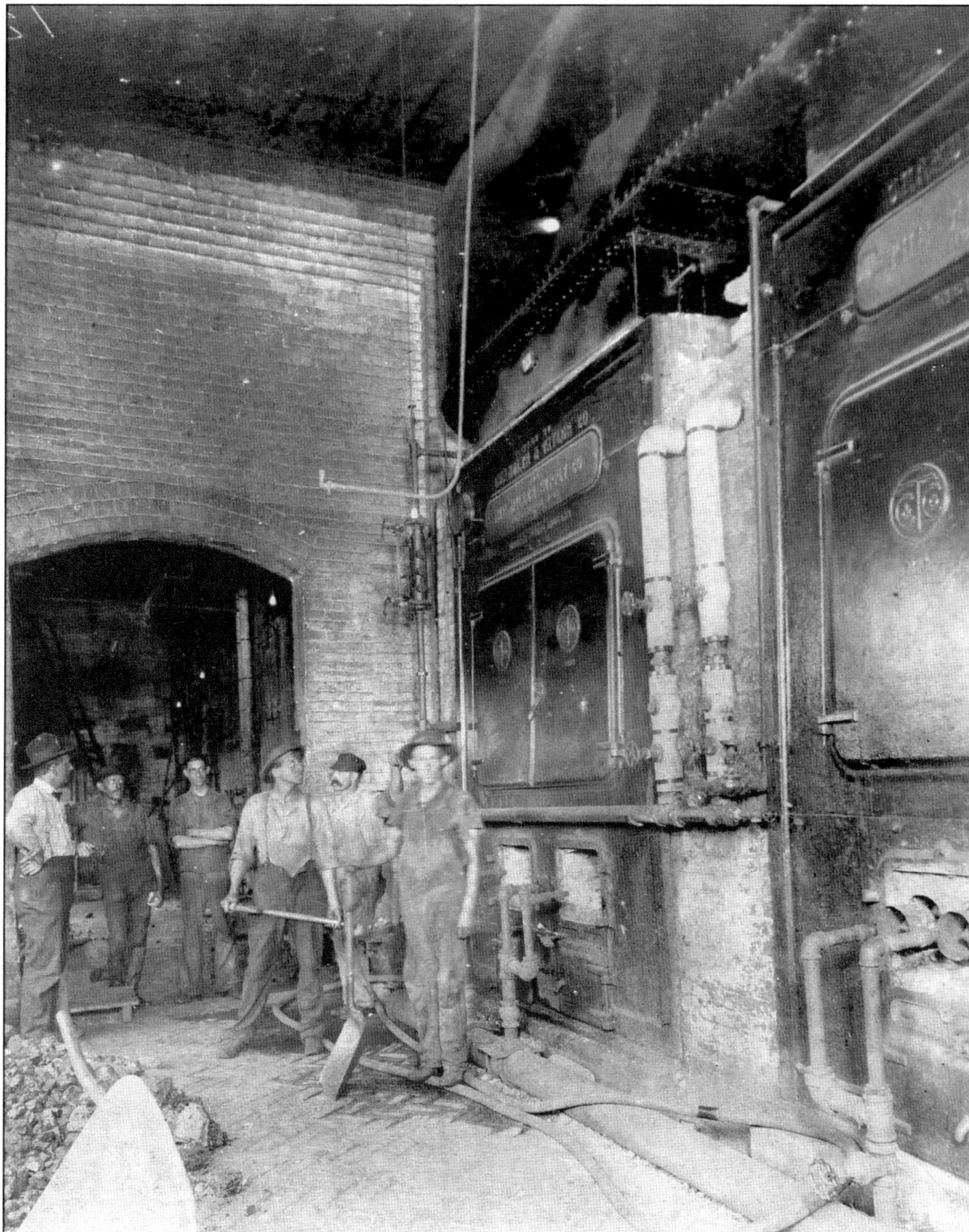

Inside the brewery in the 1890s, the employees were hardworking, and these boiler workers endured extreme heat all year-round. One of the stages of brewing beer was to boil the mash. The boilers had to be at extreme temperatures. These furnaces above were kept going all the time. The only time they were shut down was for cleaning or maintenance. Demand for the product exceeded expectation.

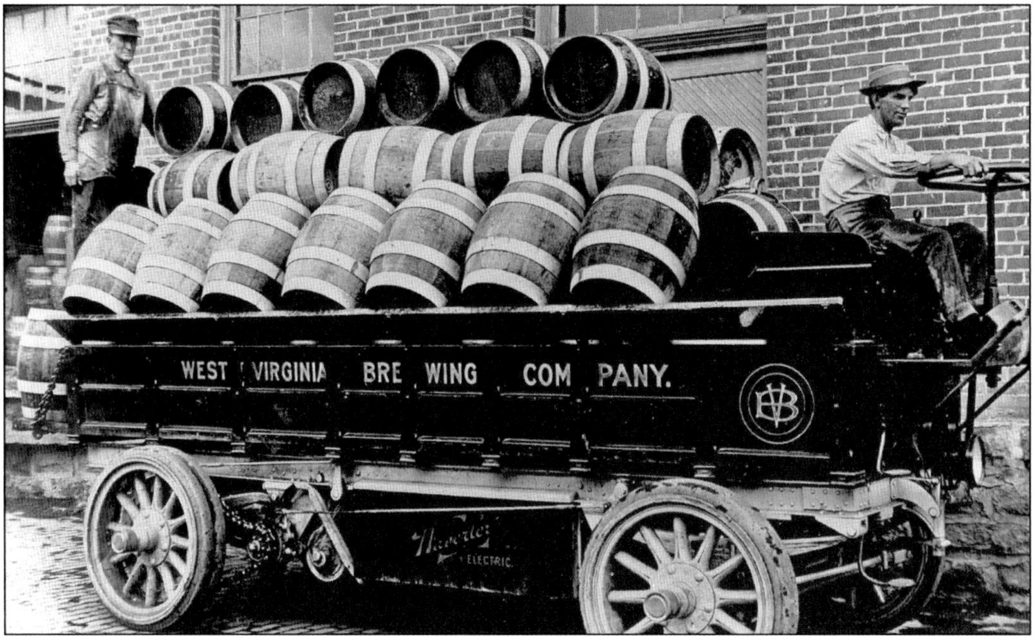

With the cooperation of the City of Huntington, Third Avenue was paved except for a two-block area between First and Third Streets West, which was a section of town called Neutral Strip. It was not a part of Huntington nor Central City. When Neutral Strip and Central City were annexed as a part of Huntington, a completed link was made. By this time, delivery methods were changing also. This 1912 electric truck was the next step in transporting the brewery product.

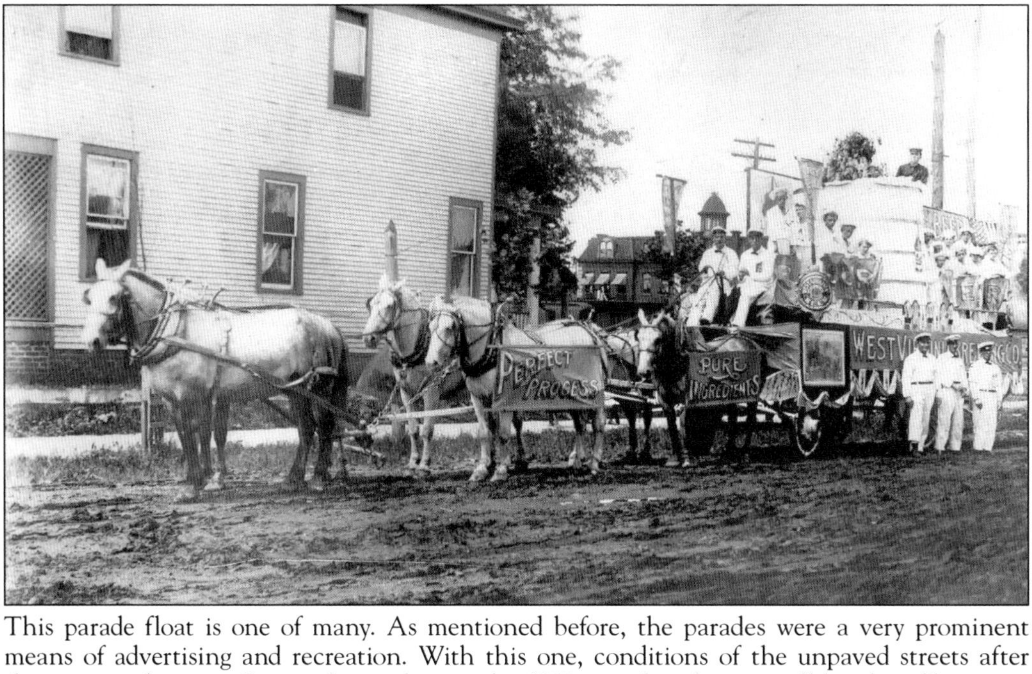

This parade float is one of many. As mentioned before, the parades were a very prominent means of advertising and recreation. With this one, conditions of the unpaved streets after the rain can be seen. Pricing for product in the 1910s was five dozen small bottles of beer in a package for $3.75 and $9 a barrel.

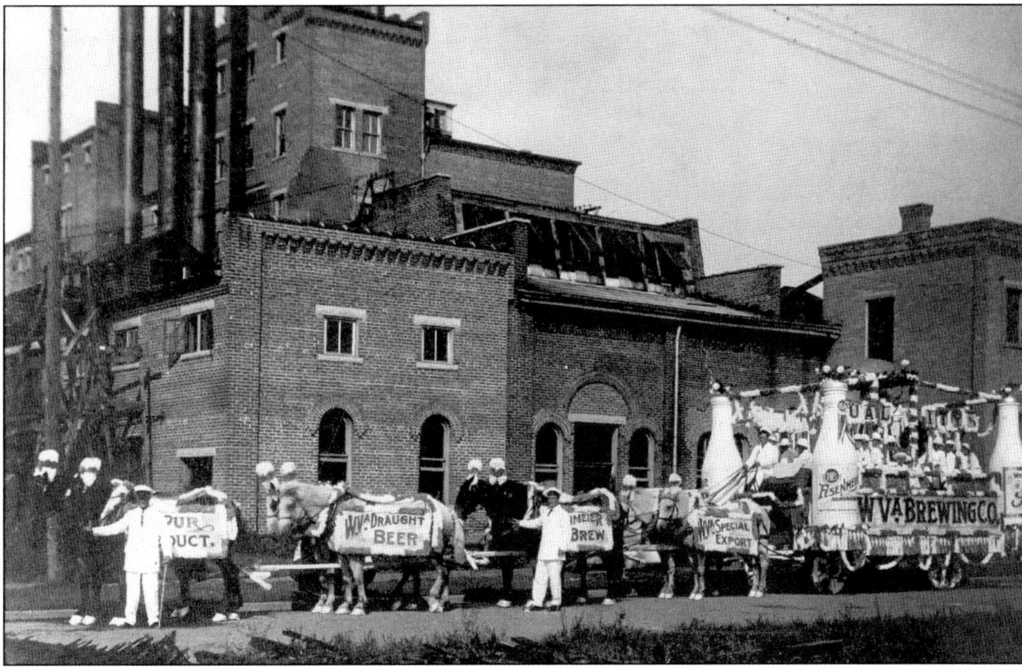

Another year brings another parade. It does appear that the street was paved here. Most streets were brick. There are several different brands of brick, and brand names are stamped into the bricks' faces, many from the Central Brick Company at Tenth Street West from 1901 to 1917.

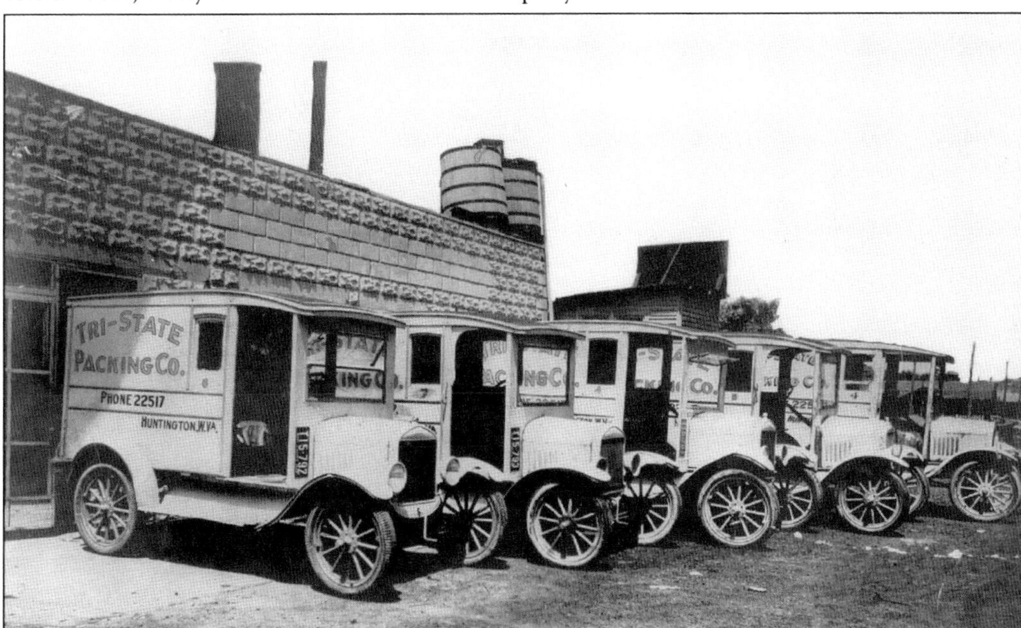

The 1913 flood caused a lot of damage to the plant. The West Virginia State Prohibition Amendment became effective in 1914. The brewery closed. Employees scattered as their livelihoods were taken away. In 1916, the brewery was remodeled into a meat packing plant, the Tri-State Packing Company. Many brewery employees were hired back and became skilled meat cutters and butchers.

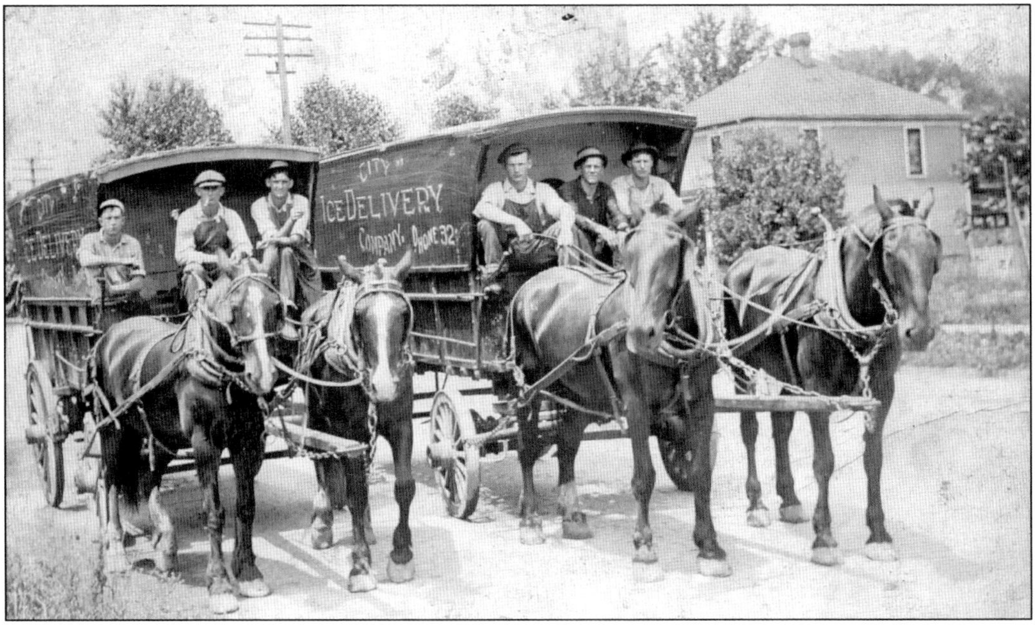

Throughout the years, the brewery had an ice plant, not only during Prohibition. The City Ice Delivery was one of the home delivery companies that took blocks of ice directly into the homes for iceboxes. Different sizes of ice blocks could be purchased, depending on the size of the icebox or the needs of the family for the week. A cardboard sign was hung on the porch with the size of ice block needed.

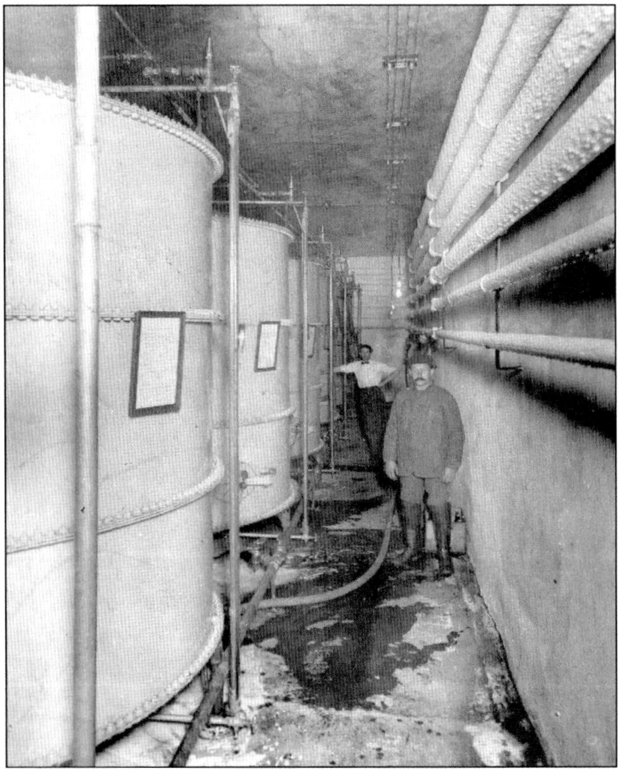

Storage tanks are very important vessels in the making of brew. Extreme care is taken in cleanliness, temperature, and pressure. The price of beer had been 15¢ in 1914. In 1934, it was down to 10¢. On May 5, 1934, Prohibition was repealed. The Fesenmeiers had held on to their business and were now ready to move forward. In the spring, they had already installed $300,000 worth of modern equipment. A million bottles (17 railroad cars) and 30,000 beer crates had been bought.

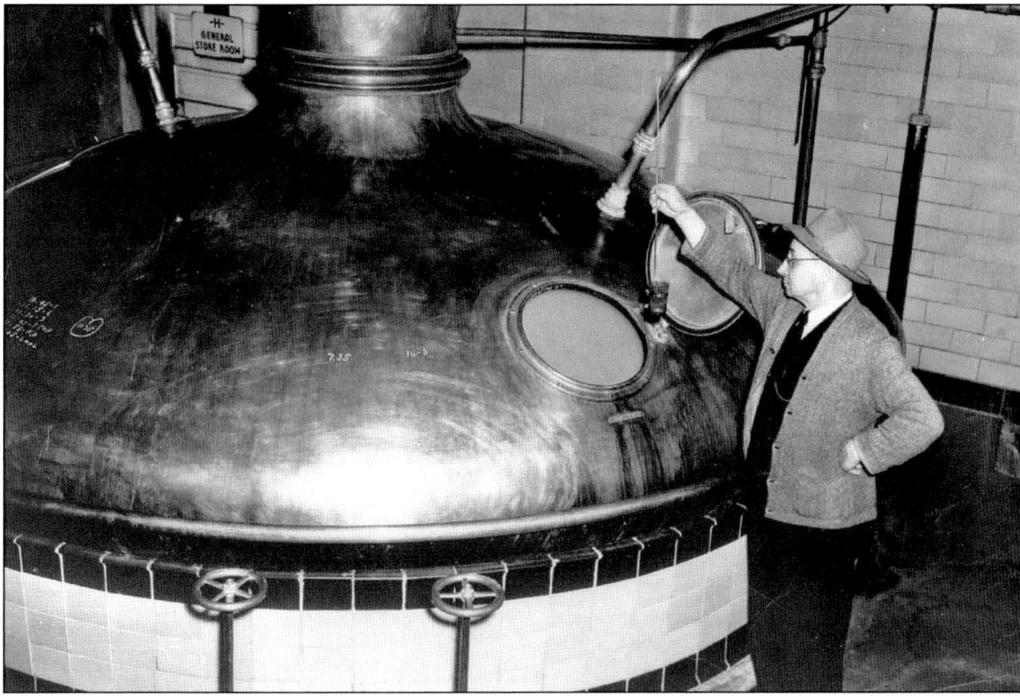

On the first day of distribution, the Fesenmeiers had a quarter of a million gallons of beer ready. At this time, the name was changed from the West Virginia Brewery to Fesenmeier Brewery. Stainless steel storage tanks were used in later years. In 1949, the Fesenmeiers celebrated their 50th anniversary with a giant fireworks display. The business also peaked that year with the sale of 60,000 barrels of beer.

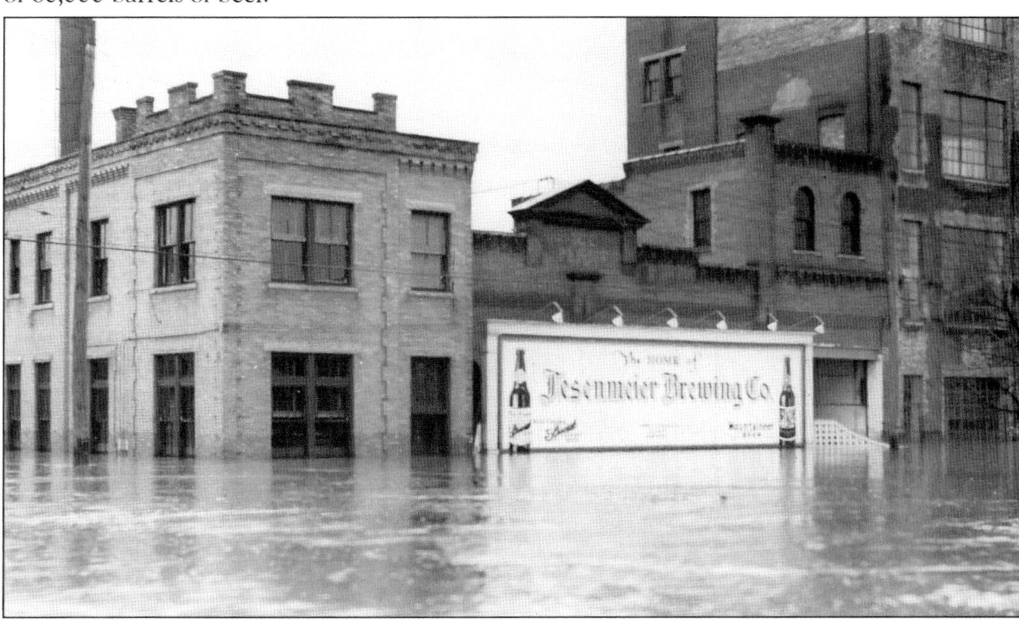

The floods in Central City were always devastating. The 1937 flood was the most damaging natural disaster to the brewery. It was after this terrible destruction to the Ohio River Valley that a floodwall was built around Huntington.

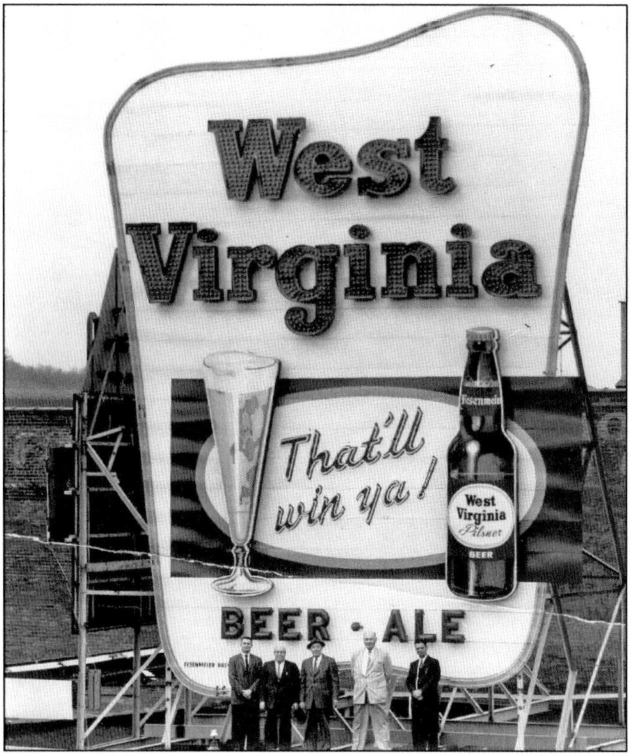

Over the years, many different brands of beer were introduced. In 1939, West Virginia Special Sparkling Ale was made to appeal to the English-type drinker. In 1941, a lighter beer was demanded; consequently Fesenmeier introduced West Virginia Pilsner Beer. There were many demands made on the use of raw materials during World War II. The brewery willingly accepted these restrictions but looked forward to normal operations to resume after the war.

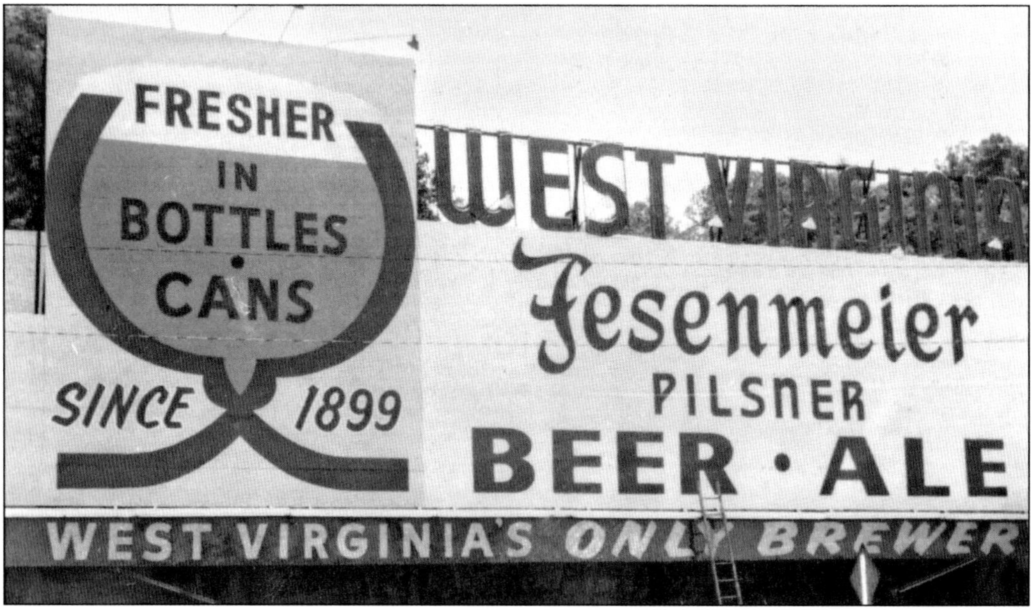

The heart of the brewery was the mixing of the ingredients. Brewing malt and hops gave the beer its bittering, flavoring, and aroma-enhancing powers. Brewer's yeast converted the fermentable sugars into alcohol. The final ingredient was the mineral content of the water, which was most important. John B. Napier reminisces in an article from the *Herald-Dispatch*, "The scent from the malt and hops . . . could be smelled from city blocks away." Meticulous containers gave the product its final home. Early bottling was difficult because of strict sanitary rules.

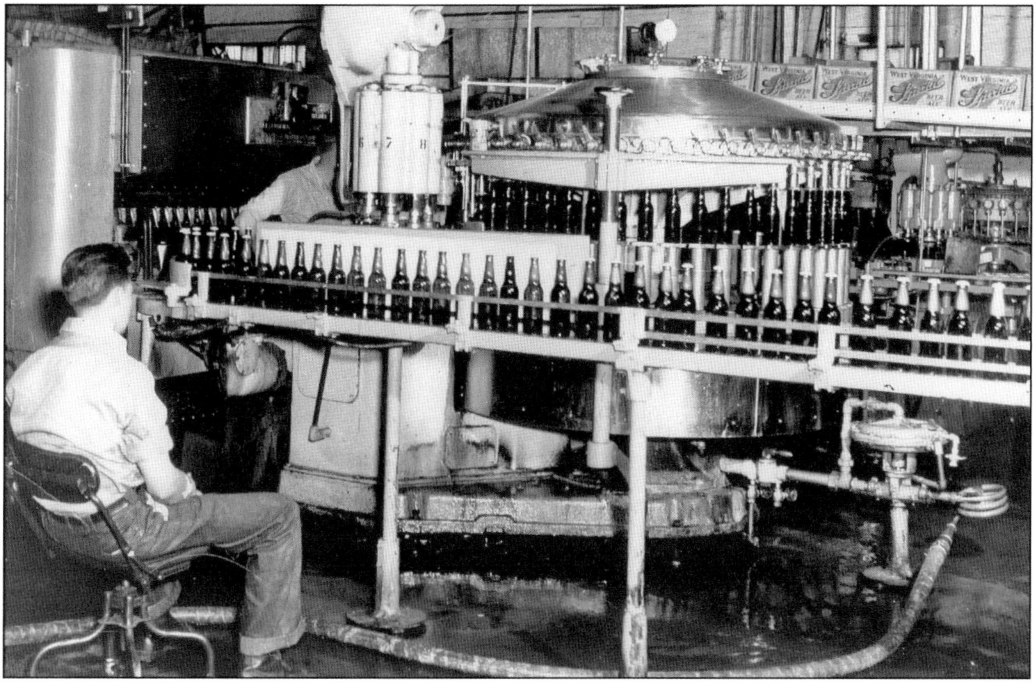

An addition was made to the bottling house after the war. Modern machinery was added for sterilizing and bottling under the most sanitary conditions at a cost of about $150,000. This more than doubled the capacity of the bottling department.

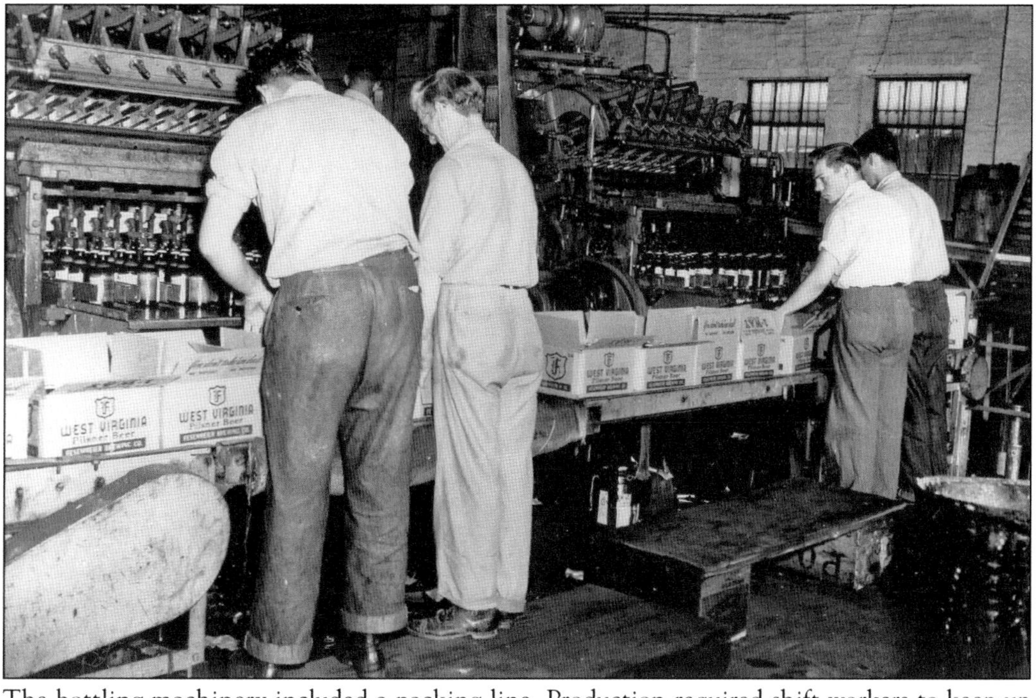

The bottling machinery included a packing line. Production required shift workers to keep up with the demand. The area of distribution had grown, so the need for more trucks and rail shipments increased.

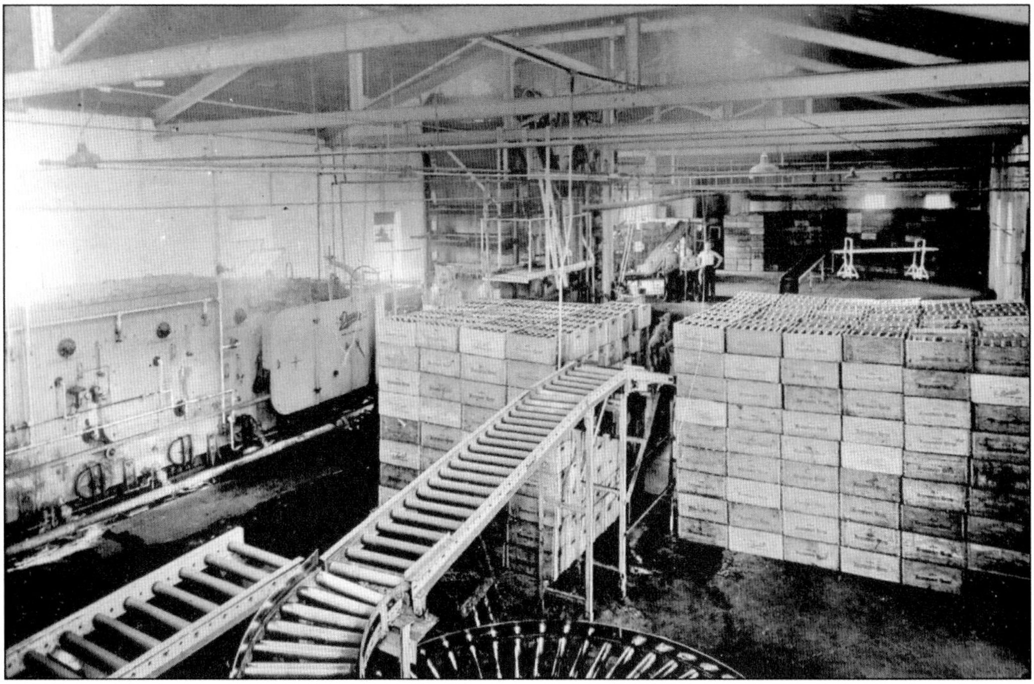

Storage was at a premium. Little space was available at the plant, so warehouses were situated in several places over the city. The production line came to the loading dock where very little product was left.

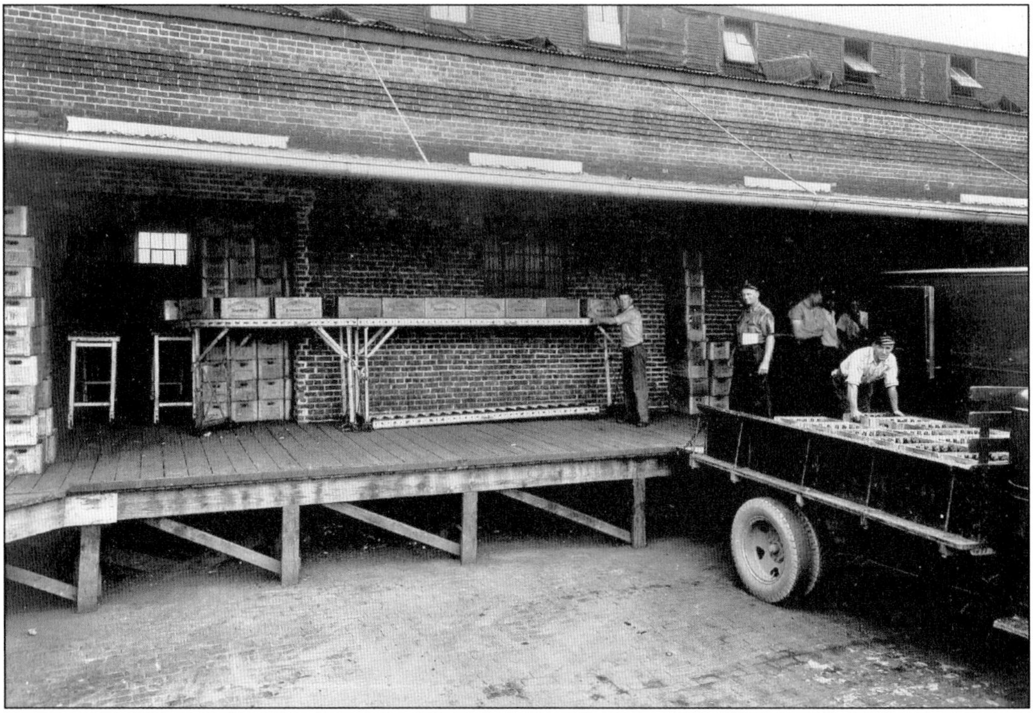

The production line led to the back of the building near Fifteenth Street West. Here cases of beer could be loaded on the trucks or railcars for further distribution.

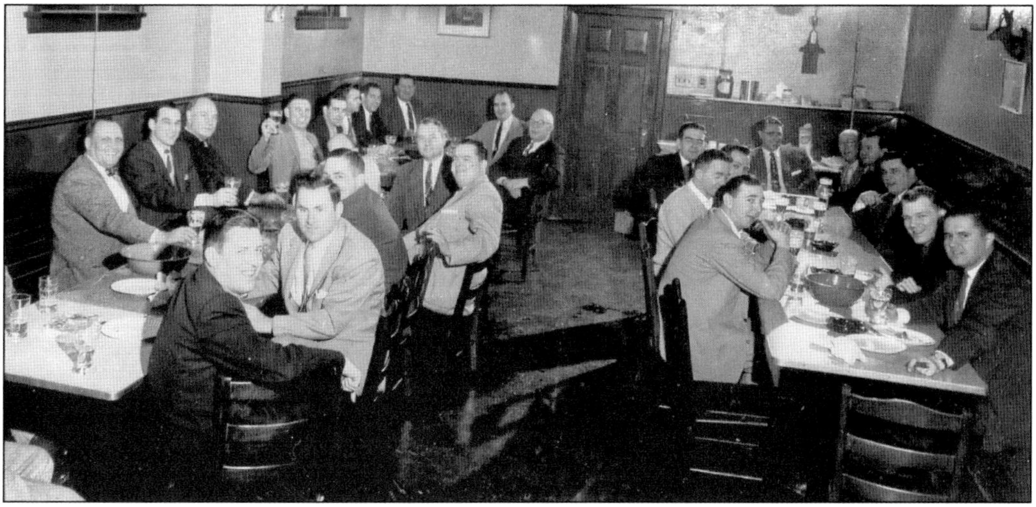

One of the renovations of the brewery included a hospitality room. Here the community, guests, and brewery workers could meet and sample the product of the day. Clarence Meisel was a young boy who lived in the neighborhood. He tells that on Friday afternoon, he would take a growler, a granite bucket with a handle, to have it filled for his father. Some days he would be invited to meet his father there. His father would sit, talk, and drink a large stein of beer with his friends. Since Clarence was too young to drink, the brewmaster would give him a stein of foam so he could drink with the fellas.

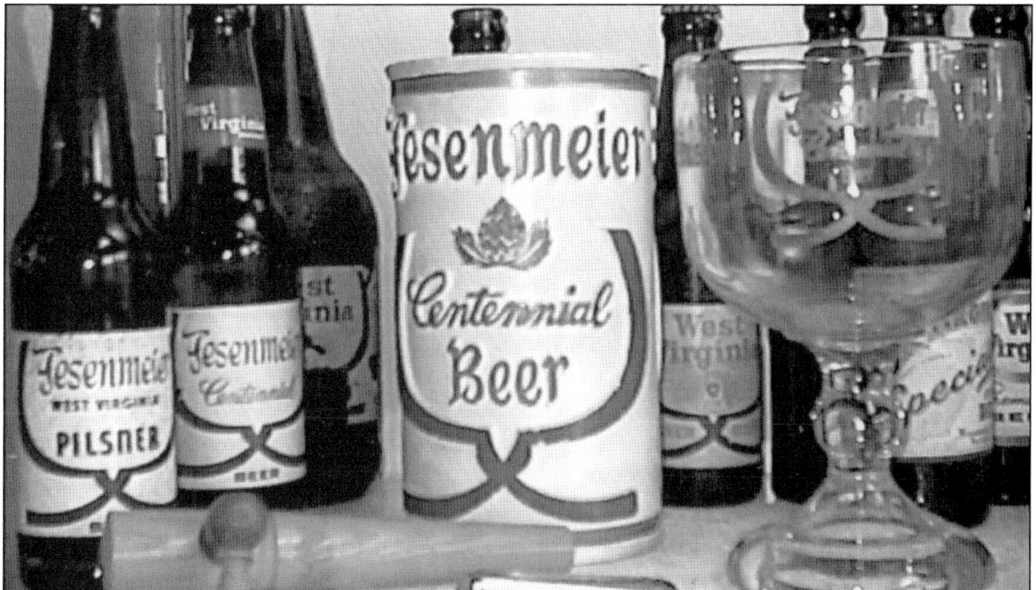

One of the most serious difficulties the brewery faced came in the 1950s when national beer companies began to swallow up the small breweries and their national advertising began taking away the local appeal. Production began to fall. West Virginia maintained 3.2 percent alcohol, while neighboring states offered full strength. Advertising became necessary but expensive. Over the years, many brands and advertising gimmicks were used. The examples above were exhibited at the West Huntington Public Library. The wooden spigot in the picture was called a spile and was used in the barrel to dispense the liquid.

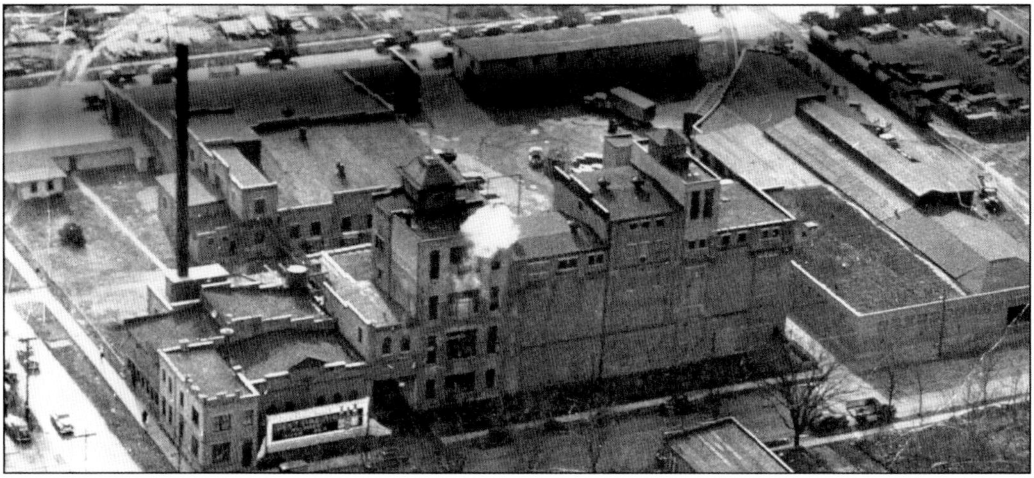

All of the original Fesenmeier family had died by the early 1960s. The fourth generation, now in control, was not as interested in being involved with the business and competing with the new challenges. Pressure finally ended the family era in 1968. The business was sold to Robert Holley and the name was changed to Little Switzerland.

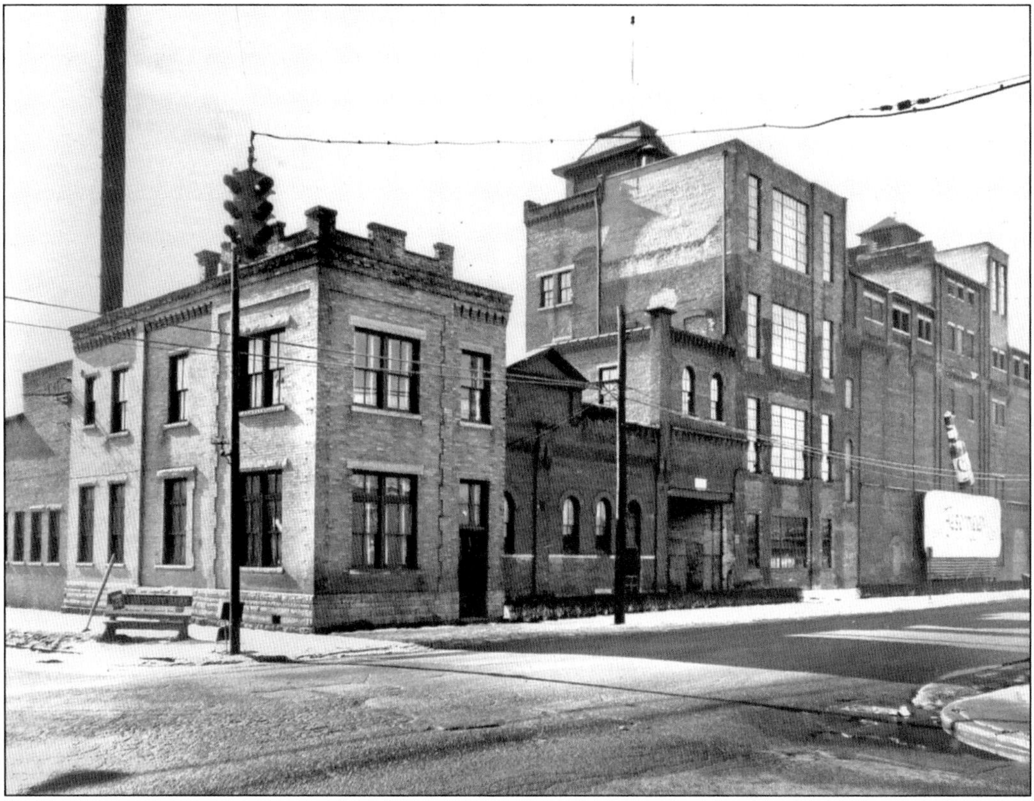

The Swiss element failed to attract tourists and new business. It was again sold at public auction for delinquent debts to a Columbus brewer who liquidated the business and closed its doors in July 1971. In 1972, the brewery was demolished to make way for a small shopping plaza.

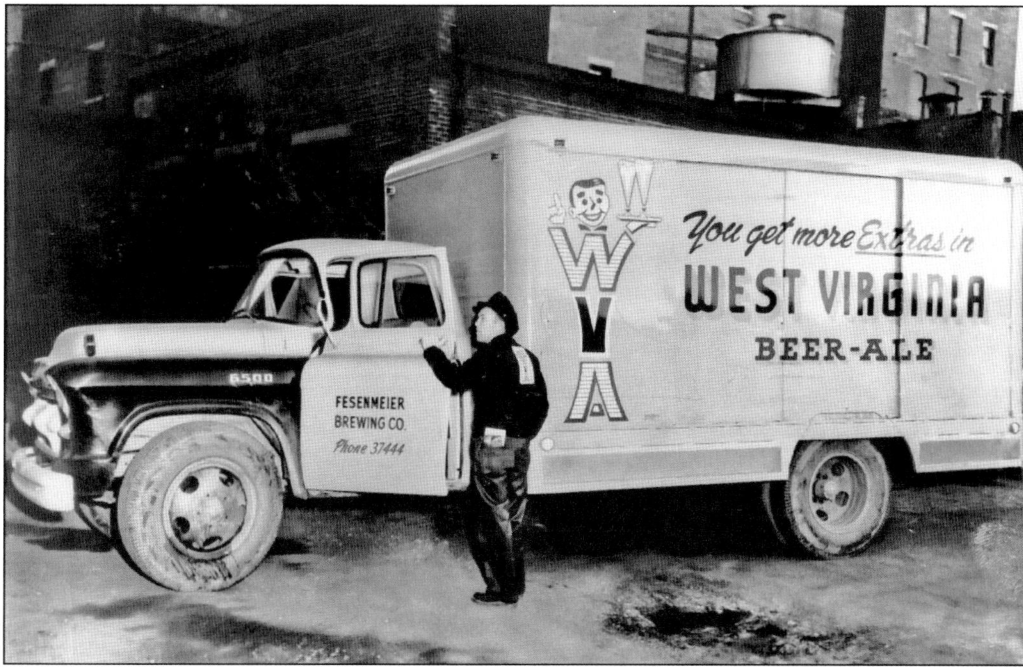

On West Virginia Day, June 20, 1994, a limited edition of a 1952 Fesenmeier Beer Truck was unveiled at the West Virginia State Capitol in Charleston and at the West Huntington Public Library in Huntington. The truck pictured above is not the exact one but one similar. There were only 1,250 made, and they were sold to collectors very quickly.

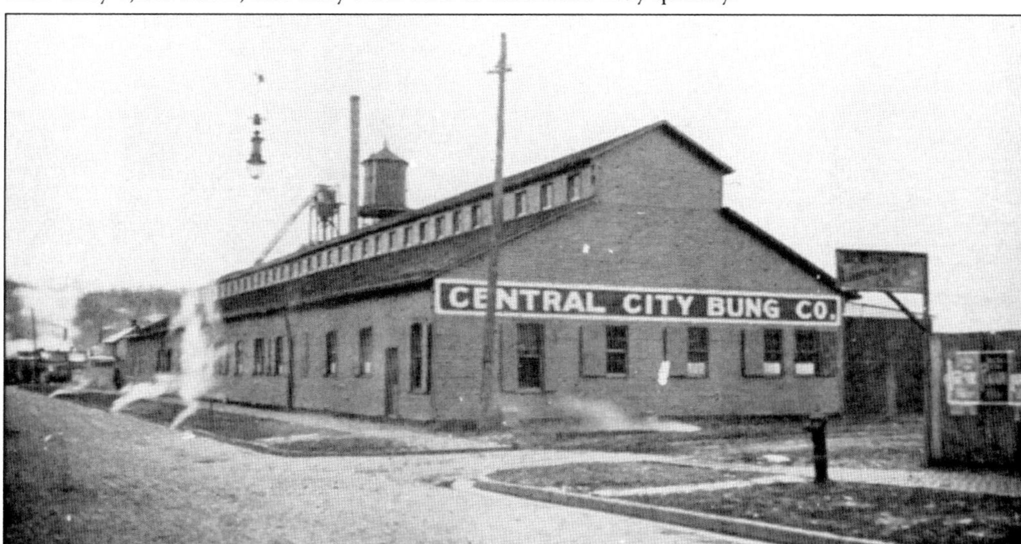

A small piece of Appalachian poplar hardwood, shaped like a cork, was used to plug the holes in whiskey and beer barrels. It was called a bung. Poplar was used because it was porous and let the liquid inside breathe. This factory, the Central City Bung Company, came to Central City after the original factory burned in Wirt County, West Virginia. When offered a whole city block by the Huntington and Kenova Land Company, John Hale accepted in 1894. Its worldwide market made it very successful. Because of the uniqueness of the product, Central City was called the bung capital of the world.

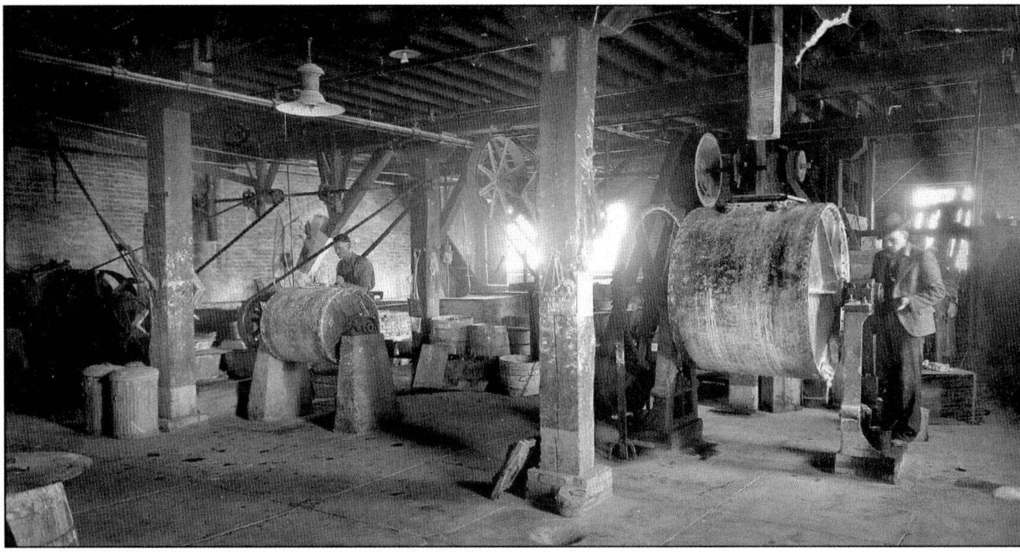

The bungs were squeezed after the block of wood was put through a stationary cutting knife. Then they were sanded by putting them in large barrels that contained an aggregate and turned until they were smooth. The plant was very secretive and limited the people allowed inside. No one with any mechanical or engineering knowledge was permitted to visit. A rumor is told that the factory made something secretive for World War I, hence the reason for 24-hour guards and bars on the windows. Most of the bungs were exported to Germany, Australia, Japan, and China. Supposedly the only other bung factory in the country was in Cincinnati, and the Cincinnati company took the business over after Prohibition. The Central City factory was closed in 1918.

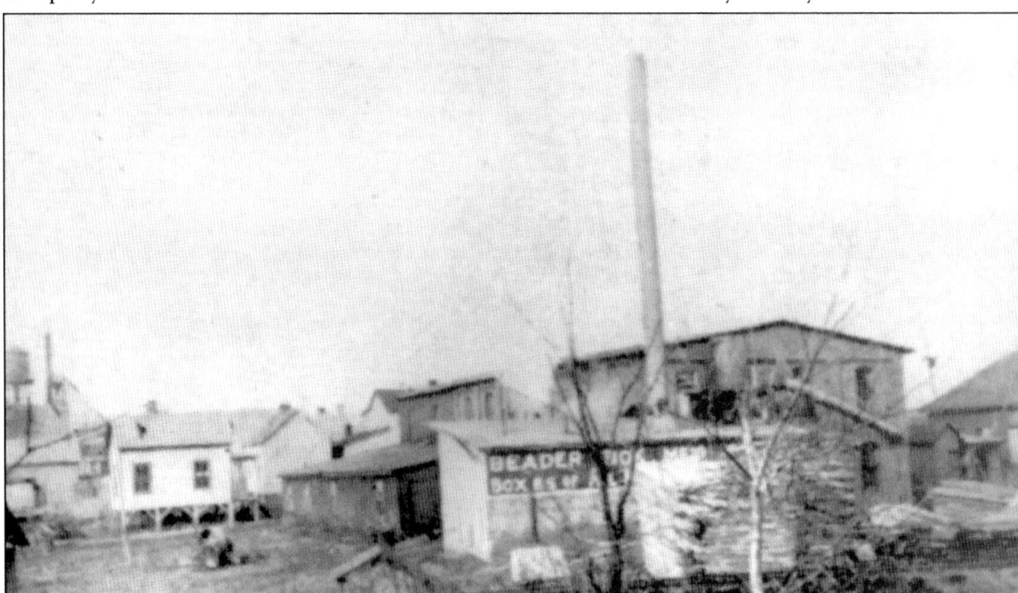

While five main industries, mentioned in the introduction, were the hub of the new town, two family businesses were founded in the 1890s and continue today. The first is the Duncan Box and Lumber Company, started as the Beader Box Company in 1895 by M. L. Duncan and his brother-in-law, J. W. Graham. They employed four persons.

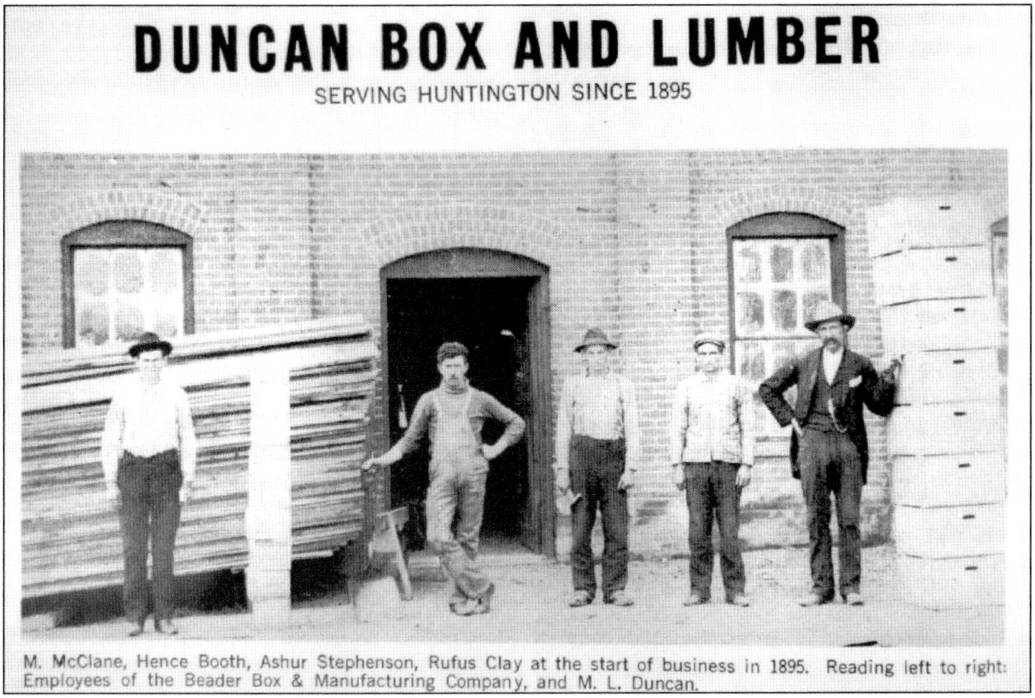

In 1917, the name was changed to Duncan Box and Lumber Company. It is said that Mr. Duncan had an unfaltering faith in the future of Central City, West Virginia, and America. The company's main efforts were building boxes for military needs beginning with the Spanish-American War in 1898.

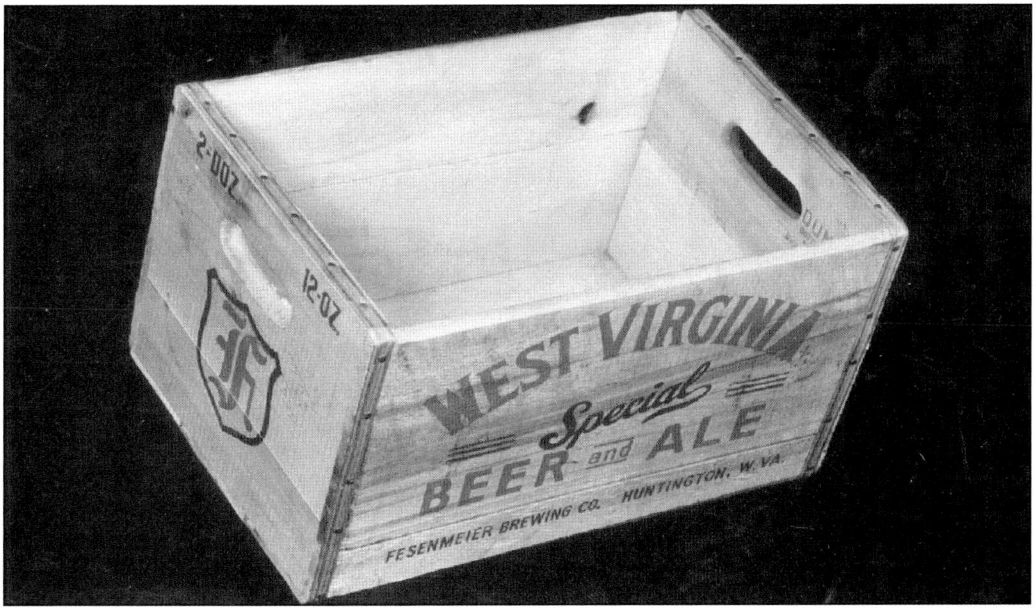

World War I and World War II also saw Duncan boxes shipped to every battlefront in the world with every kind of military needs. Beer boxes were made for the Fesenmeier Brewery, located just two blocks from the lumber company. Later they made crates for soft drinks and a variety of other boxes.

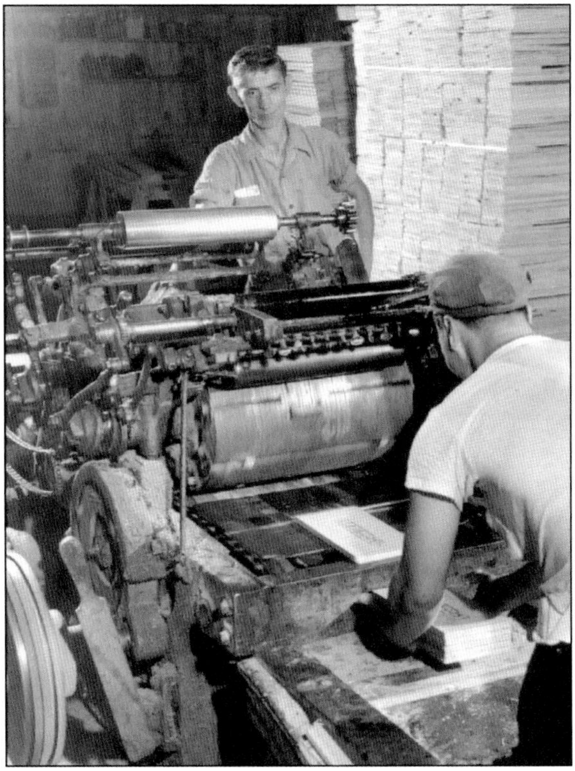

Because of the variety of boxes made, a stamping machine was used to print a label on the different boxes contracted. One of the big sellers was a Collapso Coop. This device, which can be collapsed when not in use, was used for penning poultry. It was patented in the name of H. A. Duncan just before 1929.

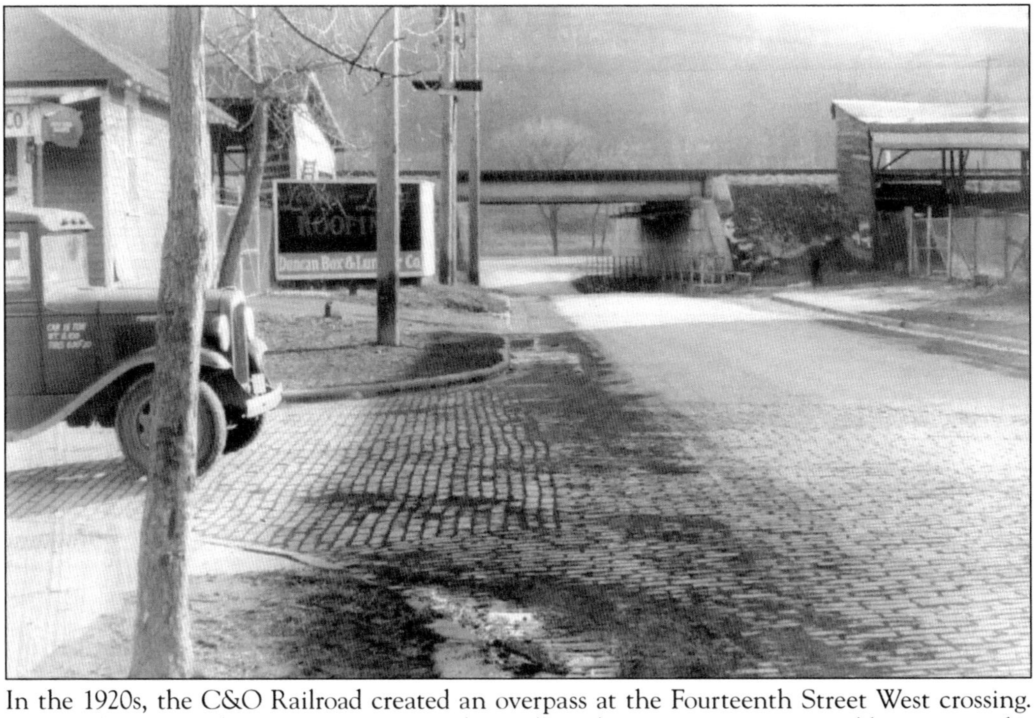

In the 1920s, the C&O Railroad created an overpass at the Fourteenth Street West crossing. The track was raised. Duncan spent several months in litigation to secure suitable access to the track because the siding had been divided when the viaduct was created.

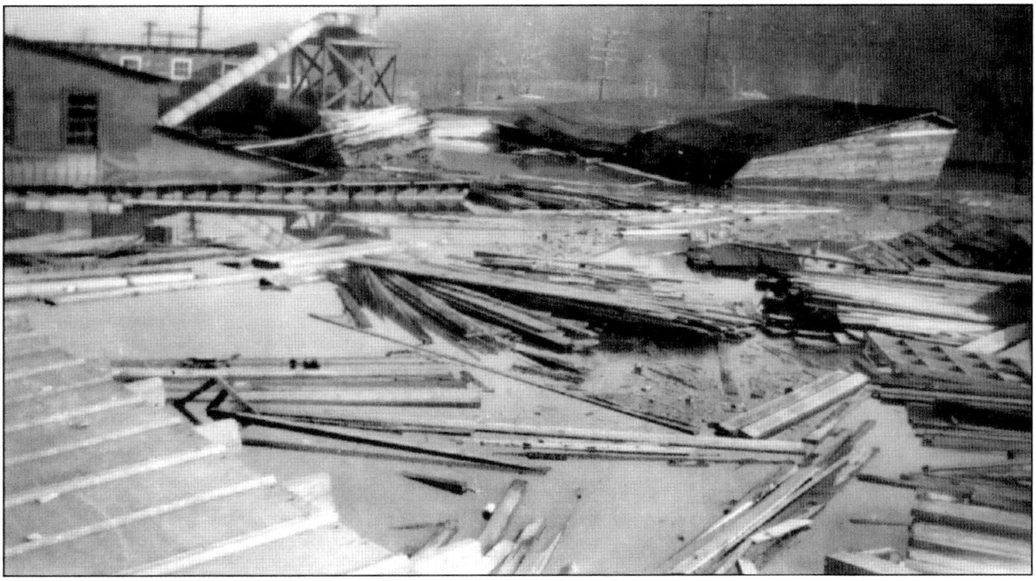

As with all the other businesses in 1937, the flood wreaked havoc with Duncan Lumber. In the above pictures, floating lumber from the stacks in the storage sheds is visible.

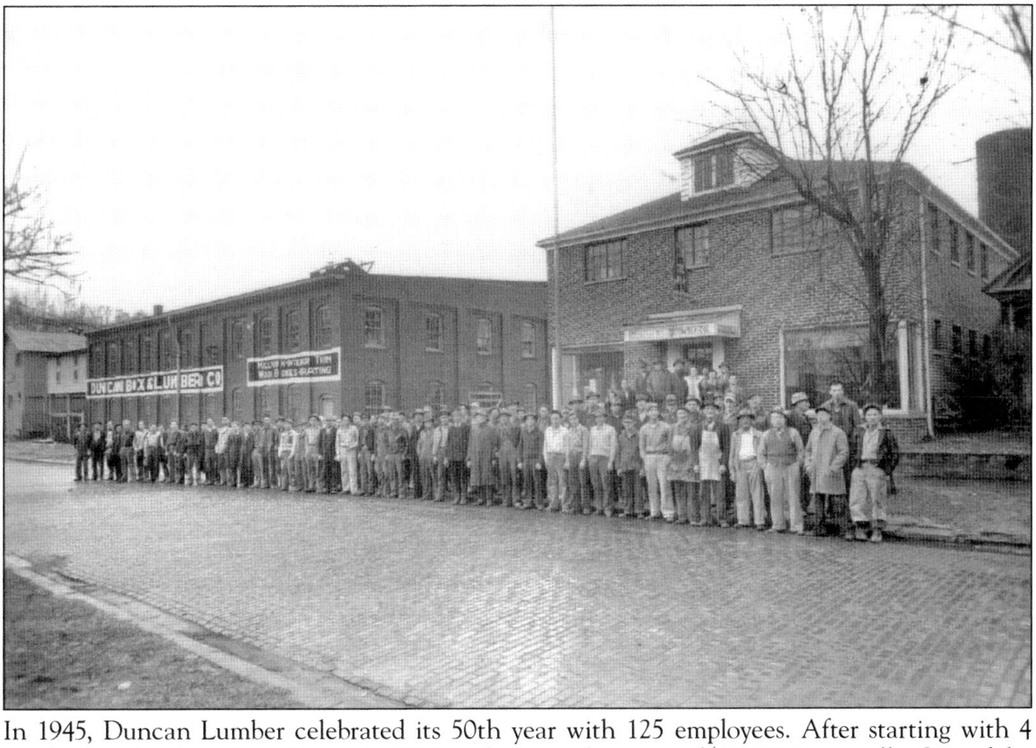

In 1945, Duncan Lumber celebrated its 50th year with 125 employees. After starting with 4 employees, the plant had 25 men in 1929 with a gross business of $150,000 annually. One of the employees, Carl Gibson, who joined Duncan in 1945, is still an employee in 2005.

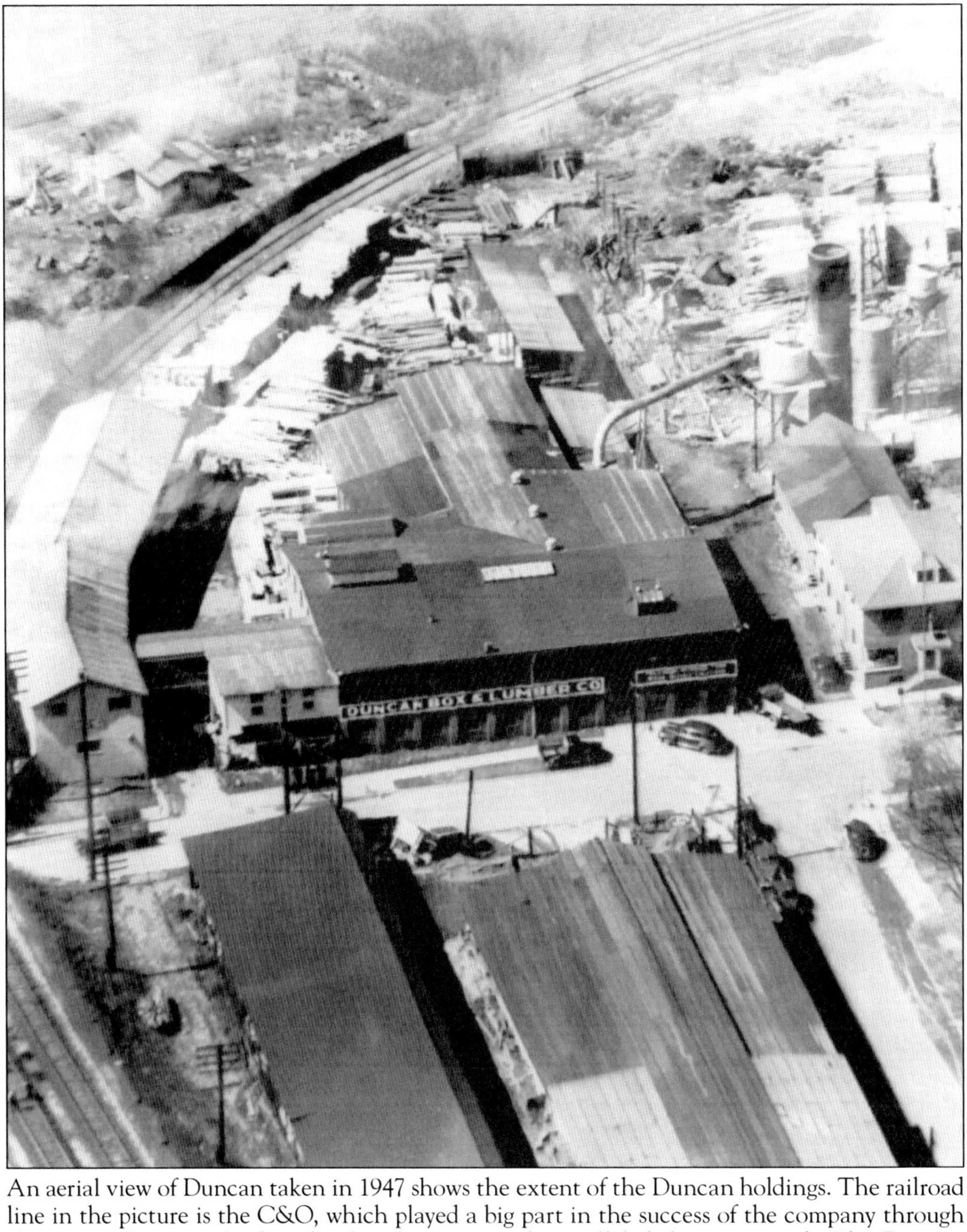

An aerial view of Duncan taken in 1947 shows the extent of the Duncan holdings. The railroad line in the picture is the C&O, which played a big part in the success of the company through the years. The special siding for the plant's use only paralleled the main track. The Duncan family still runs the business. Although the size has diminished over the years, the company is held in high regard for its 100 years of community involvement.

The second family-owned business that needs to be mentioned because of its longevity is Heiner's Bakery. The company was begun in 1904 by Charles W. Heiner in the kitchen behind a stove company at 1321 Washington Avenue. The family lived in an apartment on the second floor. Heiner took skills he had learned as a baker apprentice, and with courage to make it on his own, he opened his own bakery. Katie Heiner, Charles's wife, helped in the kitchen, and a business was born. Shown here with an unidentified woman (left) is Charles W. Heiner and his wife, Katie, at an airport at Virginia Beach, Virginia.

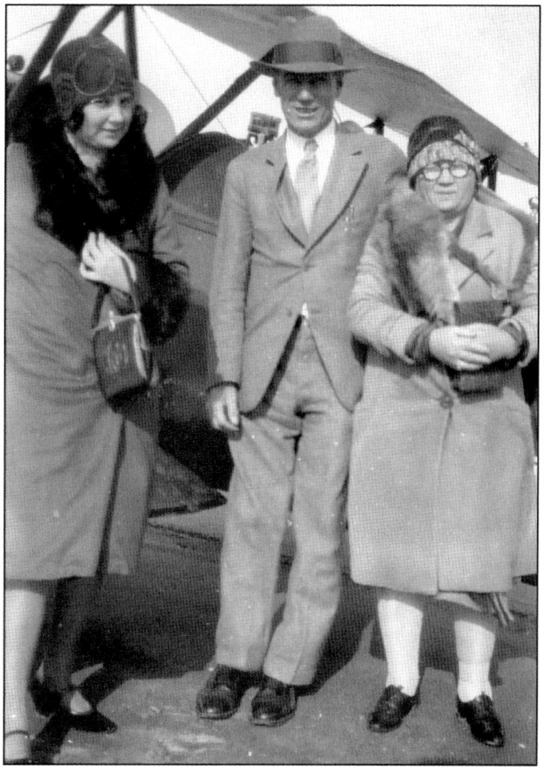

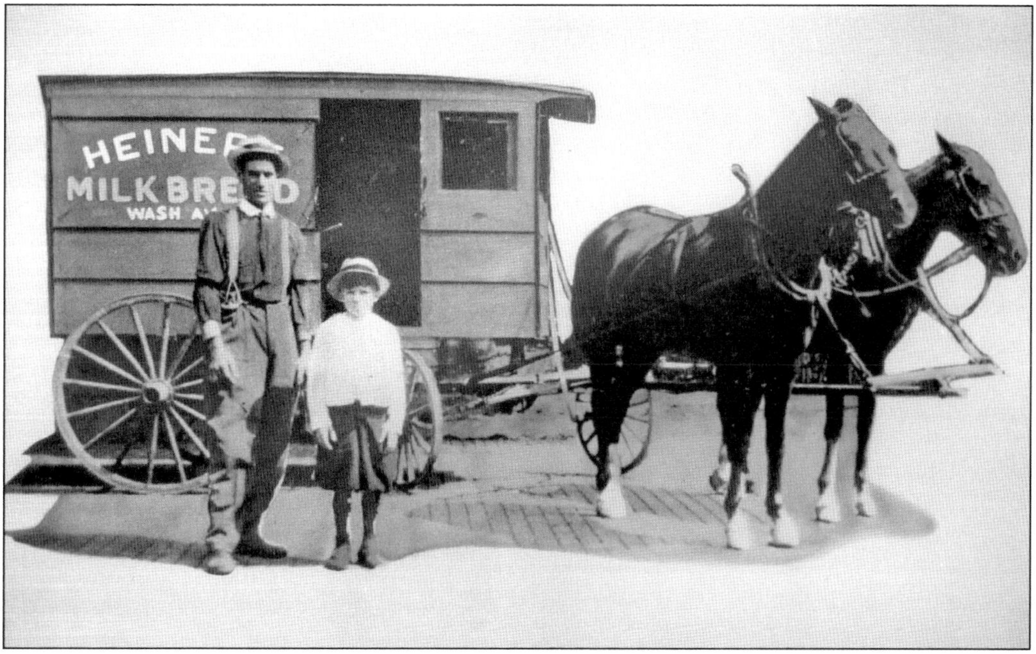

Probably the most famous picture of the Heiner's business is this one of Charles and his son. Earl Sr., c. 1912. After a very early morning of baking, Mr. Heiner would load up the wagon and begin daily deliveries. Since most ladies baked their own bread at this time, the idea of the home delivery of someone else's bread was a big risk but was very innovative.

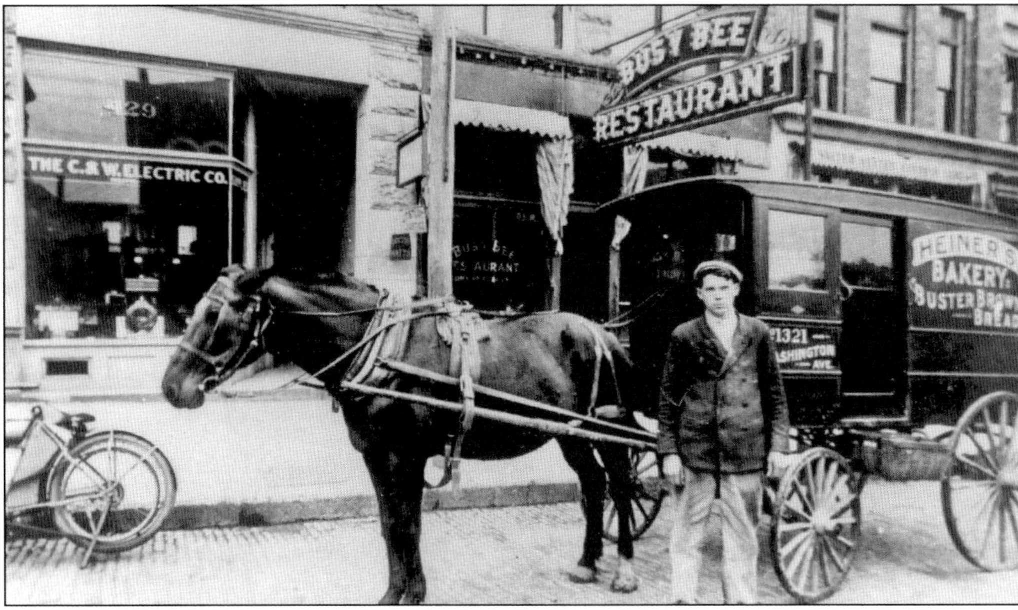

After a few years, the business was expanding. This employee was delivering bread to a restaurant in downtown Huntington. Notice the Buster Brown bread label on the delivery wagon. Heiner's had a philosophy that has remained through the generations: when you sell a loaf of bread for 5¢, make sure there is 5¢ worth of value in it.

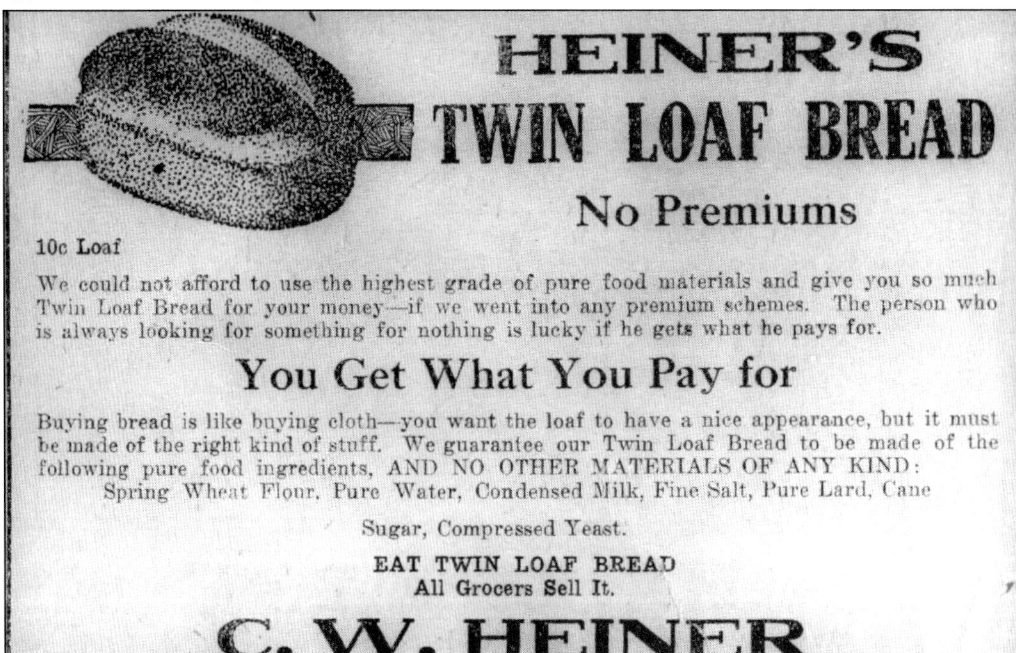

Advertising in any business is essential. This was one of the early newspaper advertisements that illustrates the Heiner's pledge of quality. The addition of pies was a time-intensive project. Earl Jr. tells, in an interview in the *Huntington Quarterly Magazine*, that his father, Earl Sr., would get up very early and prepare the fruit before he went to school. After school, Earl Jr. would come home and make the pies.

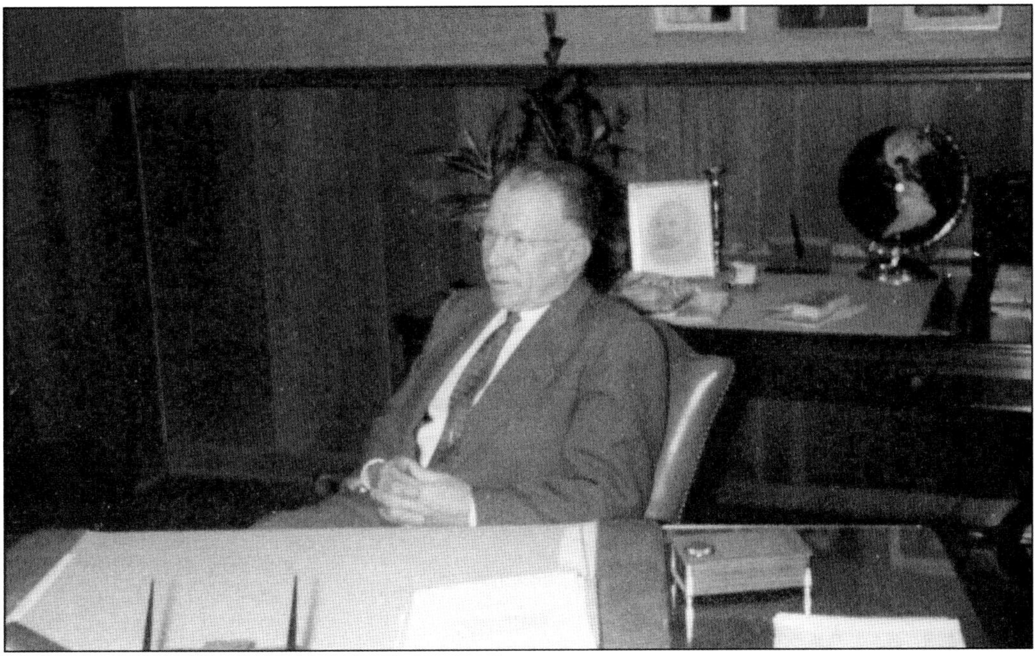

Earl Heiner Sr. brought the business to new heights. From 200 pounds of bread a day in 1905, the company produced 12,000 pounds in 1930 and 50,000–60,000 pounds in 1991. Earl Sr. turned most of the business over to his son, Earl Jr., in the late 1980s. The picture above was taken in 1957.

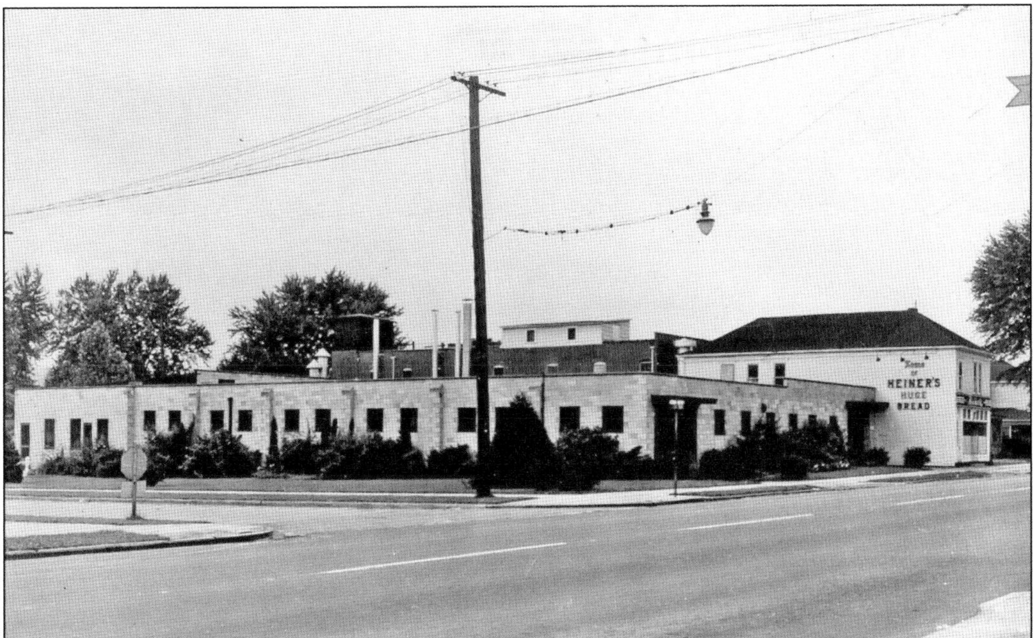

An addition was built to Heiner's in 1943. The plant now surrounded the original building where it all started. The plant had been inhibited through the years because of a city alley that ran through the property. By 1976, with the cooperation of the city, Heiner acquired the alley so that a new loading dock could be constructed with 25,000 square feet.

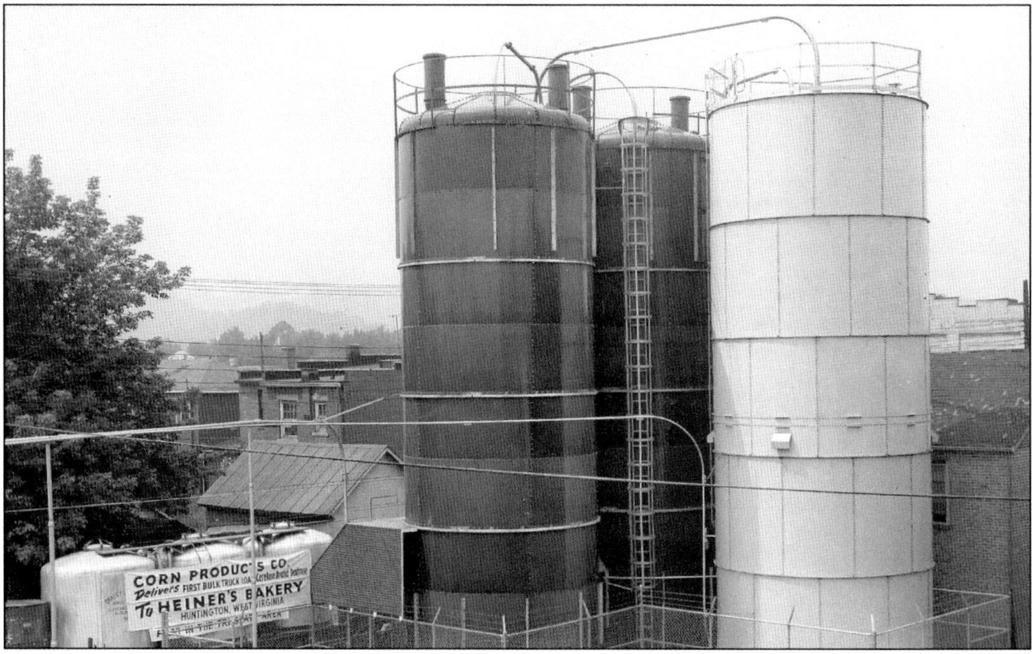

Storage tanks held much of the product between rail shipments. In the late 1980s, a pipeline was installed from the Fifteenth Street West railroad spur to the storage tanks. The products were blown through the pipeline to the tanks. When bakers can mix 1,600 pounds of dough in 14–17 minutes, 80 loaves can be baked in one minute.

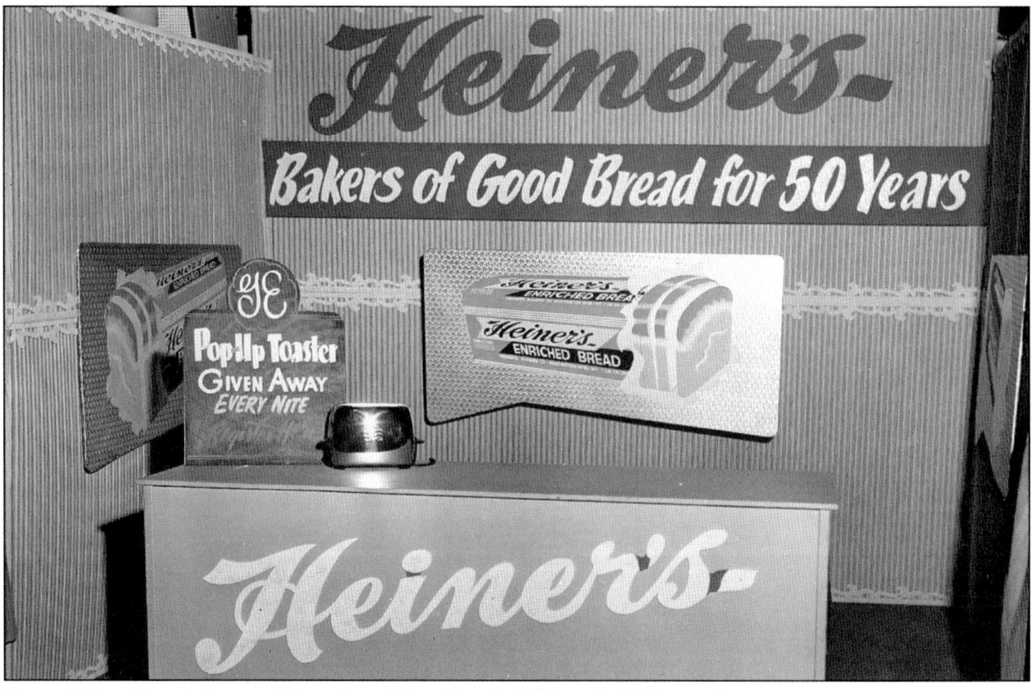

One of the gimmicks used for advertising for the Heiner's 50th anniversary was a pop-up toaster. One was given away each night during a period of time. Every housewife in Huntington was registering for this freebie because the pop-up toaster was the newest type of kitchen appliance.

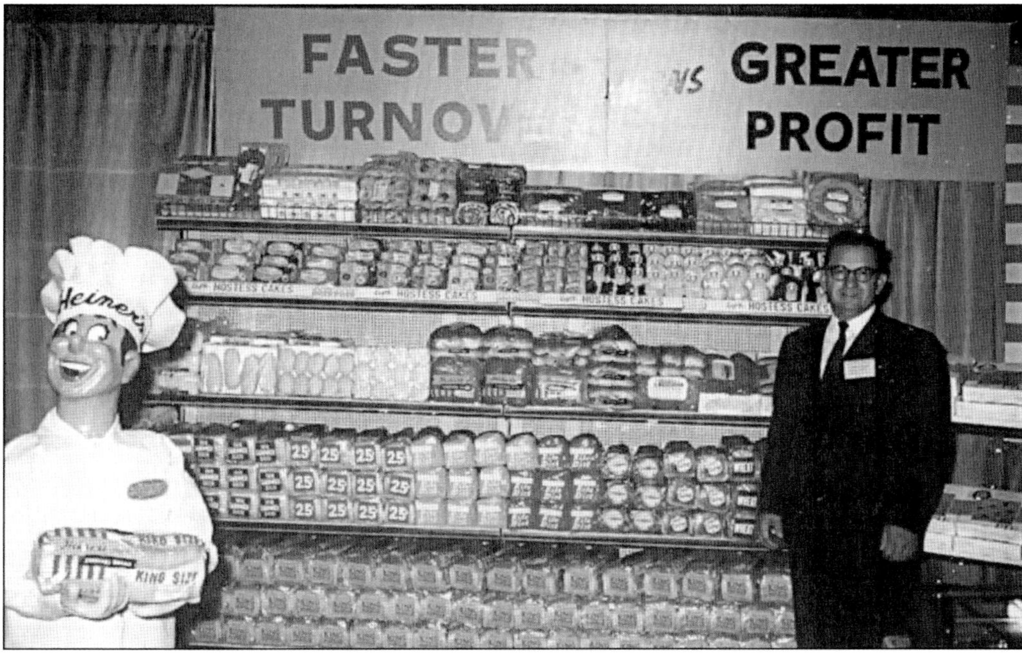

Many different names have been used for Heiner's products, like regular bread, sandwich, wheat and diet bread, pies, and buns. Keeping up with the times is one of the most popular types of bread today—the "35" loaf with the same enriched quality but only 35 calories. The employee above is Lawrence Wagner.

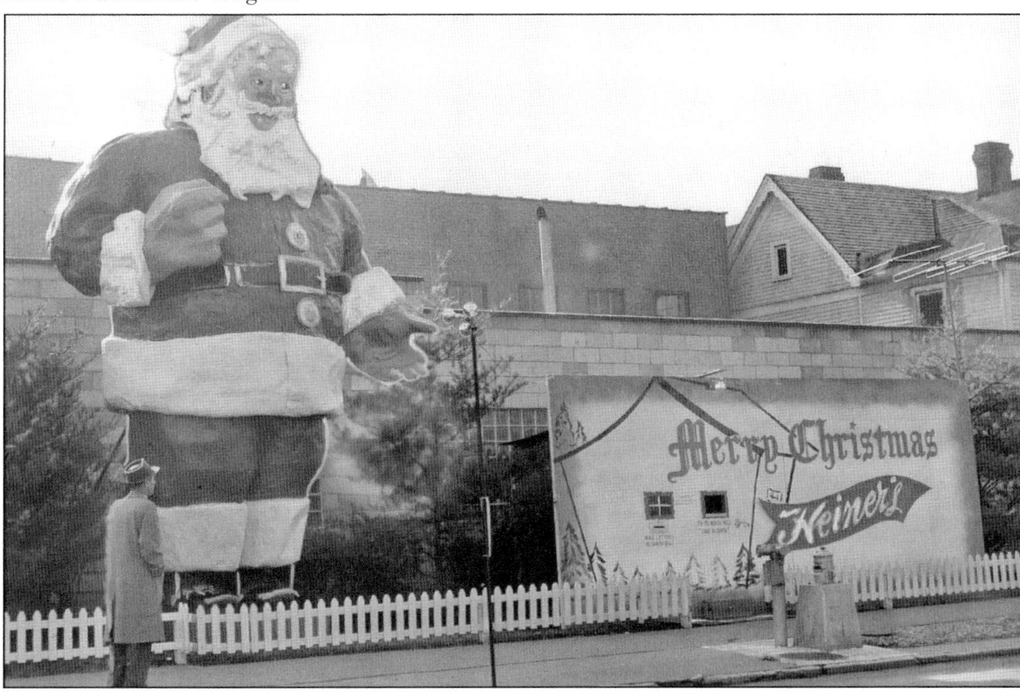

During the 1950s, one of the familiar scenes on Washington Avenue was Heiner's giant Santa. Heiner's has always been a family-oriented business. This symbol of Christmas was just one of the many community-minded things that Heiner's did.

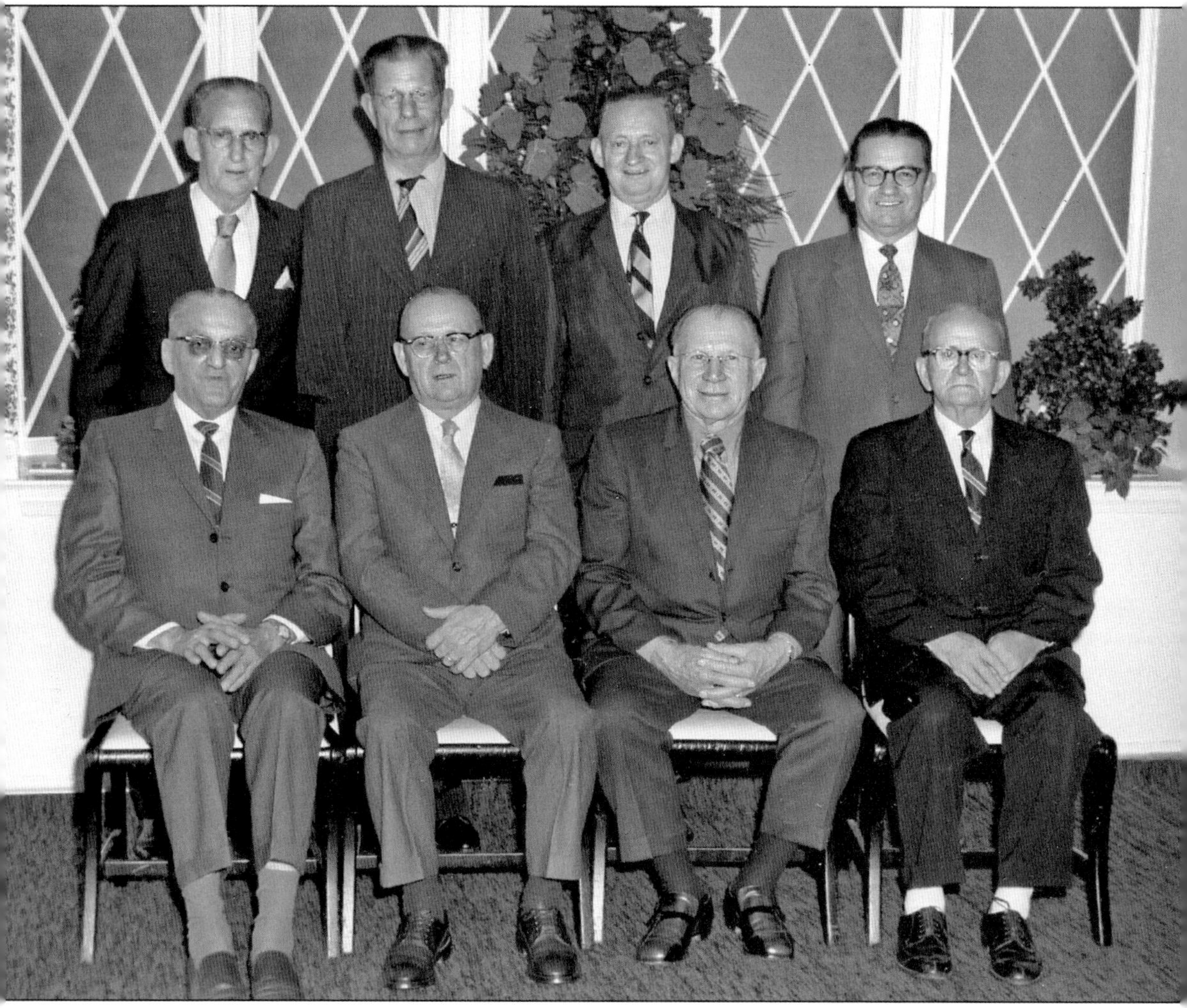

One of the most important factors in the Heiner's business was the company's relationship with their employees. Many employees were loyal enough to work there until their retirements. In 1976, 41 people had been with the company for 25 years. Another group of these employees was the Wagner brothers. The five brothers worked for the company for a total of 168 years. A dinner was held honoring some of these employees for their longevity. This picture includes three of the five brothers. From left to right are (front row) John Fleckenstein, Don Wagner, Earl Heiner Sr., and Mike Watts; (back row) Bill Hayton, Oscar Riggs, Ralph Wagner, and Lawrence Wagner.

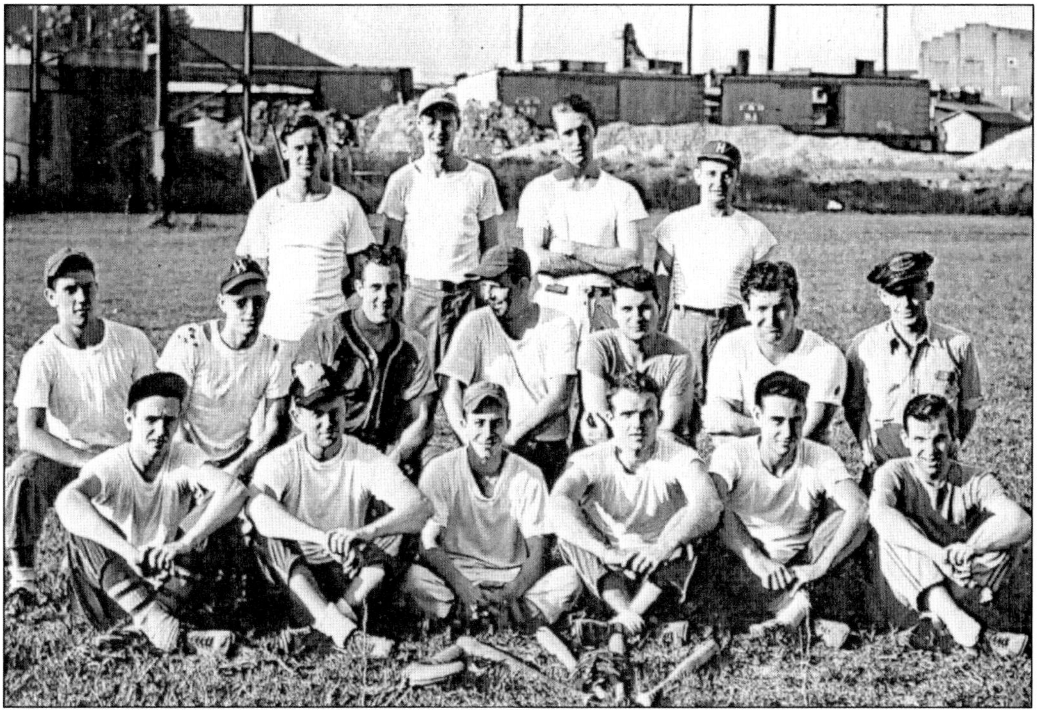

Heiner's also encouraged after-hour recreation and sponsored a baseball team. This team of employees is shown on a practice field, probably off Fourteenth Street West at Monroe Avenue.

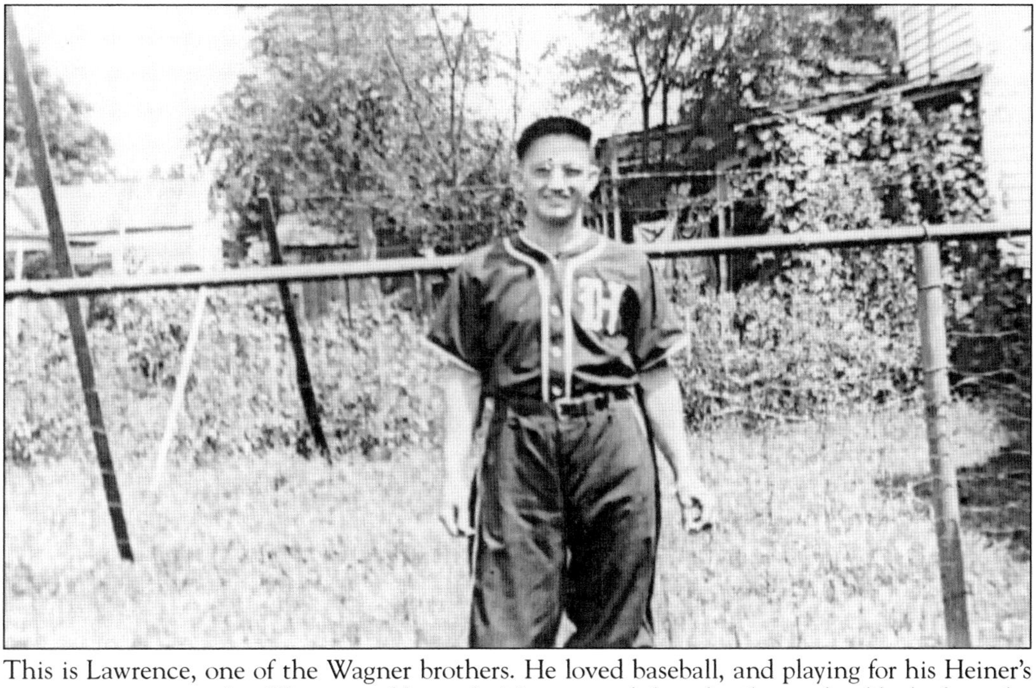

This is Lawrence, one of the Wagner brothers. He loved baseball, and playing for his Heiner's team was a great outlet. Wagner and his wife, Mina, raised their family just five blocks from the bakery, which was not an uncommon thing in Central City. Many people lived within walking distance of their employment.

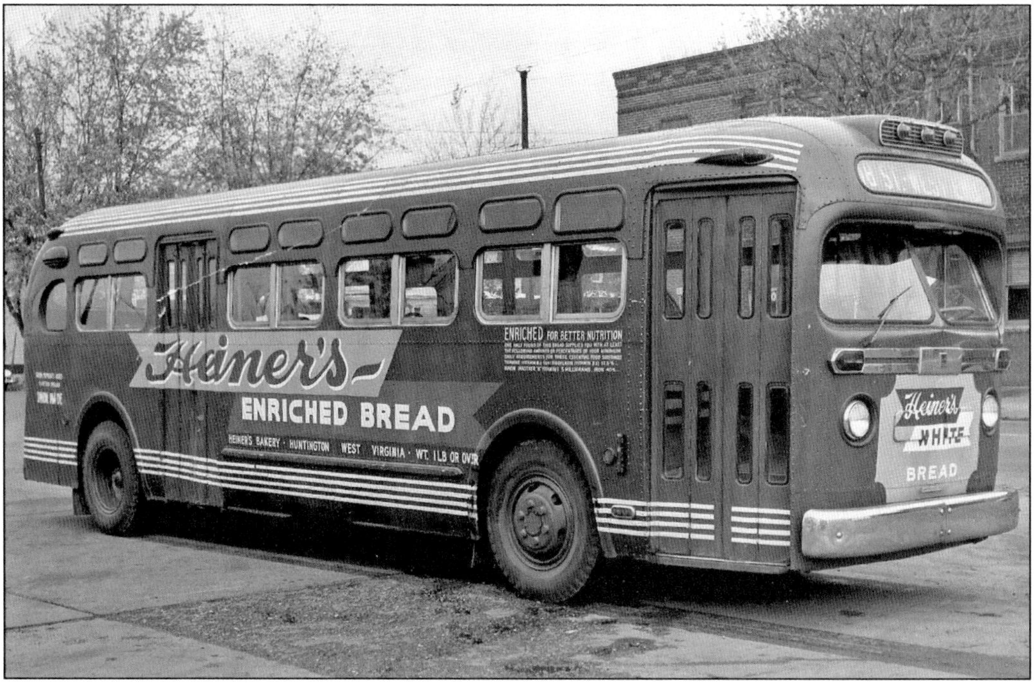

Heiner's advertising took a unique turn in the 1950s when they sponsored the painting of a bus with the Ohio Valley Bus Company. This type of advertising is seen often now on Huntington buses, now the Tri-State Transit Authority, but then it was an unusual step.

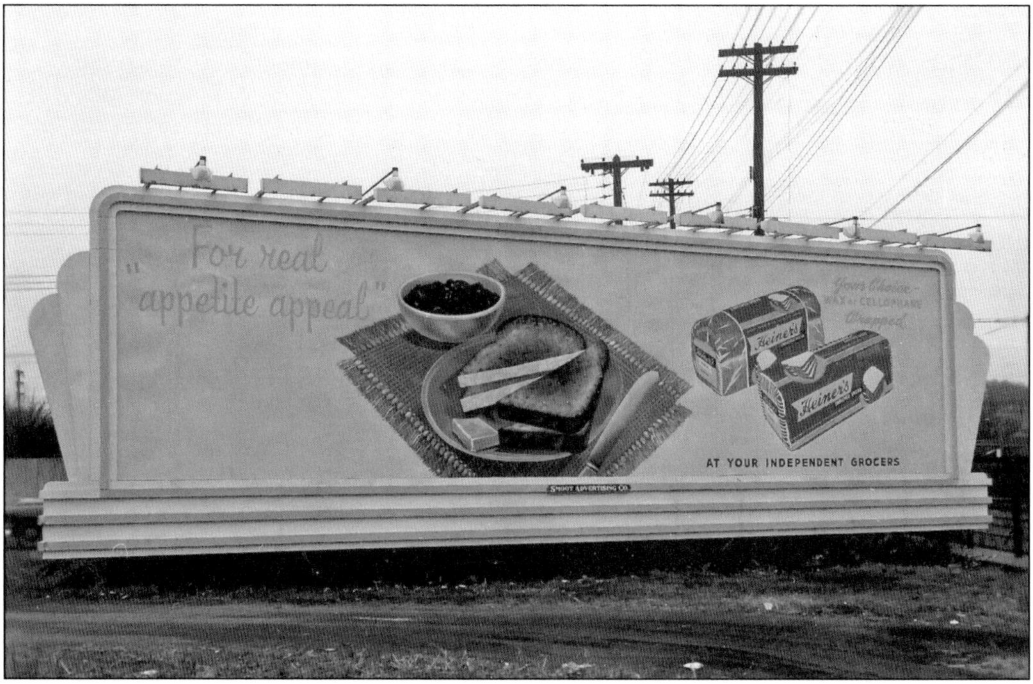

Billboards are always a popular form of advertising. Many of these have been done over the years, but this is one of the simplest, to the point, and easily read for someone passing by or stopped at a stoplight.

Three

EARLY BUSINESS

There were many small businesses that are typical for a busy little town at the turn of the century. Many would be called "Mom and Pop" businesses today. The business was a family affair. The children were as much a part of the day-to-day chores as the adults. Everyone had a duty, and all were expected to fulfill their obligation so that it all ran smoothly. The boys of the family often ran the errands and delivered goods. The girls might take care of younger children while Mom waited on customers or cooked and baked. Even if the family had a small store, Dad might be working at a local factory on shift work.

Central City was a good example of this type of community. Every block had a business of some sort, whether it was a grocery or a boarding house. Boarding houses allowed widows and older couples to rent extra rooms in order to make a living. A growing town also meant a government was needed to lead and protect its citizens. This chapter deals with the variety of enterprises it took to serve the whole community of Central City and eventually West Huntington.

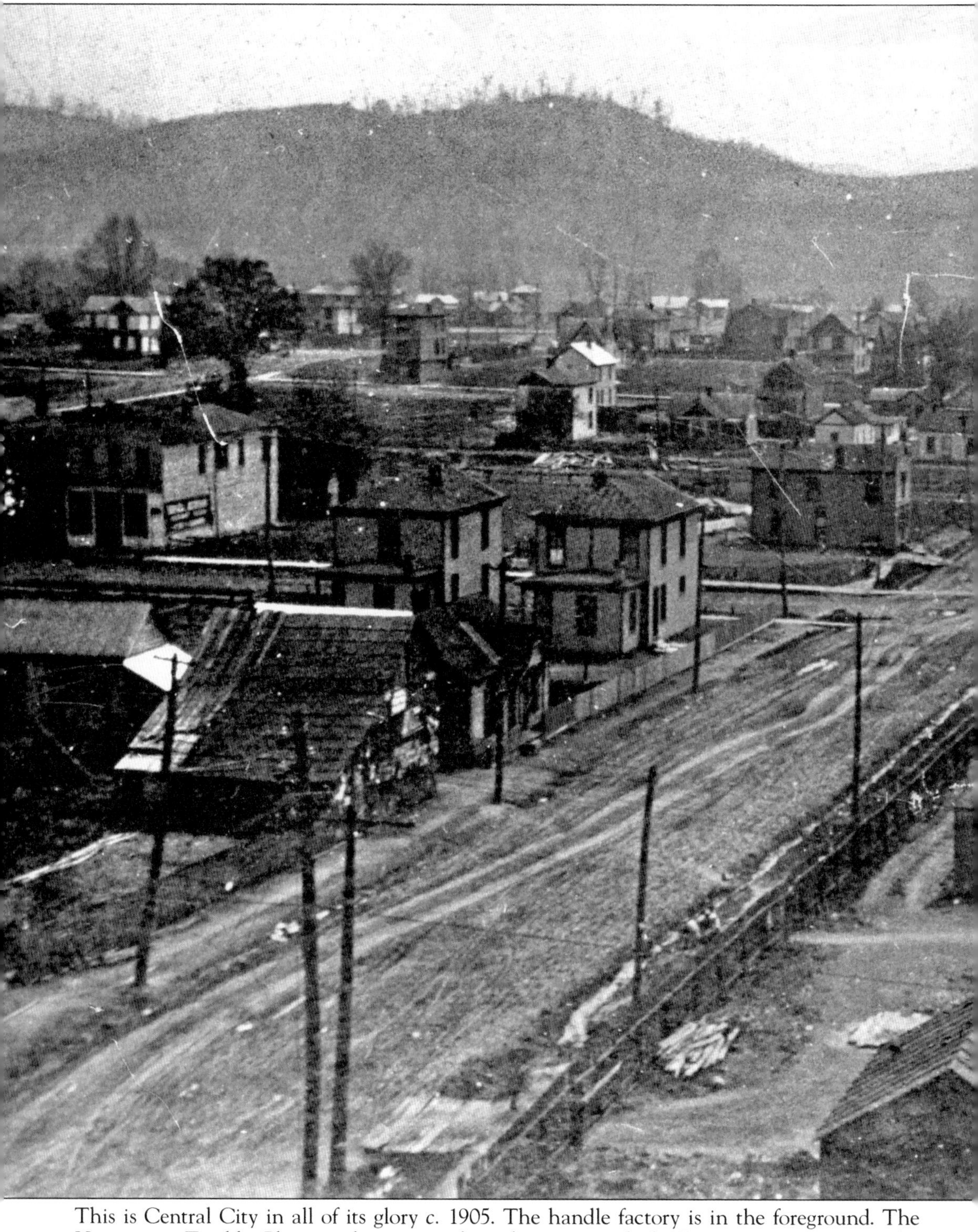

This is Central City in all of its glory *c.* 1905. The handle factory is in the foreground. The Huntington Tumbler Plant can be seen on the right center with the Fesenmeier Brewery on the top right. Note the small building in the front center. This was one of several hose houses built

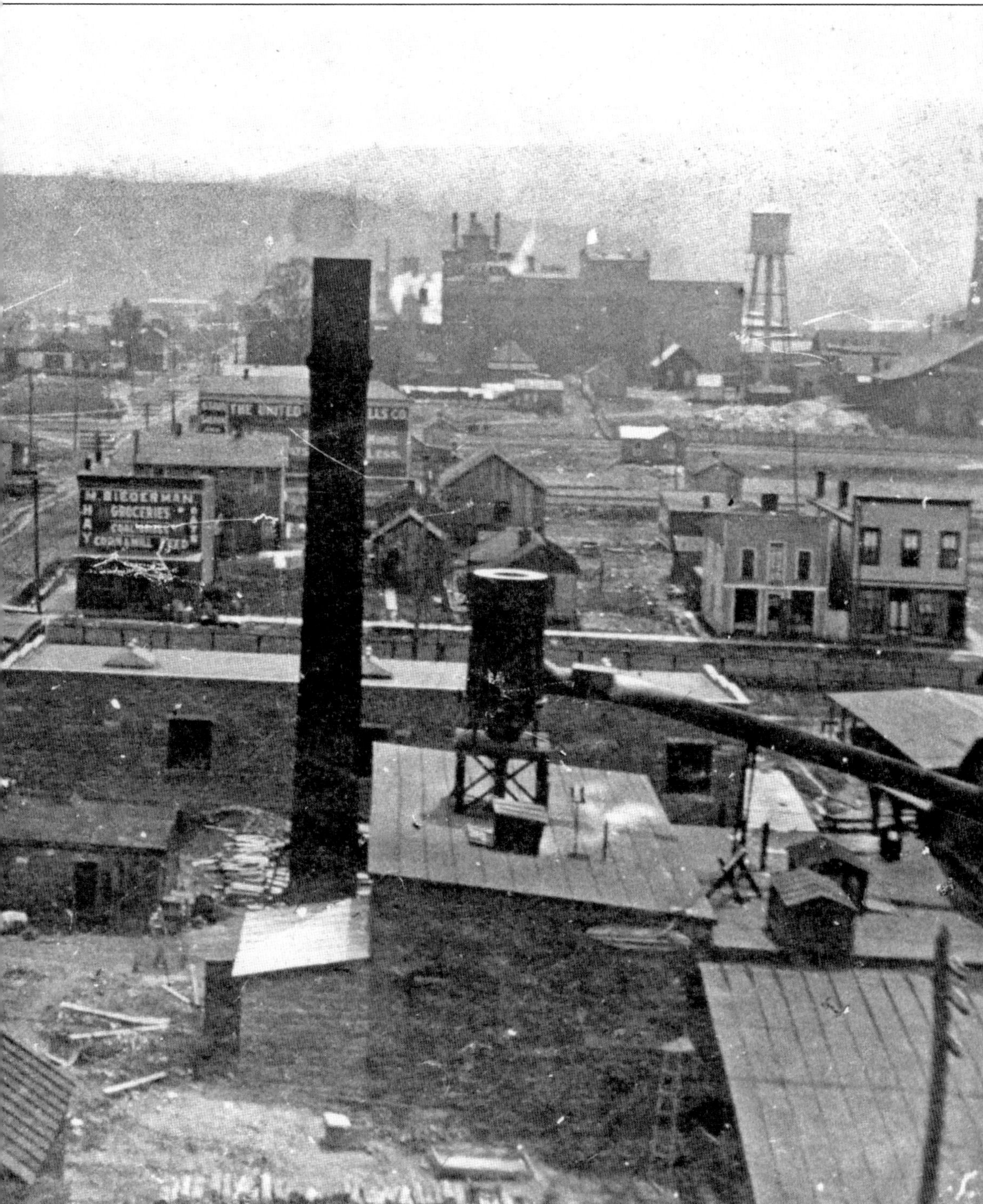

and used by the fire department to house extra fire equipment that could not be hauled on the horse-drawn fire wagons.

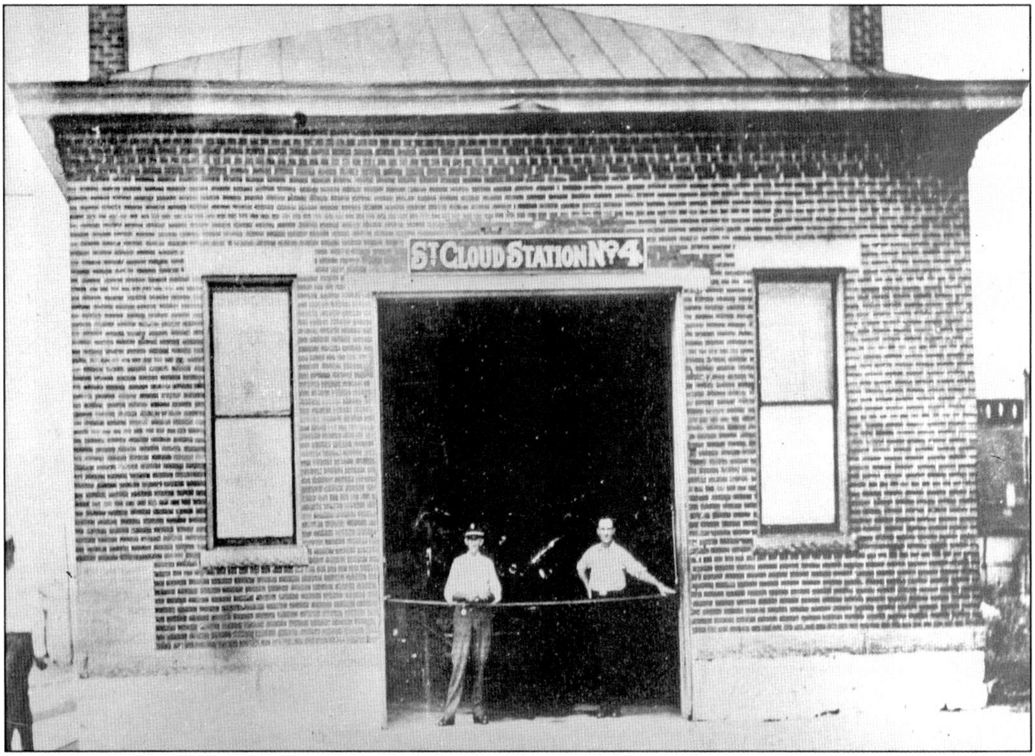

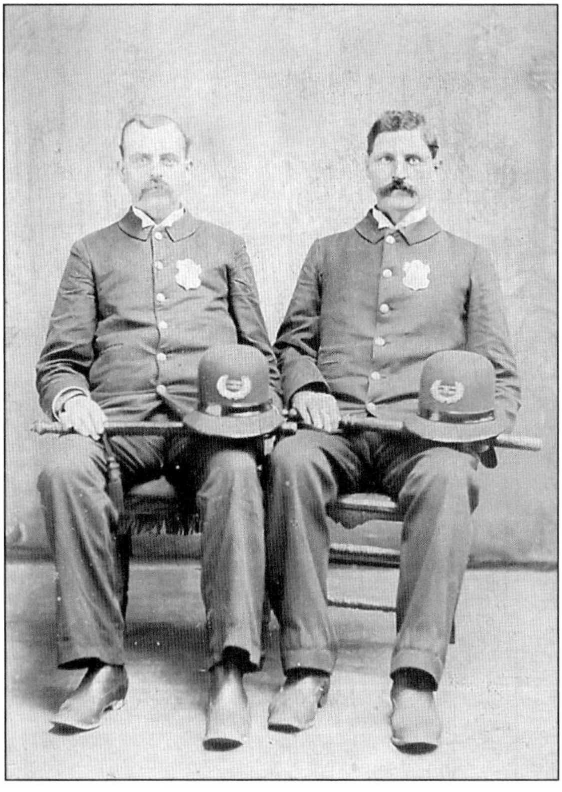

The first order of business was organizing a city council to govern Central City. The "city hall" was not built until about 1905. It was not a fire station at first but was converted later. The original plans of the city hall are available at the library but were not of reproducible quality.

The lack of order in a small town can be as challenging as a larger one. Central City was almost like a new town in the old west. Everything was starting new, and not all of the rules that were needed could be anticipated. The new city council had a real job ahead, but to keep the peace, the first order was to establish a police department. Seward Griffin was the first city marshall appointed. The first policeman was Dine Ellis. According to the "Central City News" in *The Huntington Advertiser*, the two "have proved a terror to evil doers." Pictured at left are officers ? Bumgardner and Nathan Drummonds..

Shown from left to right, officers John Plymale, Joe Ball, and Sam Wellman served Central City in 1905. The duties varied from collecting taxes or escorting councilmen to a meeting if they had failed to appear to chasing stray cattle back to Huntington. But everything was not peaceful. "An interesting occurrence was witnessed on Adams Avenue. . . . Two women were participants in the event. One was armed with a hatchet and the other had a butcher knife in her hand and was skilled in carving," according to *The Huntington Advertiser.*

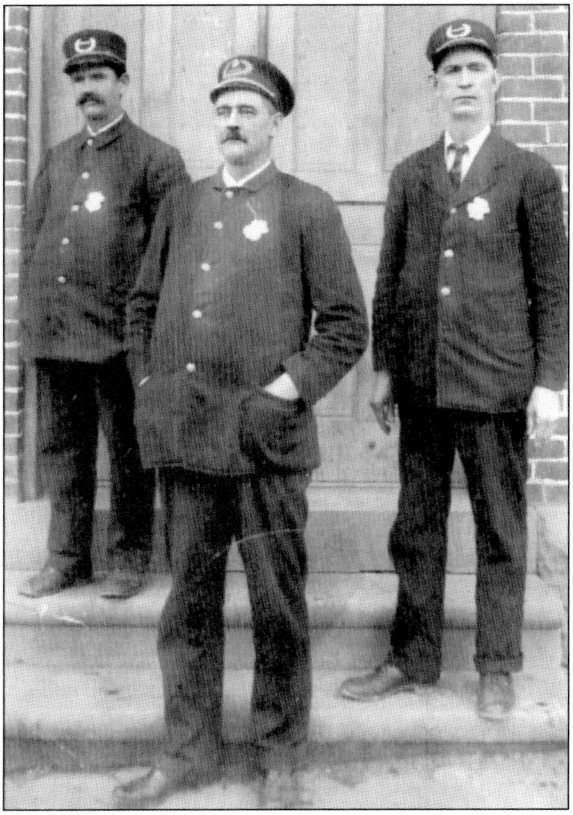

Fires were devastating to any community. A fire department was of utmost importance. Central City formed this department from the very beginning. Horse-drawn wagons were the first means of arriving at the fire. Bucket brigades were in use at this time, and the equipment was kept in the hose houses mentioned above. This picture is of the very first Central City Fire Department in its new home, *c.* 1905.

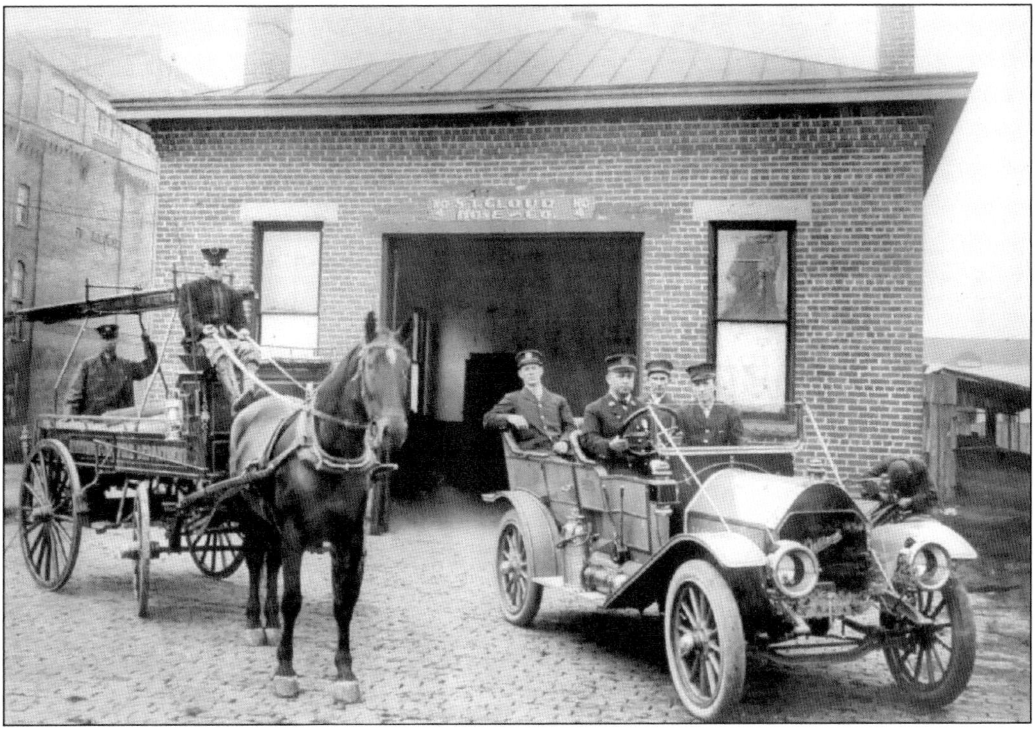

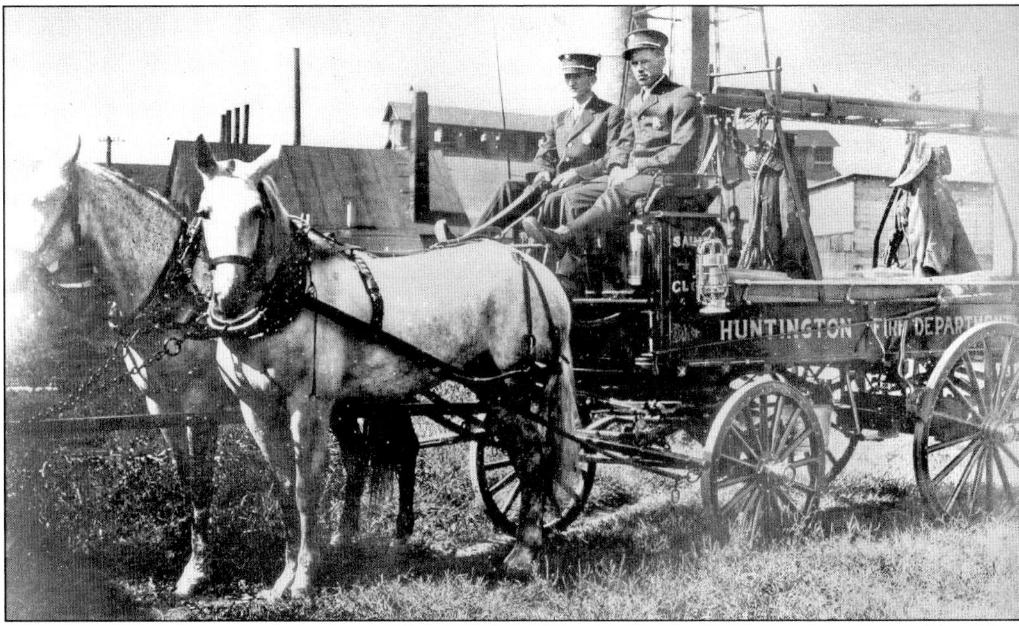

In the picture above, notice "Saint Cloud" behind the lantern. The Huntington Tumbler Plant is in the background with its water tower. When the city hall was converted into a fire station *c.* 1905, frames were built to hold the horse harnesses. These frames could be raised or lowered as needed to get the horses ready for pulling the fire wagon The horse stalls faced the windows, and you can still see where the horses gnawed on these ledges.

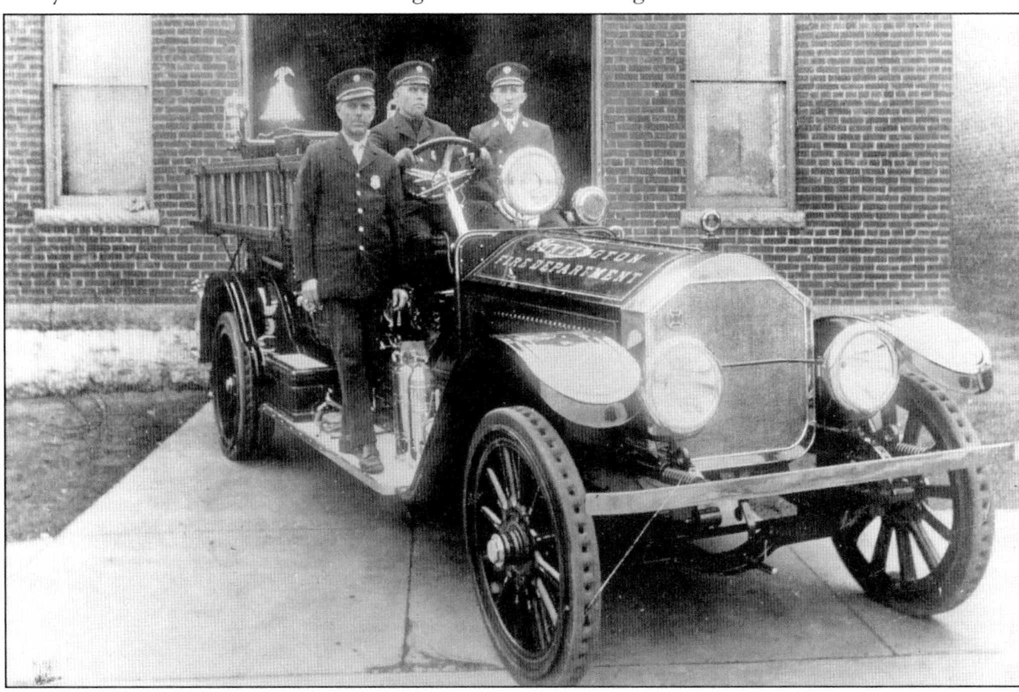

It was a great day when a motorized ladder truck was added to the department. This brought Central City into modern firefighting. When Huntington annexed Central City, this department became Station No. 4 of the Huntington Fire Department.

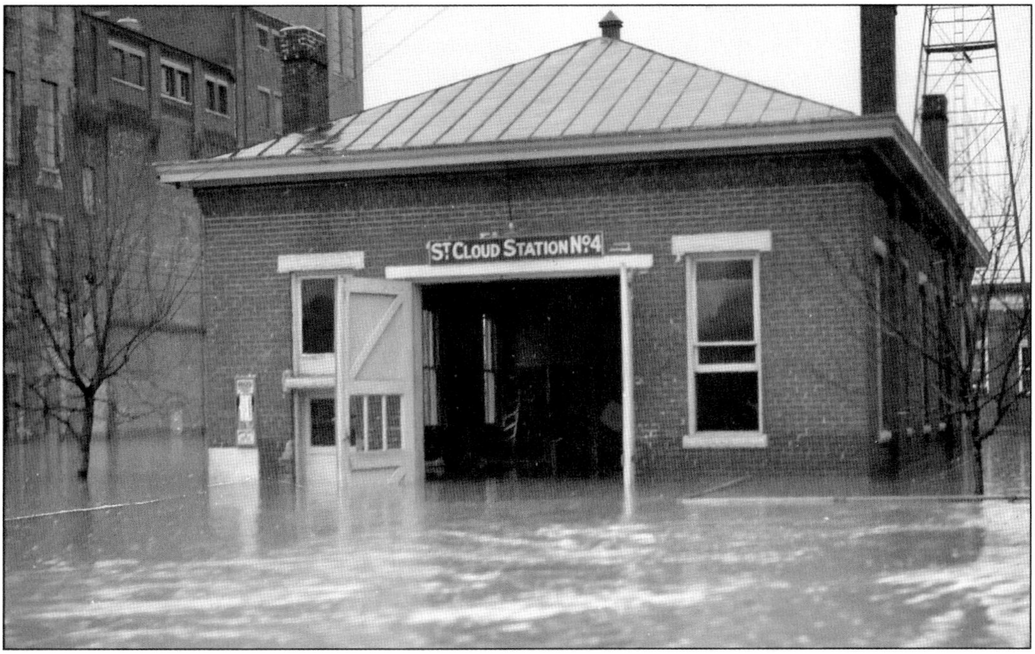

You can see here more devastation of the 1937 flood. The fire station sits on a higher plane than most of Central City. This picture shows how inundated the whole town must have been.

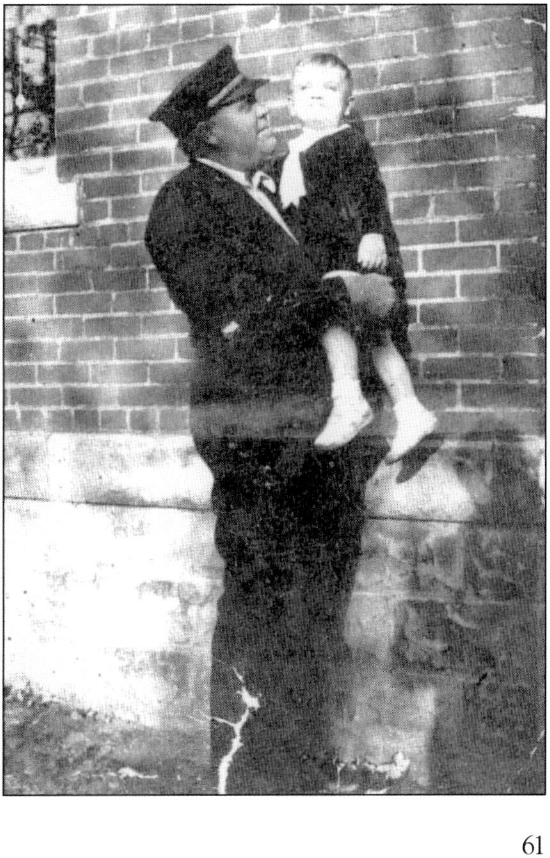

In the days after Central City, one captain of Station No. 4 was Capt. Willie Earnest "Hoggie" Watts. This is a picture taken outside the station with his grandson, Don Watts, in the early 1940s.

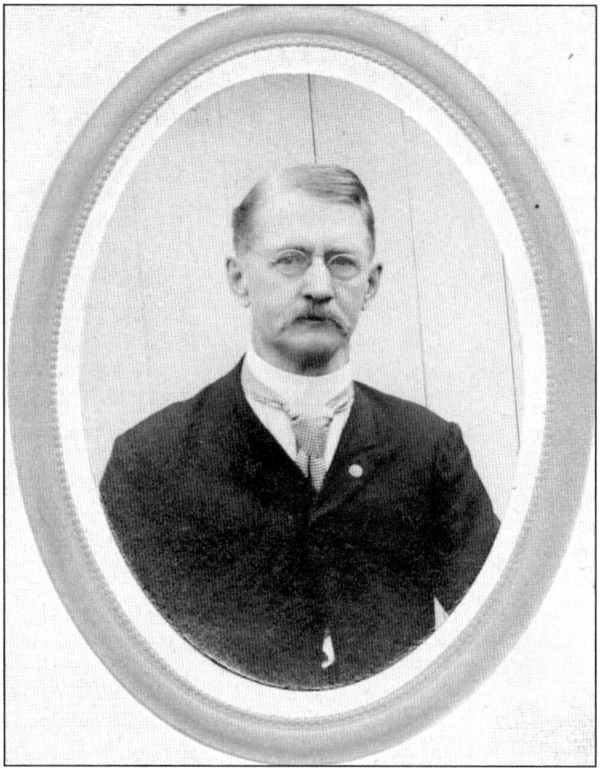

Another necessity to a new town is mail delivery. Charles Roscoe LaValley was appointed the first postmaster. He served many years in that capacity. A note in the "Central City News" column of *The Huntington Advertiser* says that as Col. C. R. LaValley was walking along Fourteenth Street, "a board on the walk was loose at one end. . . . The Colonel's left foot struck this board and he was thrown violently to the walk and painfully injured."

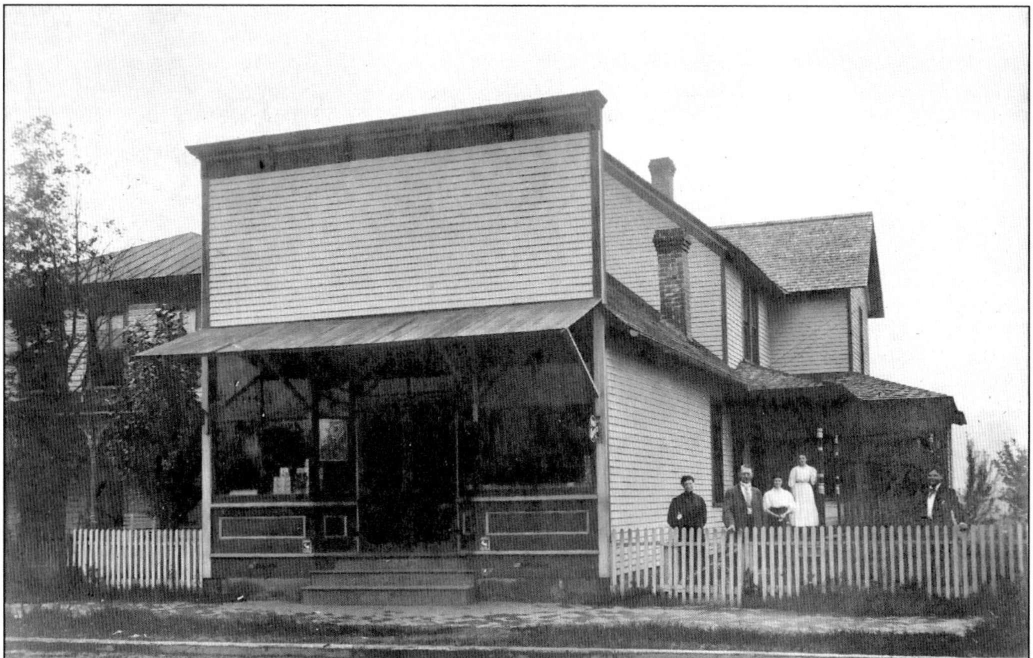

The LaValley home served as the post office. A small addition was added to the front of the home for individual mailboxes. Pictured above from left to right are Helen Sullings LaValley, C. R. LaValley, Maude Sullings, Alma Sullings LaValley, and Ernest Sullings.

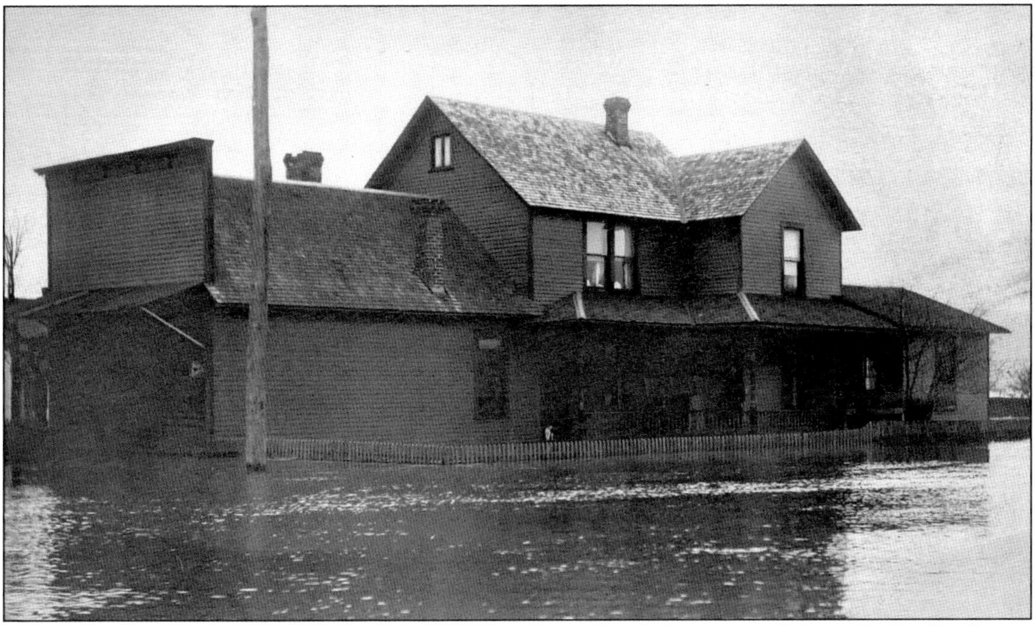

The flood of 1913 was very destructive. This picture shows the post office and LaValley home with several feet of water in the main floor. It is told that the family lived on the second floor during this 1913 flood and during the 1937 flood. A neighbor in a rowboat was chatting with the family at their second floor window during the 1937 flood. The water was receding, and when he began to leave, his boat would not move. His boat had settled on top of a car.

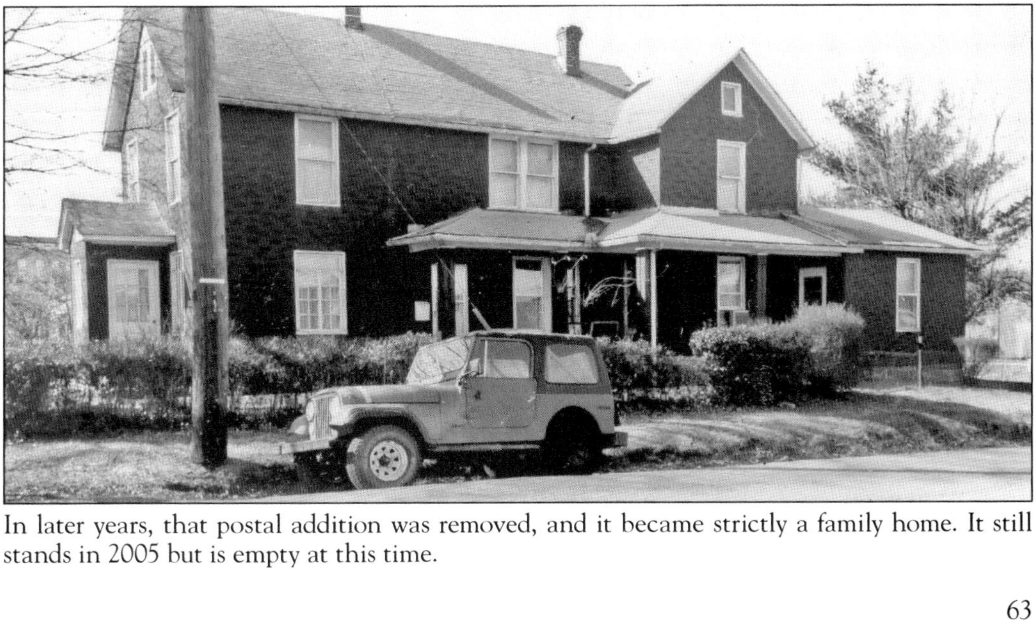

In later years, that postal addition was removed, and it became strictly a family home. It still stands in 2005 but is empty at this time.

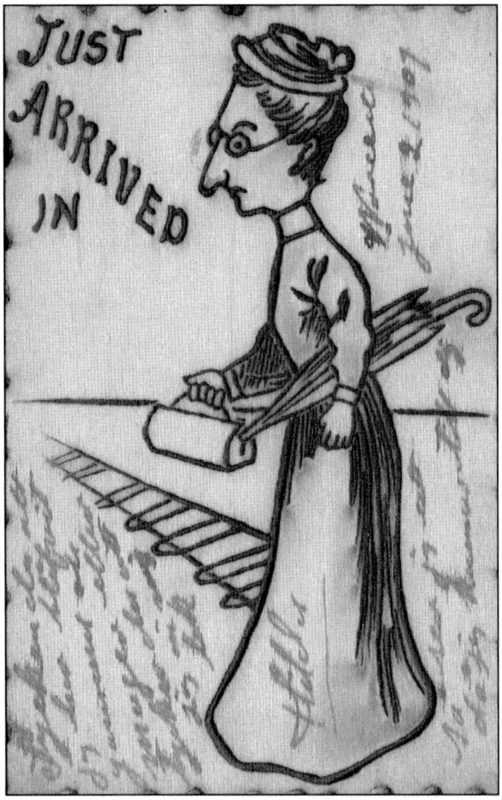

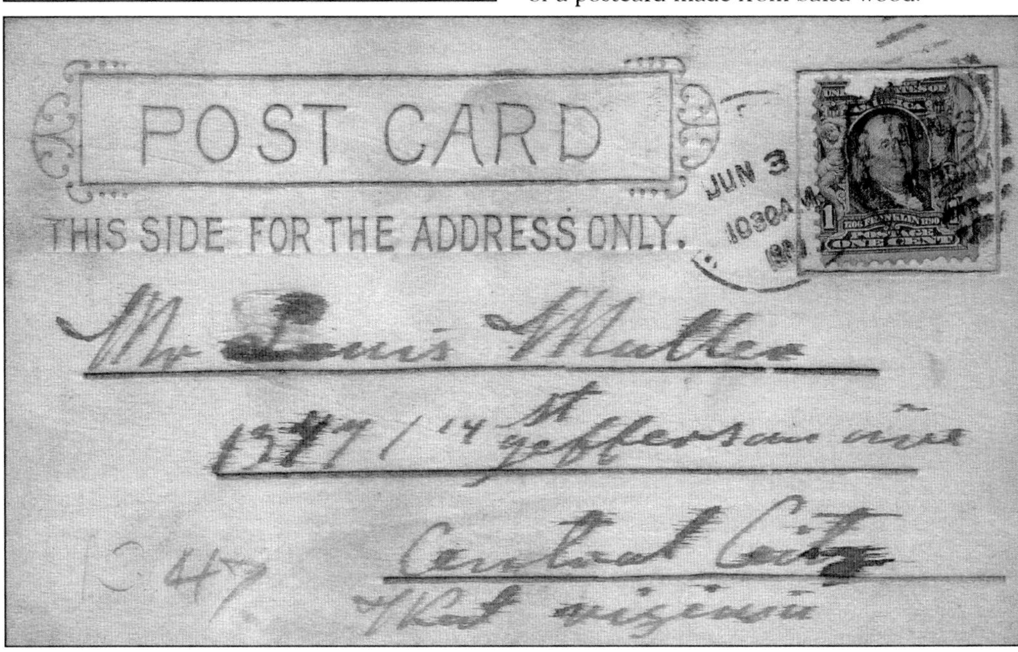

Postcards were a very popular at the turn of the century. With postage at 1¢, it was a reasonable means of communication. Some were very original. This is the front and back of a postcard made from balsa wood.

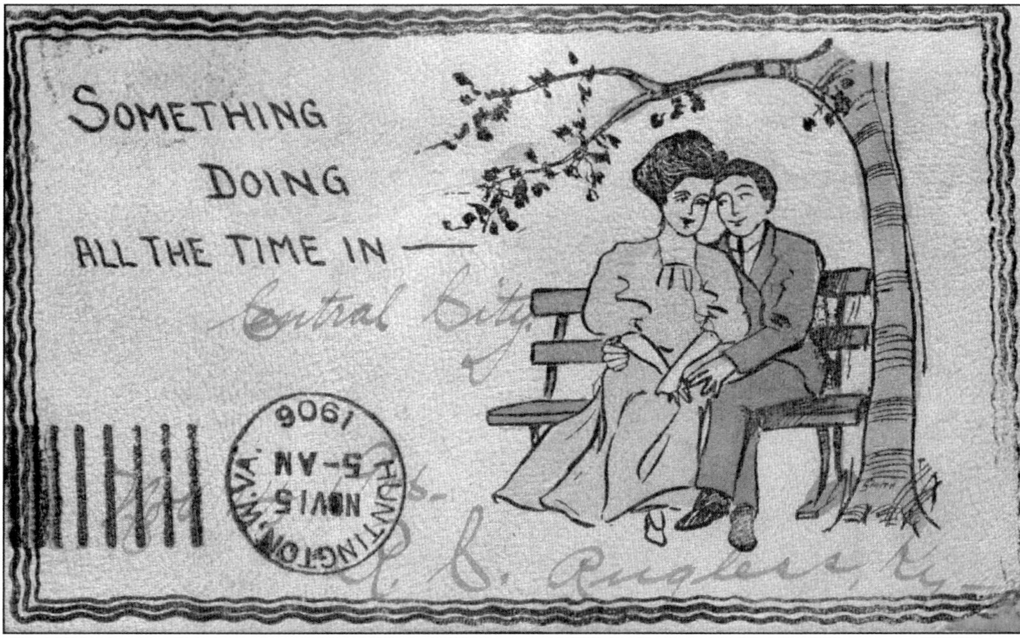

This postcard, a part of a collection from the Muller family, is made of leather. There is nothing to indicate that special handling was required of these unusual postcards. Many family pictures during this period of time were done on postcards.

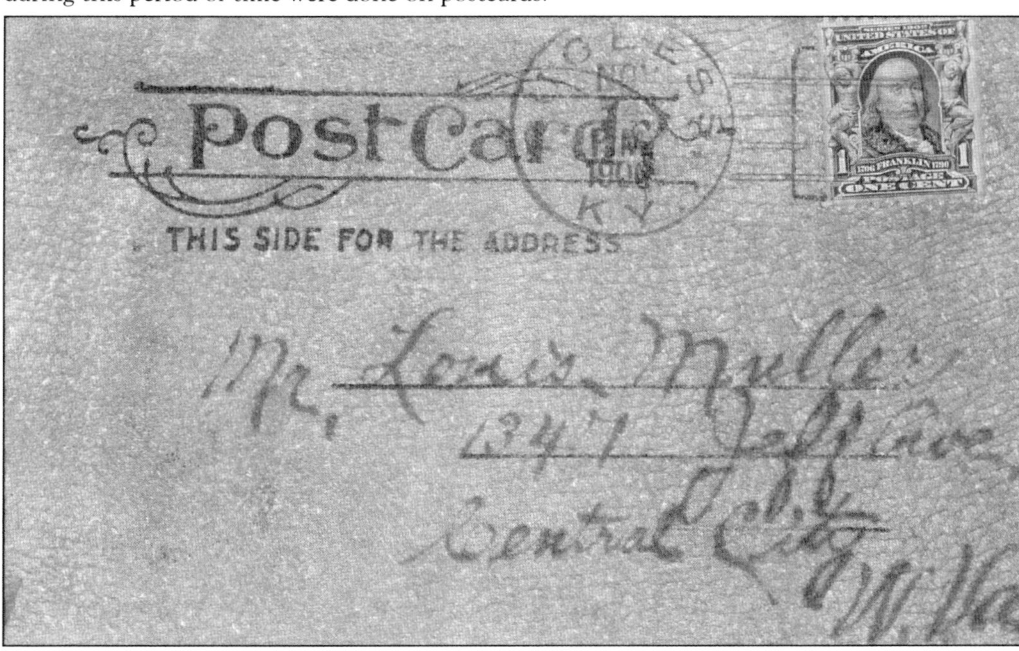

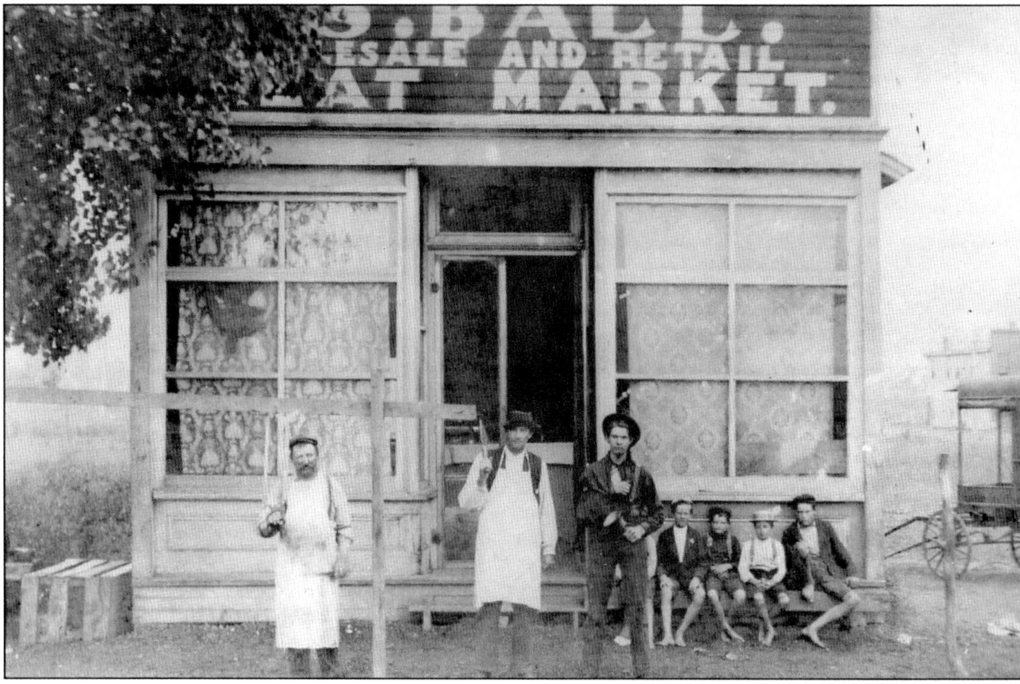

As mentioned before, the small groceries dotted all over Central City. Joe Ball, who was also a Central City law enforcement officer, owned a small grocery at 1069 Adams Avenue. Many groceries delivered if your order was larger than you could carry. You can see a buggy beside Ball's grocery that may have been used to deliver.

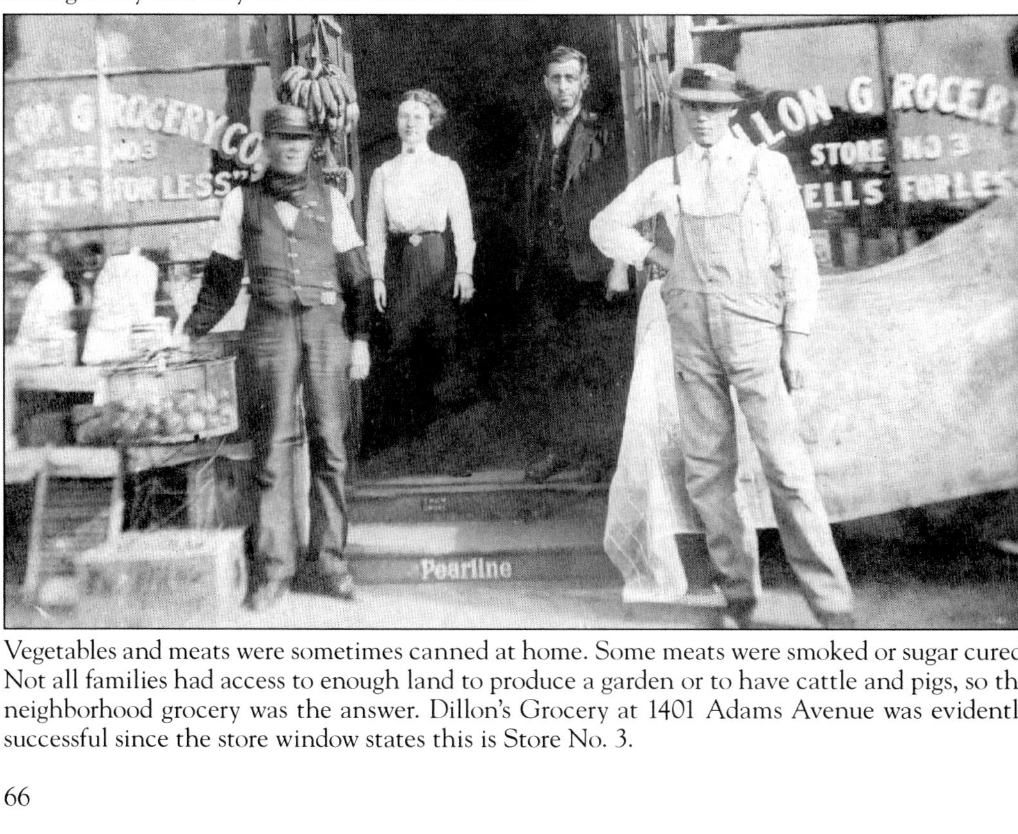

Vegetables and meats were sometimes canned at home. Some meats were smoked or sugar cured. Not all families had access to enough land to produce a garden or to have cattle and pigs, so the neighborhood grocery was the answer. Dillon's Grocery at 1401 Adams Avenue was evidently successful since the store window states this is Store No. 3.

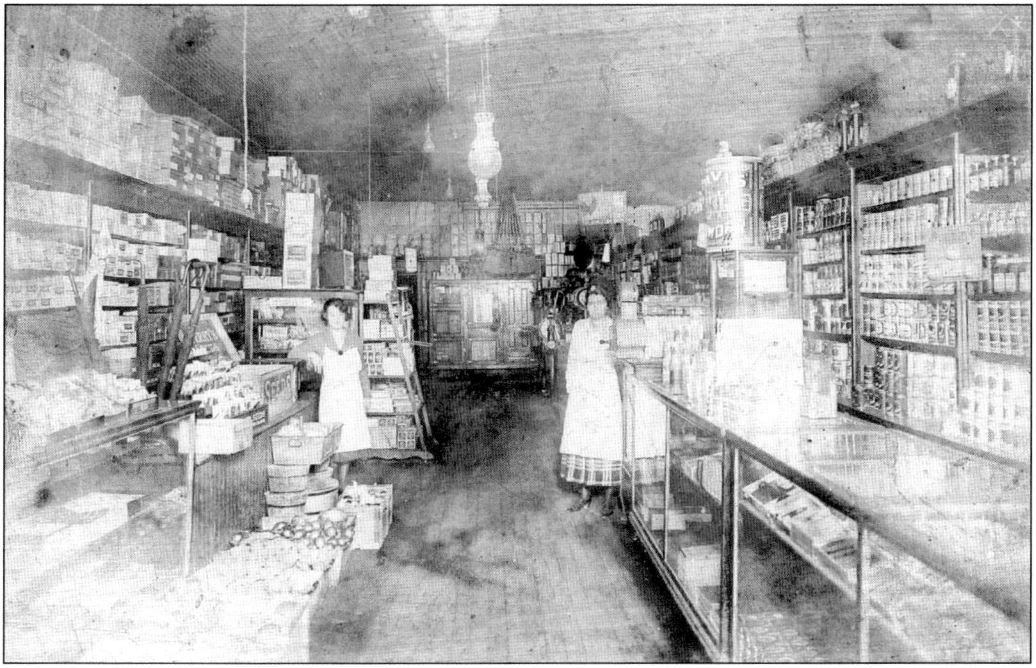

Dillon's Grocery became Beiderman Market in 1906, then Wright-Beiderman Grocery. As in most of these stores, the grocer retrieved your requests. You told them what you wanted or gave them your list and they filled the order. A newspaper article in 1907 says Mr. Dillon "serves his customers in a gallant way by selling them food while standing in (flood) water knee deep."

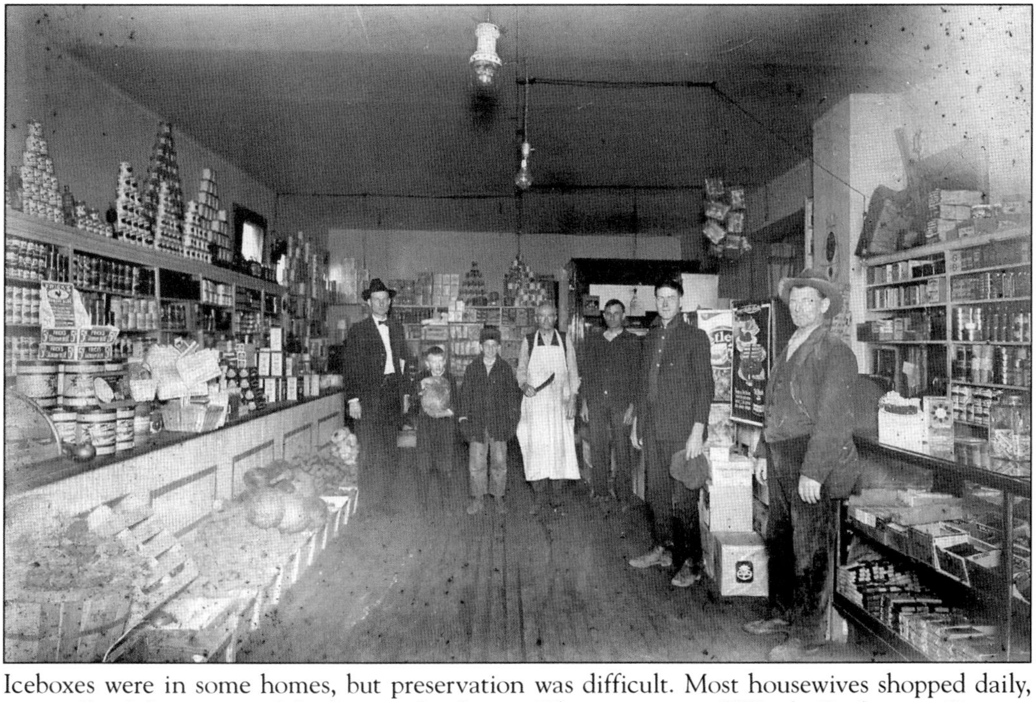

Iceboxes were in some homes, but preservation was difficult. Most housewives shopped daily, especially if they required fresh meat for dinner. This picture is of Wright-Beiderman Grocery c. 1929. The man on the far left is Oscar Watts, a streetcar employee.

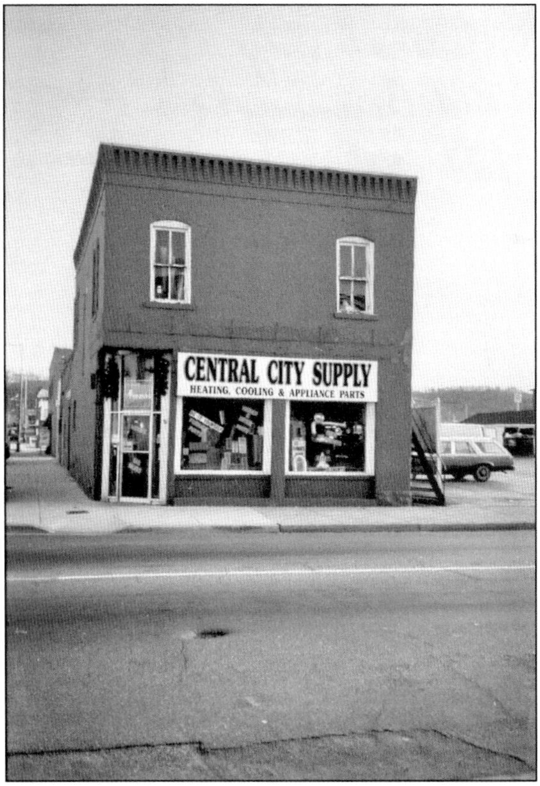

Some unknown years later, Wright-Beiderman Grocery became Cunningham's Drugstore. In the 1990s, it was Central City Supply, a heating and air-conditioning concern. In 2004, it was torn down and is now a parking lot.

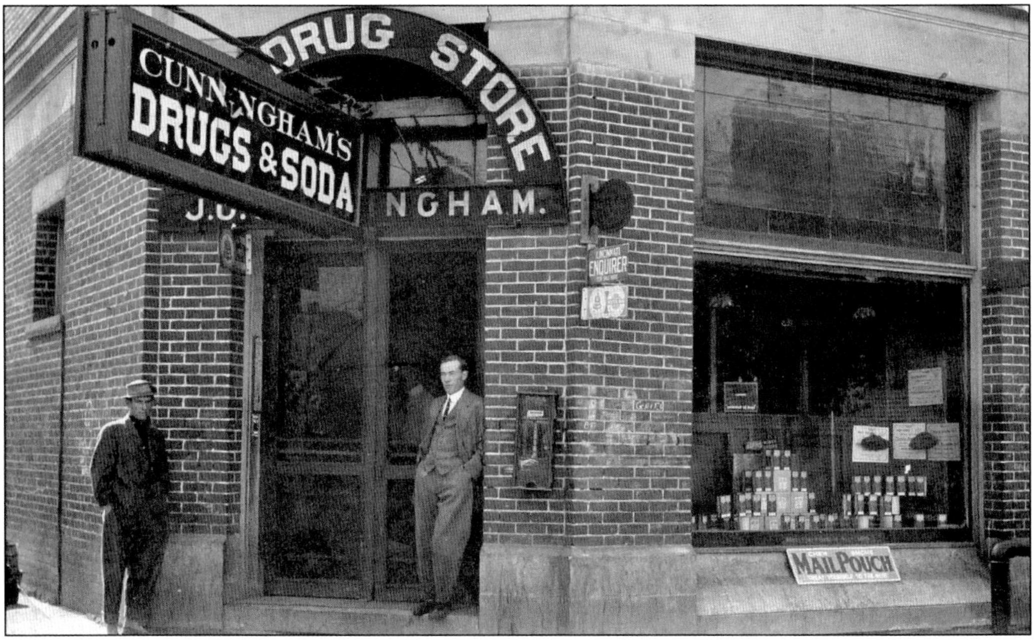

Cunningham's Drug Store began in Hotel Central. By moving to 1401 Adams Avenue, they were directly across the street from Hosey's Drugstore. These two were friendly competitors. Hosey's went out of business in the early 1970s. Cunningham's went out of business in the late 1980s.

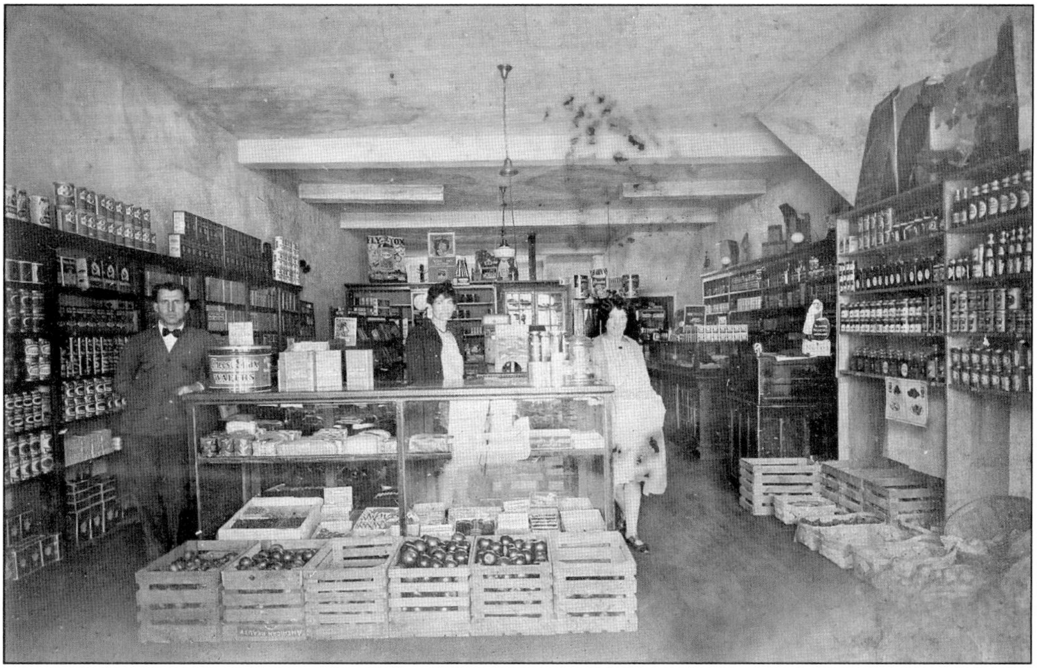

Just up the street from Wright-Beiderman was the Reliable Market at 1339 Adams Avenue. Notice how neat the shelves were. Pictured here from left to right are Ernest and Ruby Thorne and Eva Miller Watts *c.* 1929.

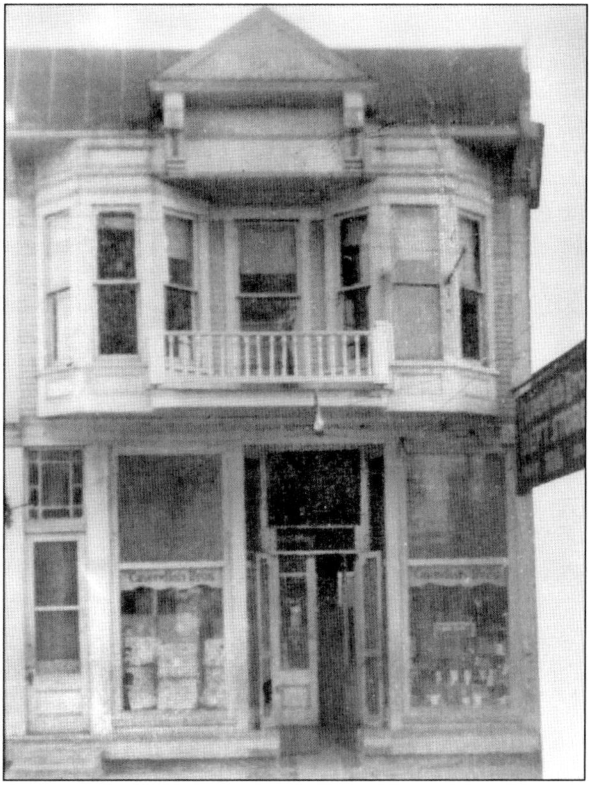

One of the prominent families of early Central City was the Cavendish family. They built homes there, and one of the early department stores, Cavendish Brothers Department Store, was owned by this family. This store, located at 13 Adams Avenue, was opened by J. Rankin Boone in 1904 and bought by the Cavendishes in 1911.

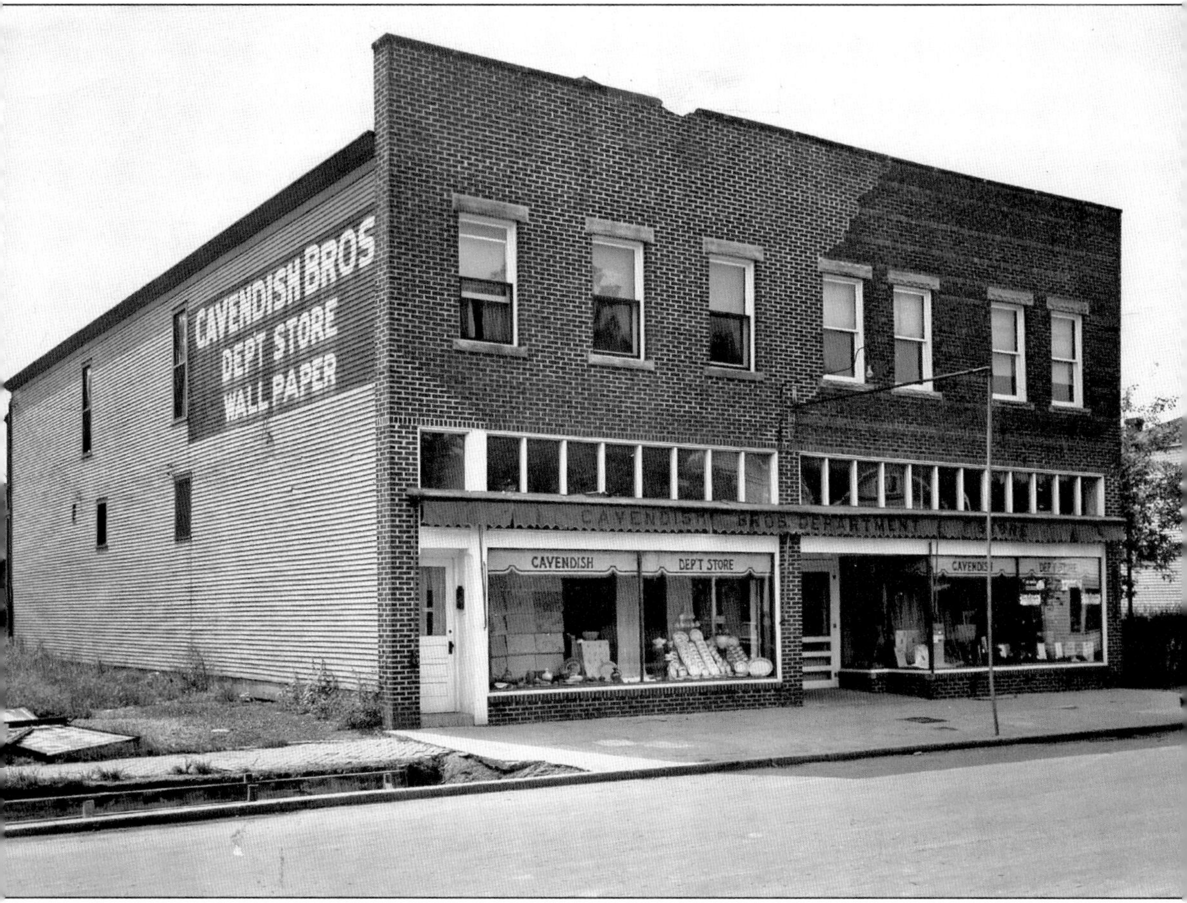

The original Cavendish Brothers store was expanded with an addition and a brick front. Peggy Boone Cyrus worked 60 hours and six days a week for her uncle and earned 21¢ an hour. She was just thrilled to have a job.

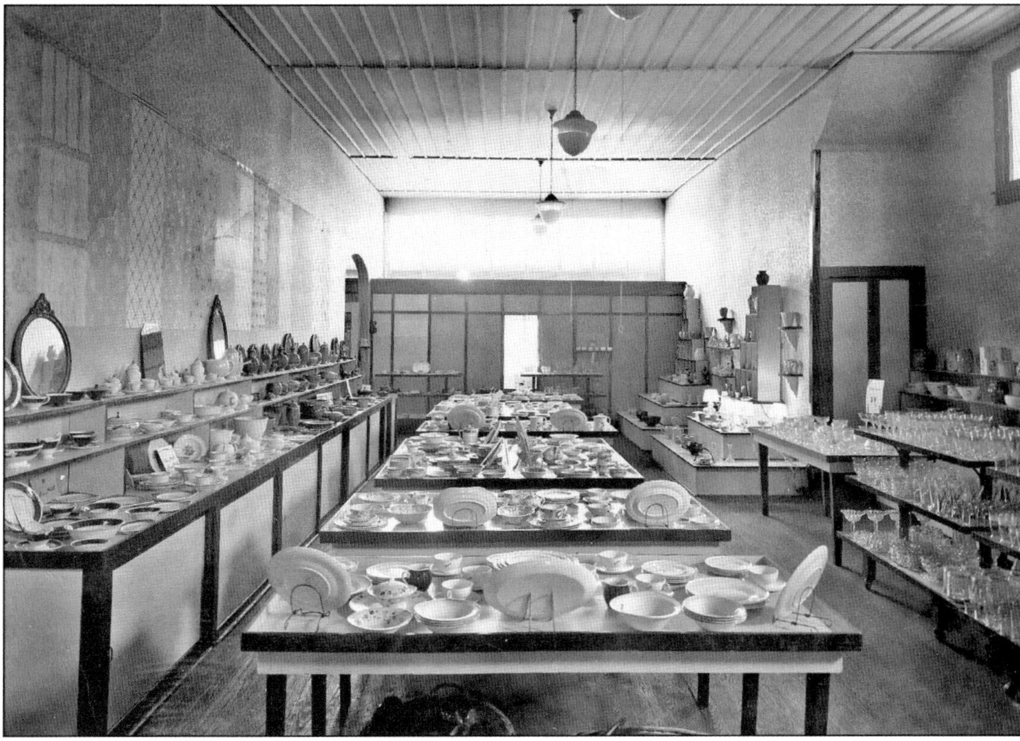

Cavendish's sold dishes, wallpaper, and all kinds of household necessities. Central City homeowners purchased much of their home supplies from this congenial family. The cover of this book is from the very early days.

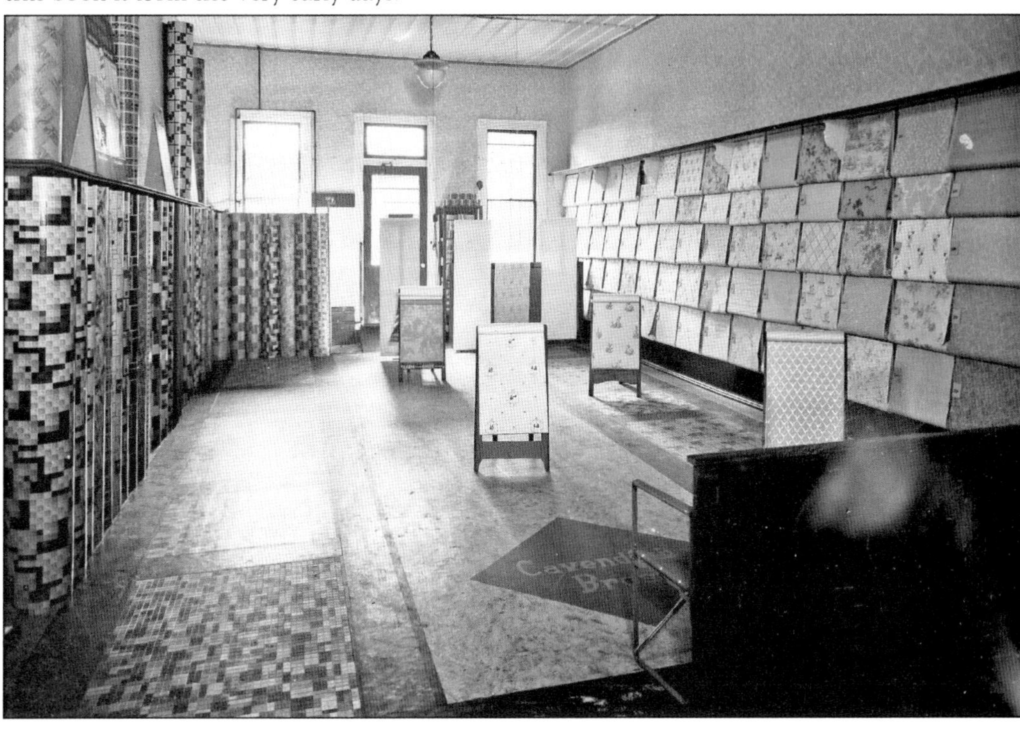

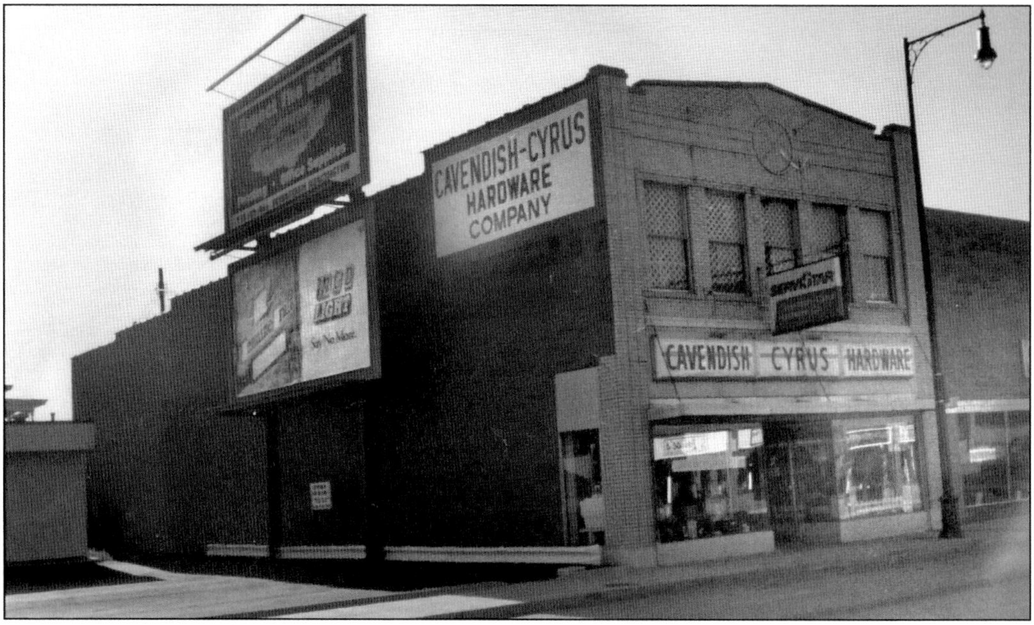

In 1928, Peggy's husband, Evan Cyrus, opened the Cavendish-Cyrus Hardware Store. This hub of hardware in West Huntington continued with the help of their daughter, Sally, until 1995. It was located in the 500 block of Fourteenth Street West. Although this store began after Central City, it was a continuation of the hardware section of the Cavendish Brothers Department Store.

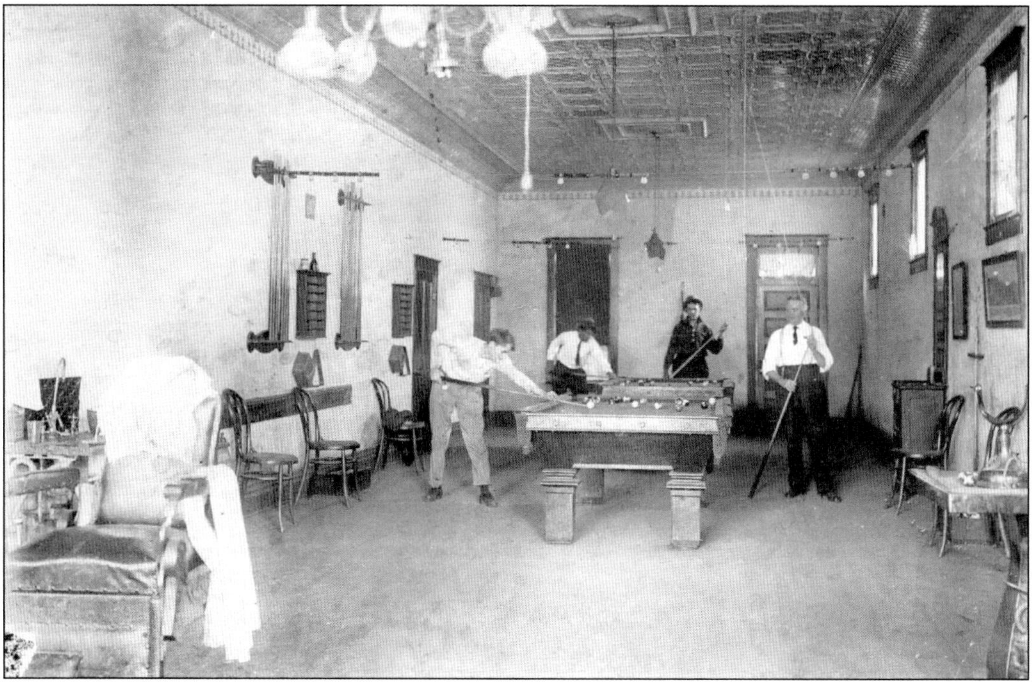

This shop is believed to have been in the 400 block of Fourteenth Street West *c.* 1929. One of the most well-known barbershops in West Huntington was Shannon's. Oscar Shannon not only had a wealth of information but kept pictures of note through the years. He had quite a collection.

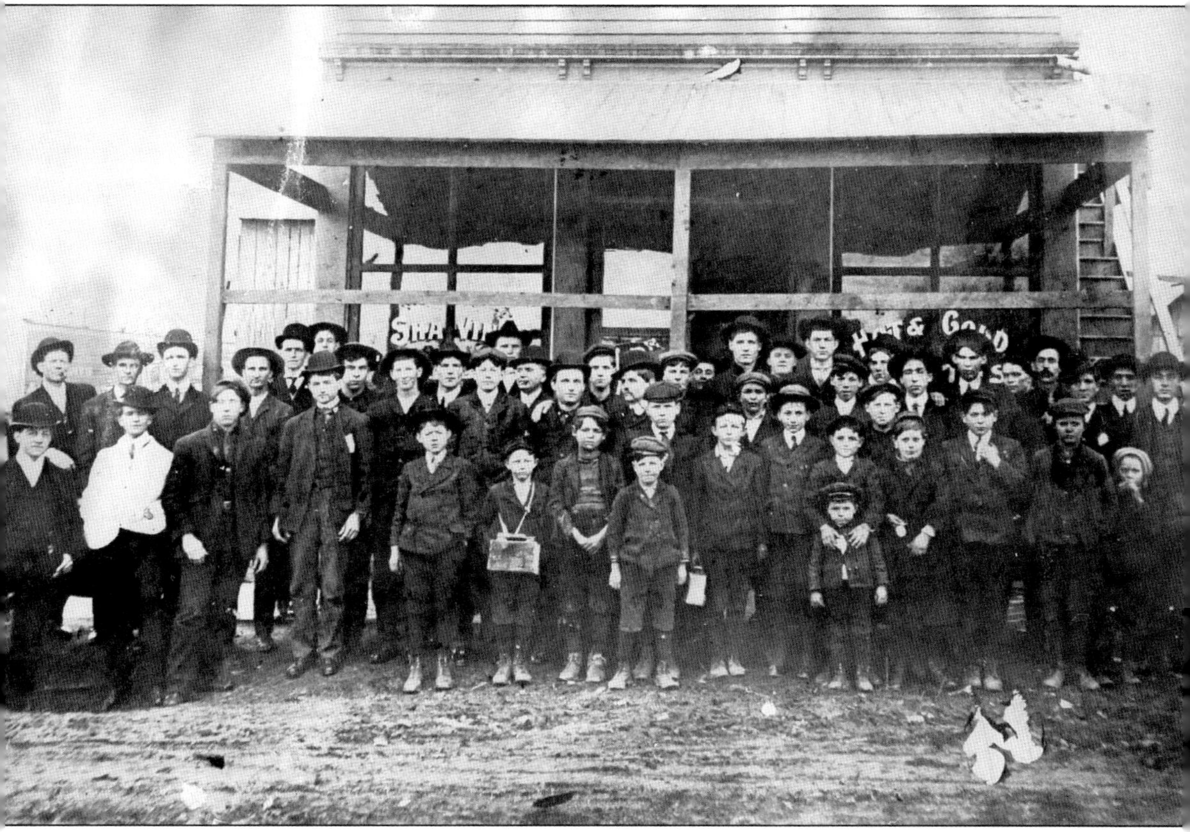

A popular place for haircuts, shaves, pool, and gossip was the local barbershop. The occasion for this image is unknown, but it certainly must have been an important one. The time of this gathering must have been in the early 1900s, since the street is still unpaved.

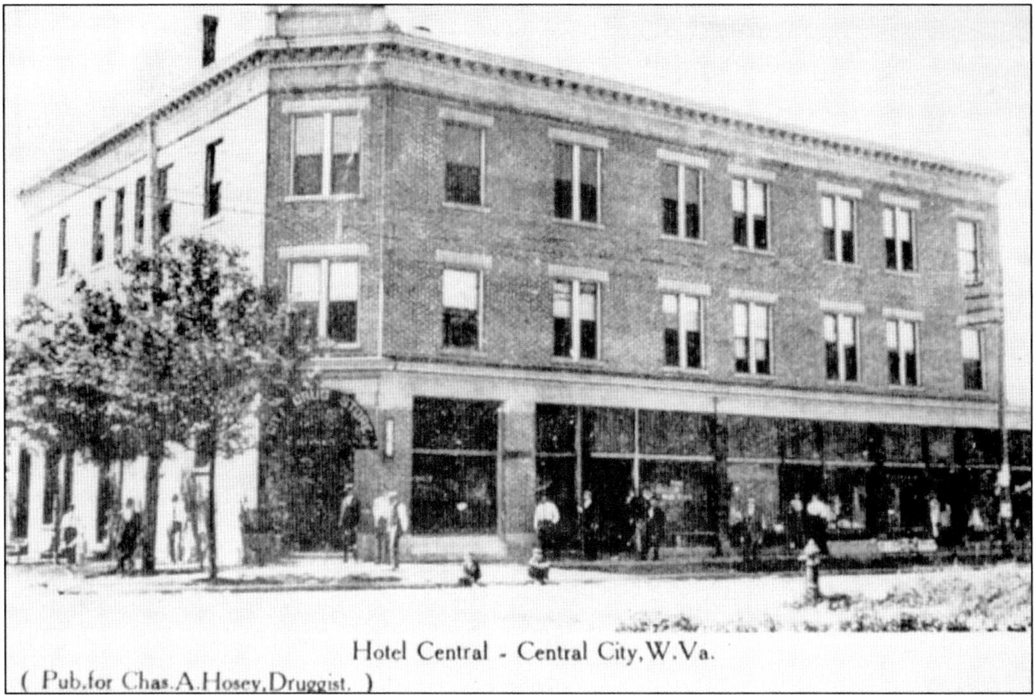

The great job market made housing scant in a new town. Besides boarding houses, the Hotel Central provided a home for single men and married men away from their families. This large building also housed several small businesses on the first floor. Unfortunately, it burned in 1911 and was not rebuilt.

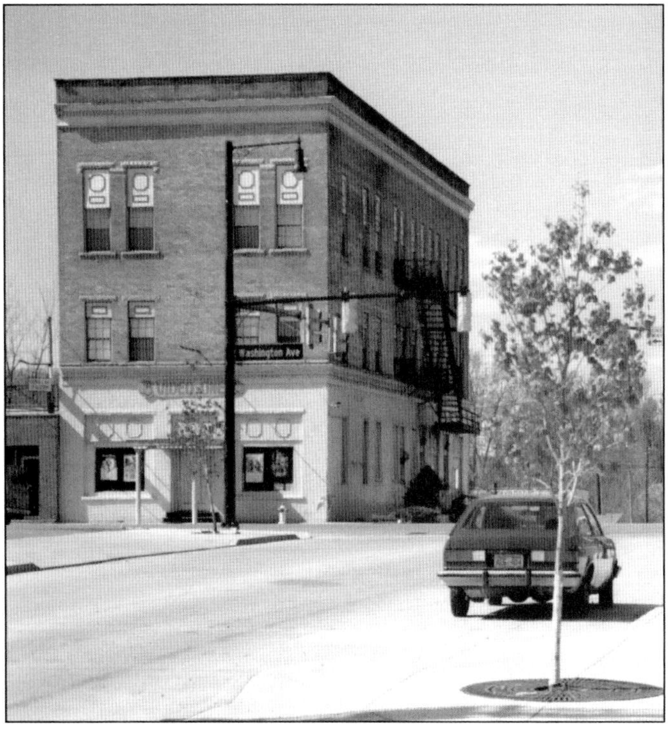

Every town must have a bank. Central City was not that fortunate. It wasn't until 1911, two years after Central City was annexed into Huntington, that a building was erected that housed a bank with offices and apartments on the second and third floors. This was as close as West Huntington would get to a skyscraper. The Central Banking Company closed after the crash of 1929, and several businesses were located there through the years. A fire destroyed it to the point of complete demolition in the early 1990s.

Every town also needs a doctor. Central City was blessed with several through the years. One of the most beloved was Dr. George Waldeck. His home was at 1159 Adams Avenue, and his office was at 1237 Jefferson Avenue.

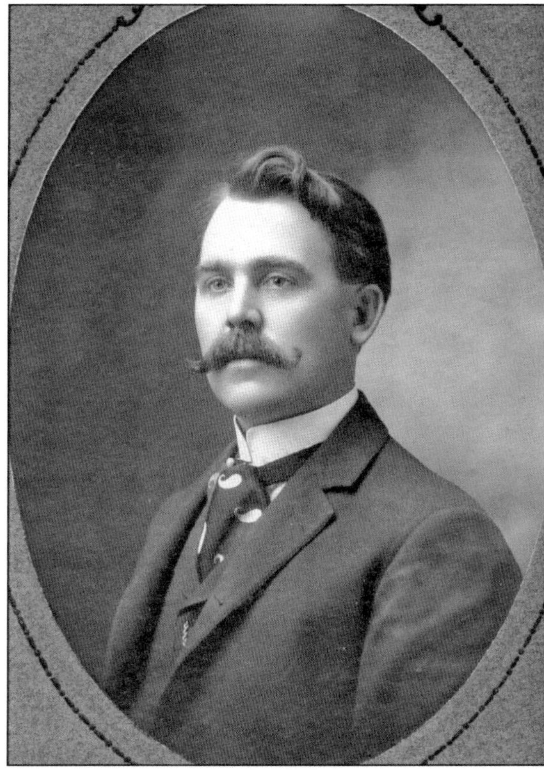

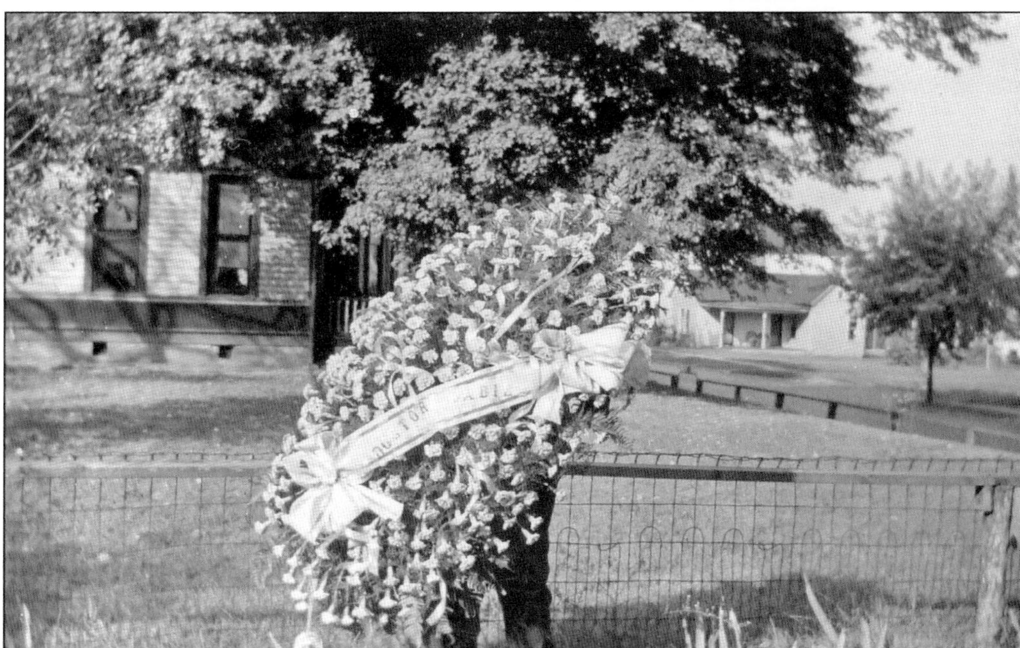

When Dr. Waldeck died, he was honored in a very unusual way. A spray of flowers was present with a bud for every child he had delivered. The exact number of buds is not known, but as you can see, it was large.

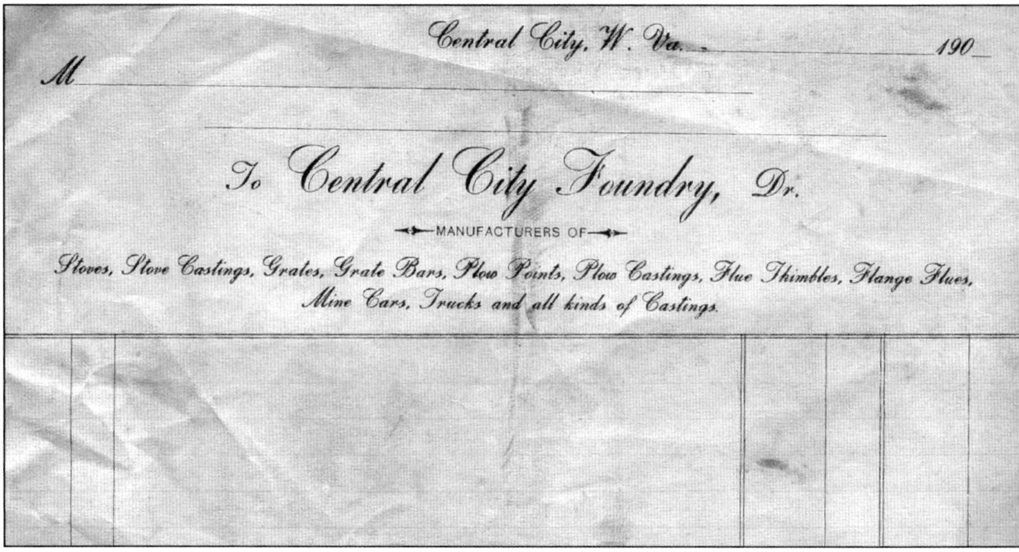

Central City, W. Va. 190

M

To Central City Foundry, Dr.

MANUFACTURERS OF

Stoves, Stove Castings, Grates, Grate Bars, Plow Points, Plow Castings, Flue Thimbles, Flange Flues, Mine Cars, Trucks and all kinds of Castings.

The Central City Foundry, as advertised on the letterhead, made stoves, plows, flues, and mine cars. West Virginia Foundry, which might have been the forerunner for the Central City version, made stoves for the B&O Railroad cars.

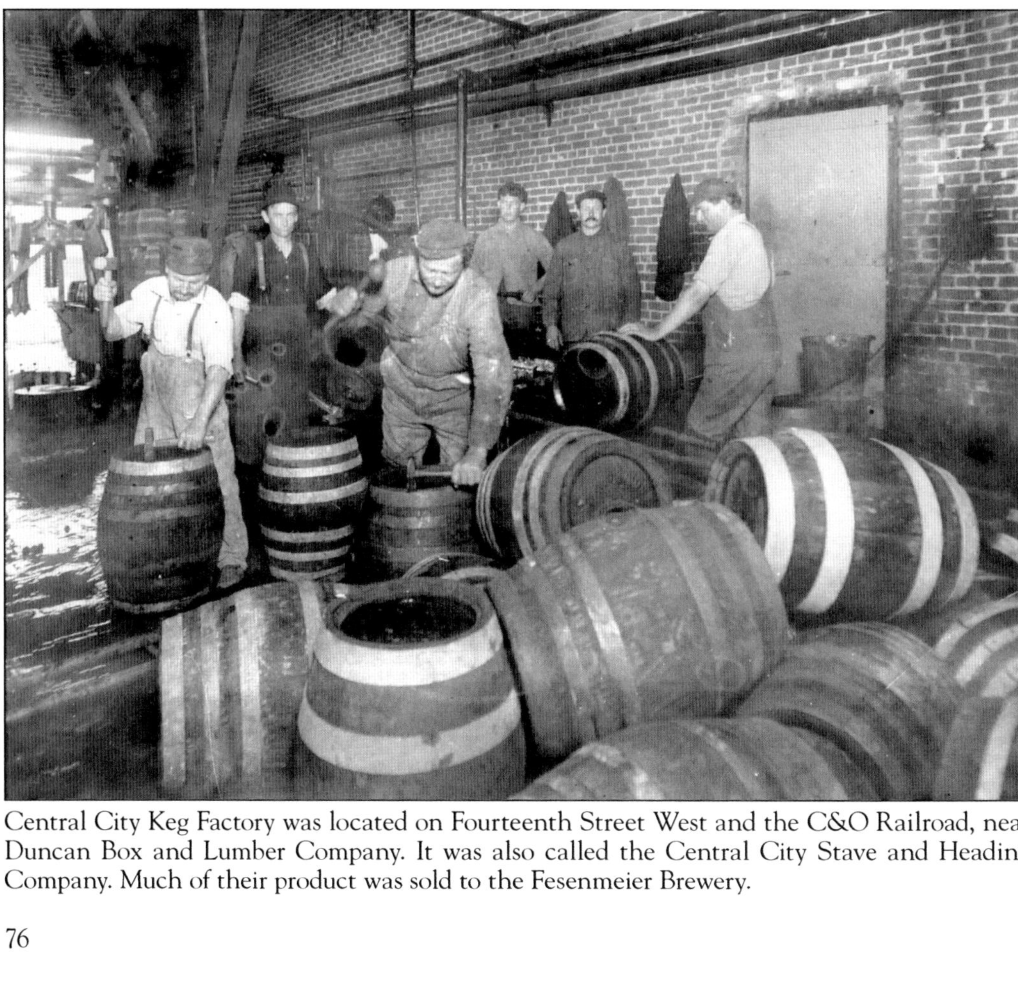

Central City Keg Factory was located on Fourteenth Street West and the C&O Railroad, near Duncan Box and Lumber Company. It was also called the Central City Stave and Heading Company. Much of their product was sold to the Fesenmeier Brewery.

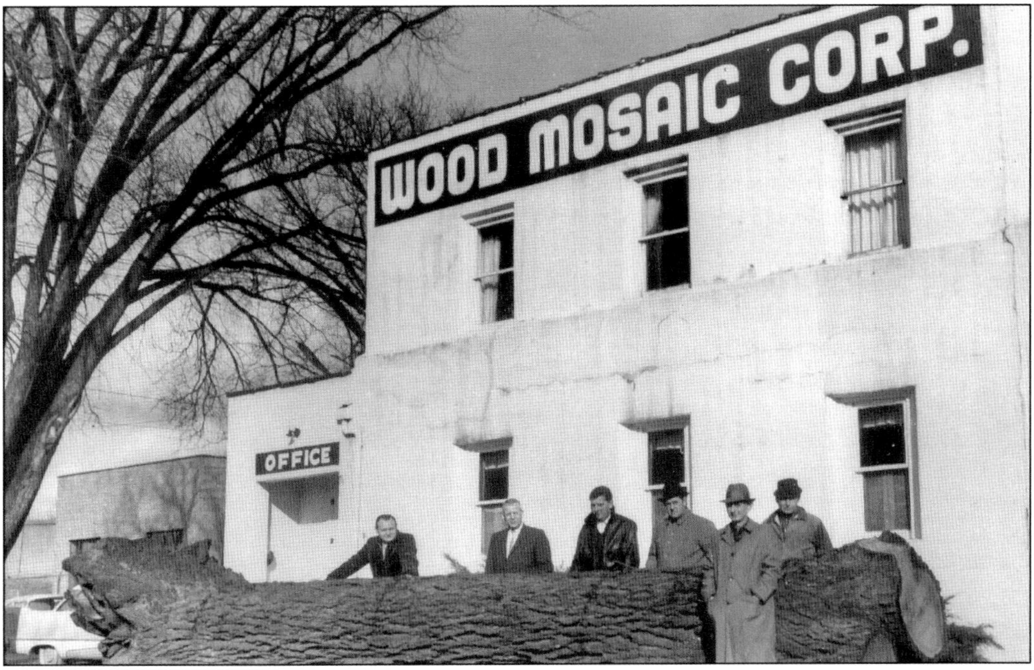

Central Veneer Company was incorporated in 1895. Their specialty was crossbanding veneer from poplar, oak, and walnut. The company traded in Canada as well as the United States. The company used the latest equipment of the day and employed 35 people. In 1917, William Seiber sold the business to Wood Mosaic Poplar Veneer Company. They enlarged the business and employed 60 people.

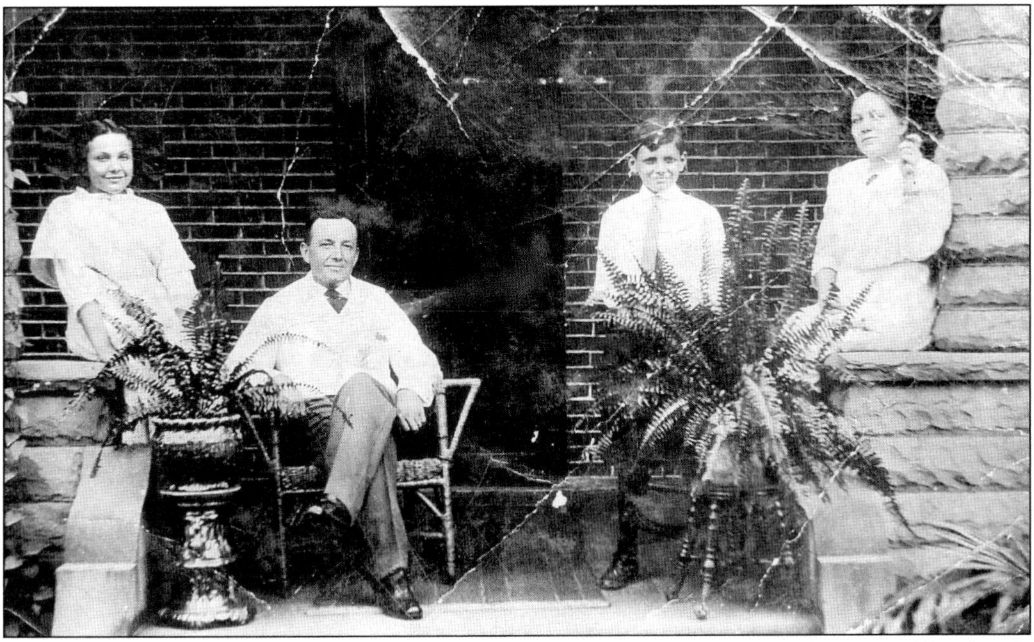

William Seiber was the mayor of Central City when the city hall was built. He and his family resided at Twelfth Street West and Washington Avenue. The house stood until the late 1980s or early 1990s. This picture is the Seiber family on the front porch of that home.

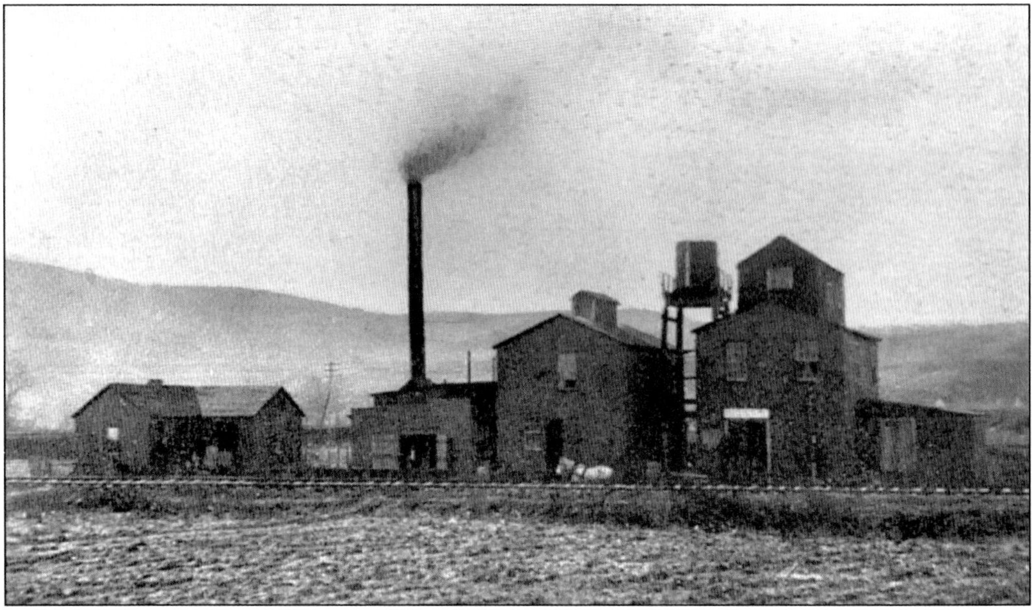

The Blue Springs Distillery was one of the earliest businesses but remains rather obscure as far as facts. It was located at Fifteenth Street West and the C&O Railway, according to the city directory.

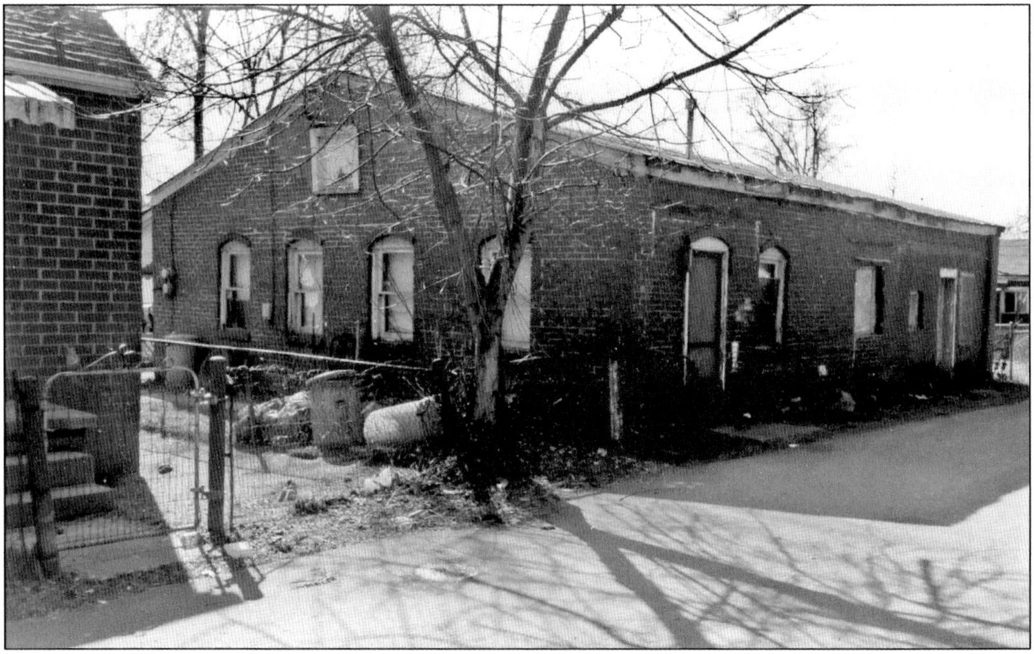

Licking River Lumber Company originated in 1902, occupied four acres, and employed 60–80 people regularly. They had large timber holdings and sawmills. This office building still stands at 8 1/2 Alley between Madison and Monroe Avenue. Calloway Lumber also in this same area was a successor to Baker and Spitler Lumber. They specialized in hemlock lumber. Licking River specialized in oak.

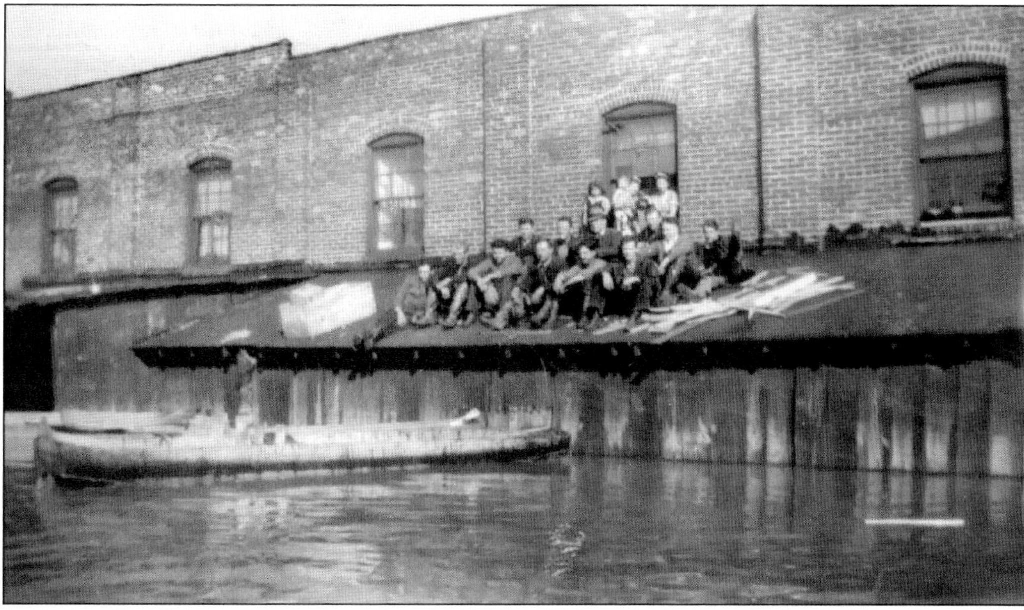

Phillips Manufacturing Company built church altars, office and drug fixtures, and showcases. They were located at Fifteenth Street West and Jackson Avenue. This picture was taken during the 1913 flood.

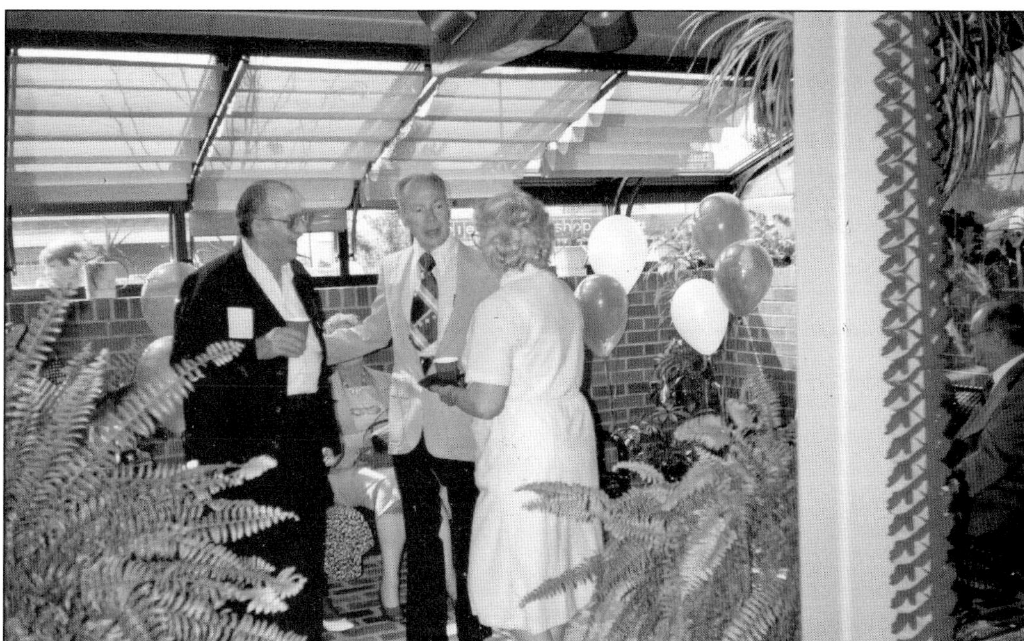

One of the most unique and colorful men known in West Huntington was Bill Sliger (left), pictured here with Dr. Will Neal, and Charlotte Sliger at the opening of the West Huntington Library. Sliger was the grandson of two lumbermen. Sliger Lumber and Shore's Planing Mill were both important to Central City. The Sliger Mill on Virginia Avenue and later Seventh Avenue closed in the early 1990s after 100 years.

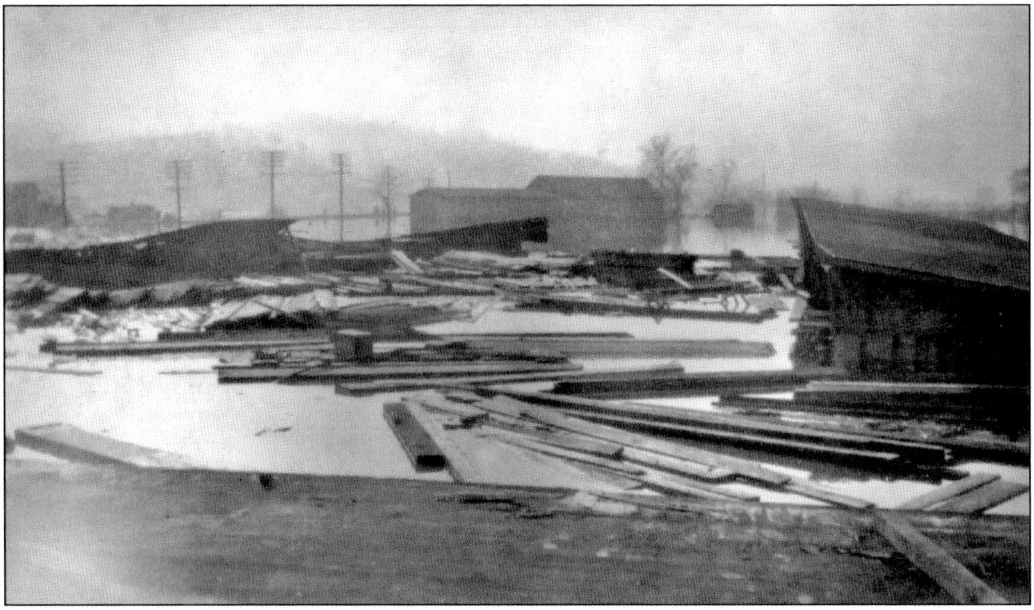

Bill worked for his grandfather Sliger and actually rode the last log rafts from their sawmill at St. Albans down the Guyandotte River to the Ohio and to the Sliger Mill at the riverfront in West Huntington in 1928. Bill Sliger supplied copies of two early newspapers, *Central City Chronicle* (September 29, 1902) and the *Central City Courier* (March 30, 1894), to the library plus a lot of wonderful oral history.

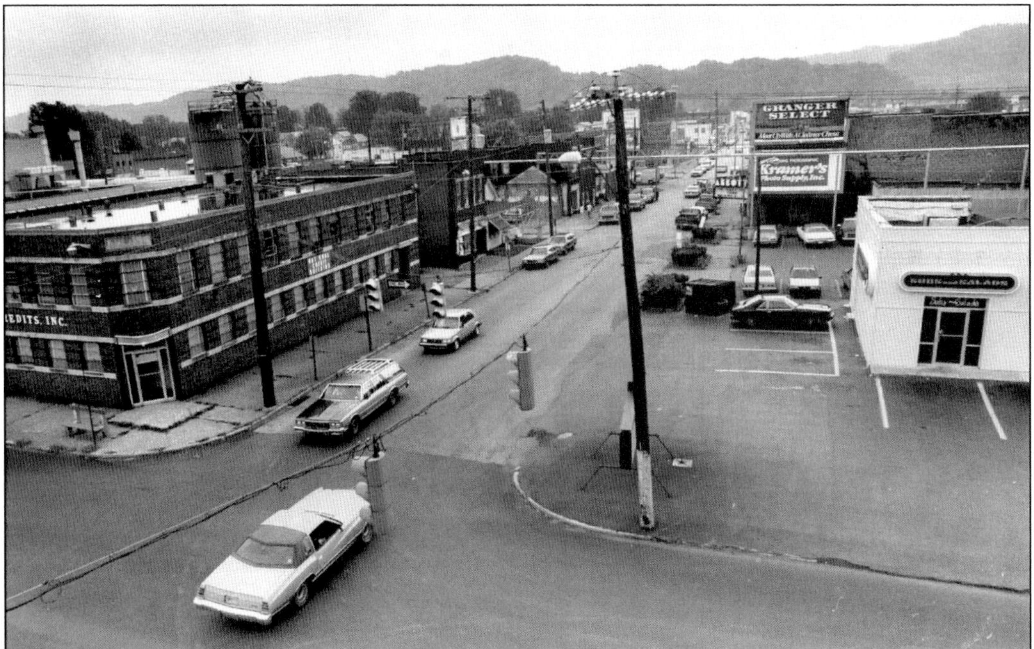

This picture of what was Central City and is now called West Huntington was taken in 1987, just before renovations began. The tumbler plant, water tower, and brewery are obviously absent in the upper right-hand corner. Many stores were empty or were bars. The neighborhood was avoided by many people.

Four

Transportation

Much of the existence of Central City depended upon transportation. Industry can not exist without a means of moving the product from factory to market. The success of Central City was due to the ideal hub it became because of the ready transportation. The Guyandotte and Big Sandy Rivers emptied into the mighty Ohio River. Huntington to the east was the railroad center that opened the east to the west.

Local transportation became more of a problem than getting the commodities out of the area. Streets were muddy and impassable during certain times of the year. Moving packages, boxes, and product to the rail and river had to be overcome. The rail spurs on Fifteenth Street West proved to be a very helpful link. To move passengers, the electric railway, which eventually became the bus system, was a great boost to Central City. The center for the local cars and bus maintenance was the bus barn built at Nineteenth Street West.

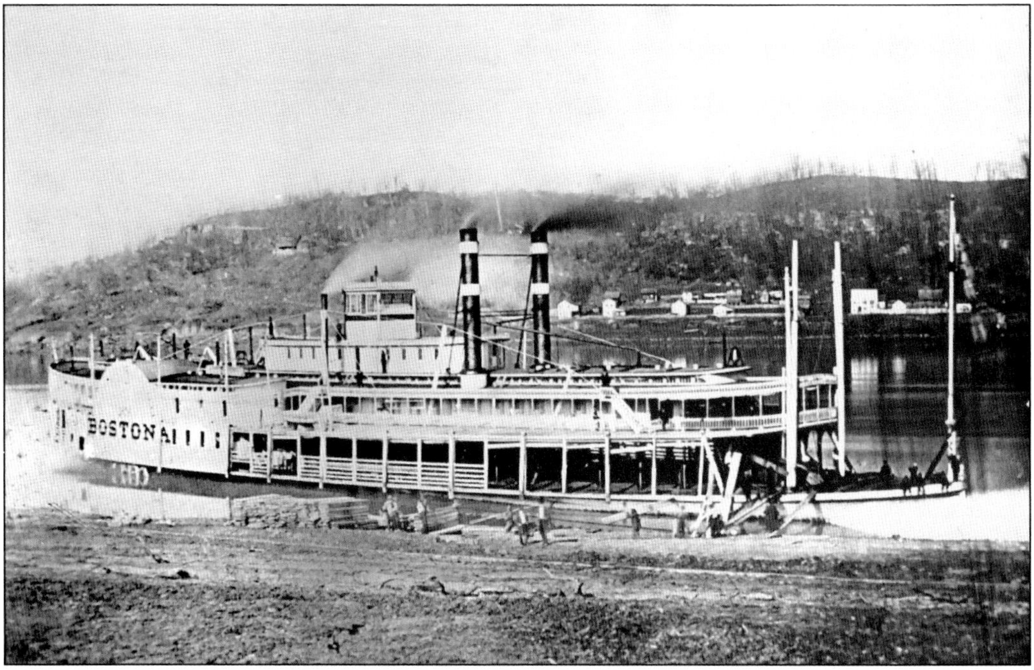

Steamboats stopped at Hull's Landing at the foot of Fourteenth Street West. River travel was very popular not only for shipping goods but also for passengers. It was getting to be quite a shipping center for the surrounding country. These larger boats, like the *Bostonia*, moved tows of loaded coal barges out of Huntington during the 1890s.

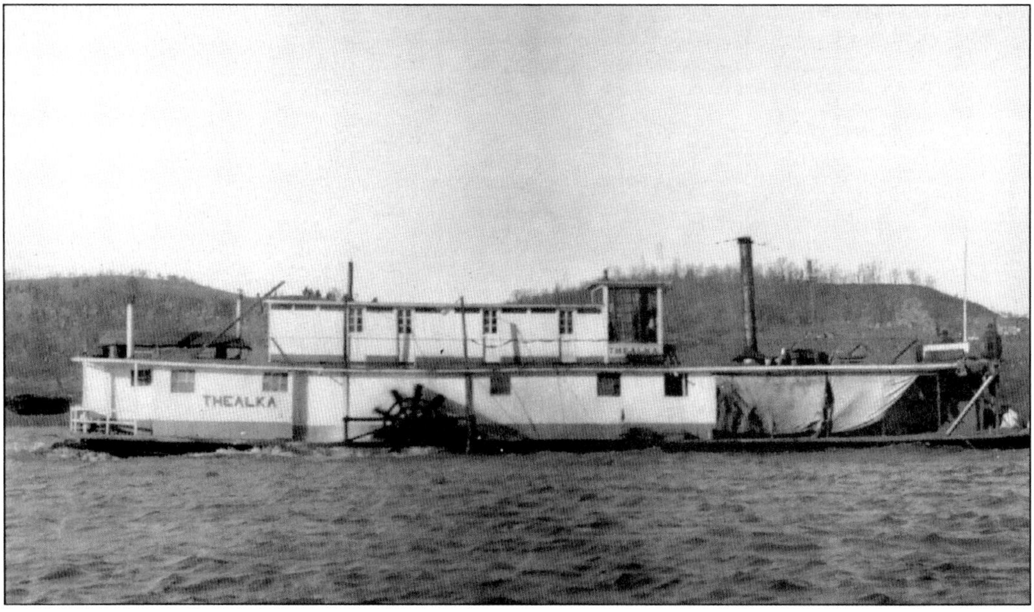

The whole riverfront, from the Guyandotte downriver to Catlettsburg, Kentucky, was busy with loading docks, steamboats, ferries, and rowboats. This is a picture of a packet boat, the *Alka*, taken at Johnston's Landing. Packet boats were used mostly for the delivery of goods. On September 11, 1895, in *The Huntington Advertiser*, the "Central City News" column wrote, "The business at the wharf has been good for several days past."

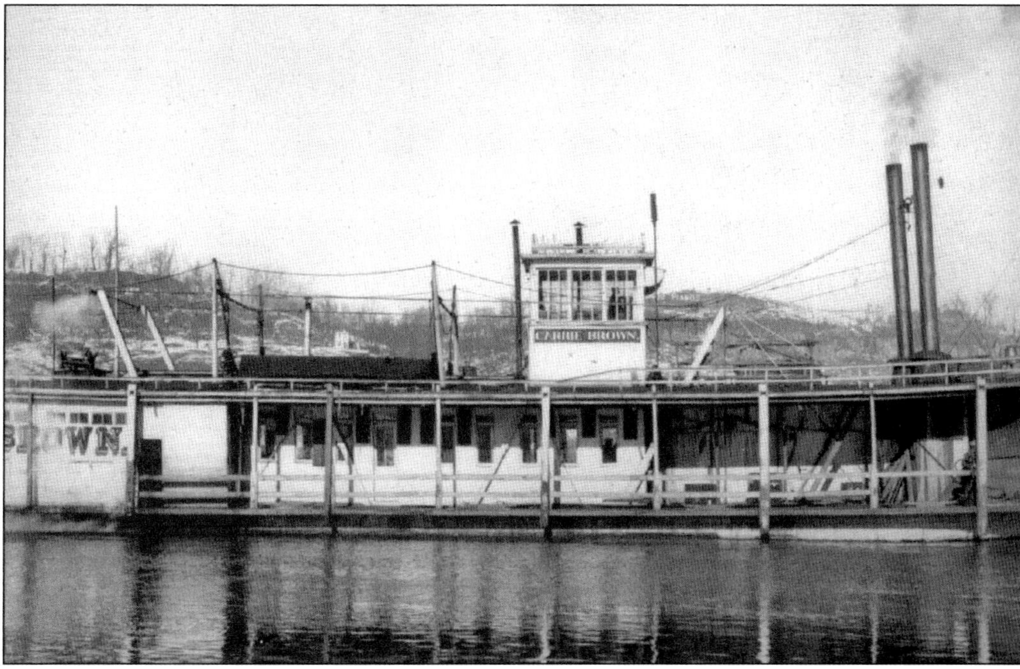

River travel was so important that local newspapers printed the schedules of arrivals and departures of steamboats. The boats each had their own steam whistle signal. They might have three short and two long sounds or one long and two shorts. People who lived along the river could identify which steamboat was arriving by their whistle. Above is the *Carrie Brown*.

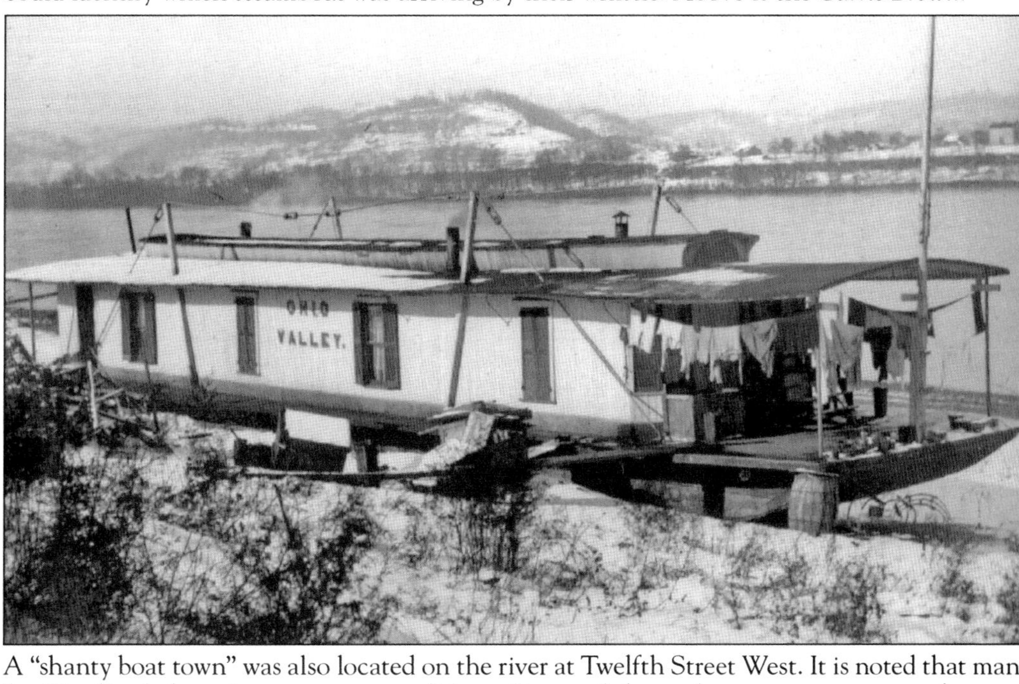

A "shanty boat town" was also located on the river at Twelfth Street West. It is noted that many families lived there in very poor conditions. Some of the early newspapers reported several crimes in that area. This picture shows the *Ohio Valley*, the home of the notorious "Cotton Top" Richardson, according to a written statement on the back of the original picture.

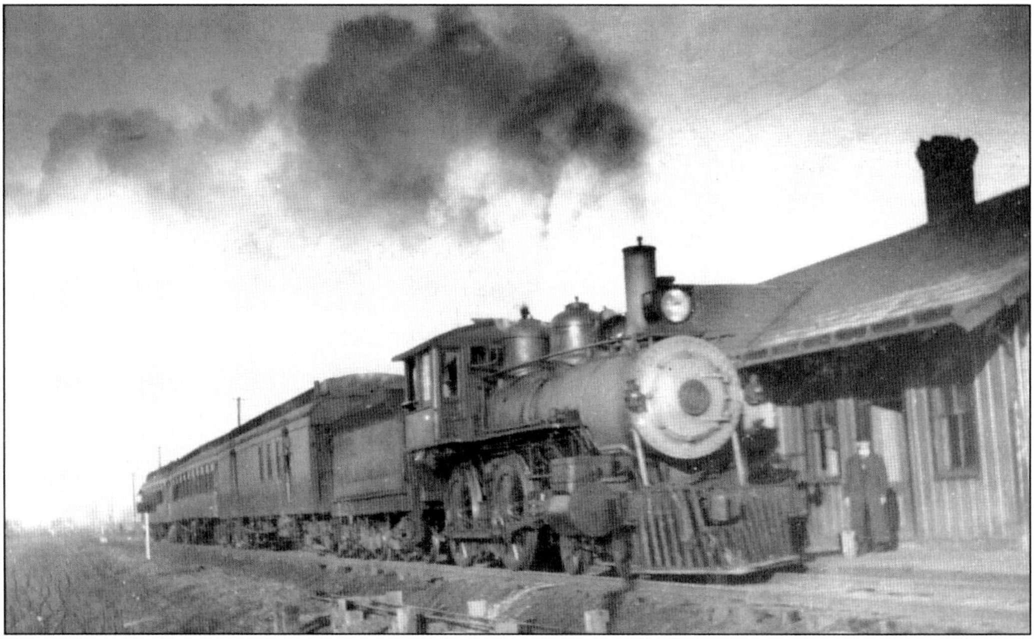

With the railroad already the reason for the existence of Huntington, the rail lines became an integral part of shipping and passenger transport for Central City. The C&O had a passenger station at the Fourteenth Street West and Van Buren Avenue. This picture is of the Central City B&O Station that stood approximately where the Central City Gazebo is today.

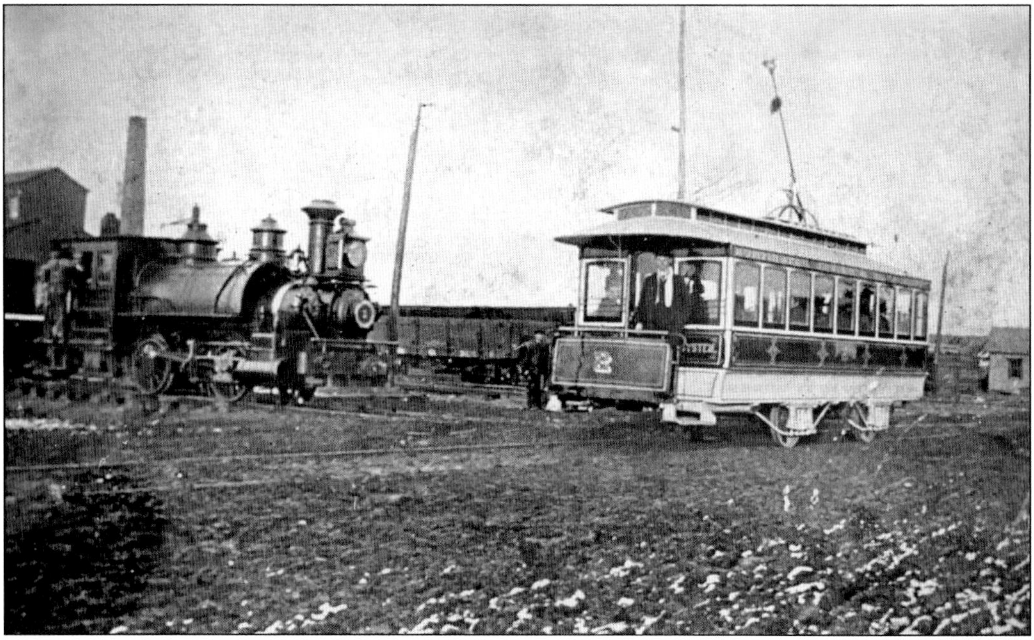

One local passenger train ran from Guyandotte, West Virginia, to Catlettsburg, Kentucky, and back, called the "dummy train." It was not kept on a strict schedule because of the many stops along the way; thus it was called the dummy. It is shown here making a connection with the city electric streetcar. Many people traveled from Charleston to Catlettsburg to buy as much whiskey as they could carry in a suitcase.

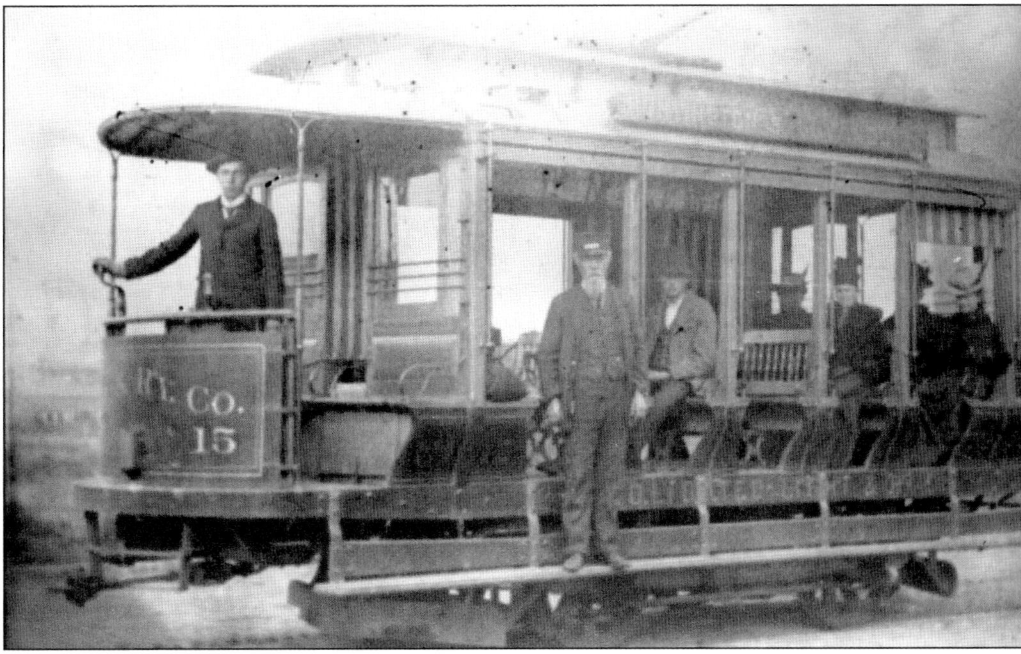

The Huntington Electric Light & Street Railway Company was chartered on June 13, 1888. It was said to have been the second electric streetcar line in the world, according to notes written by Leonard Samworth Jr., grandson of Fred Samworth, a former president of the Ohio Valley Electric Company. The City of Huntington granted a franchise to the Huntington belt line to extend to Central City in 1892.

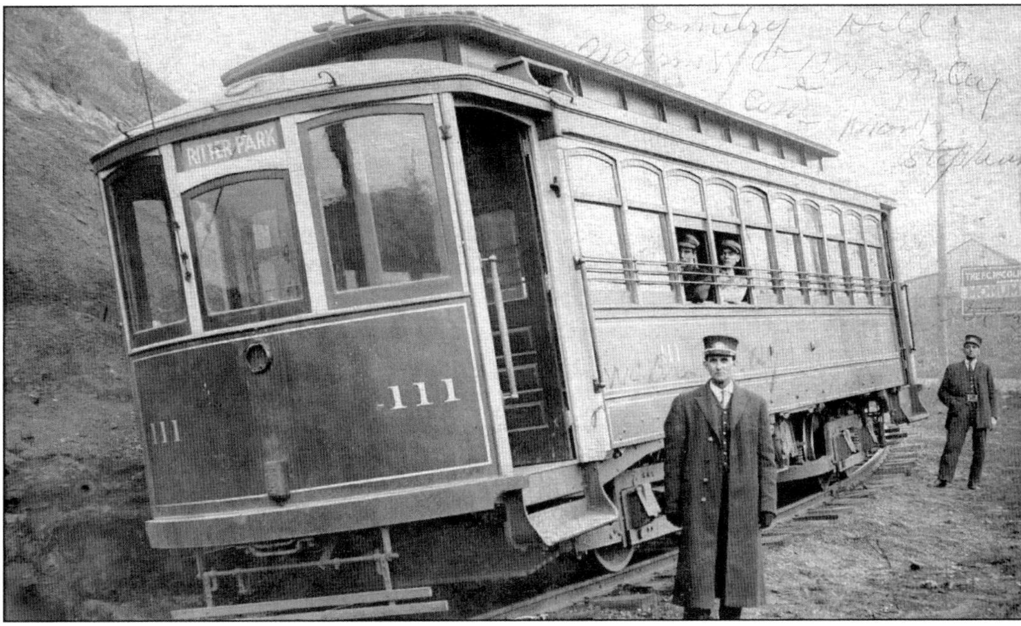

This line was run to Central City in 1892 by the newly named Consolidated Light and Railway. Pictured above standing on the ground from left to right are motorman W. C. Bromley and conductor Frank Stephens. Z. T Vinson, who was one of the organizers of the Huntington and Kenova Land Company, acquired the Consolidated Light and Railway Company in 1899.

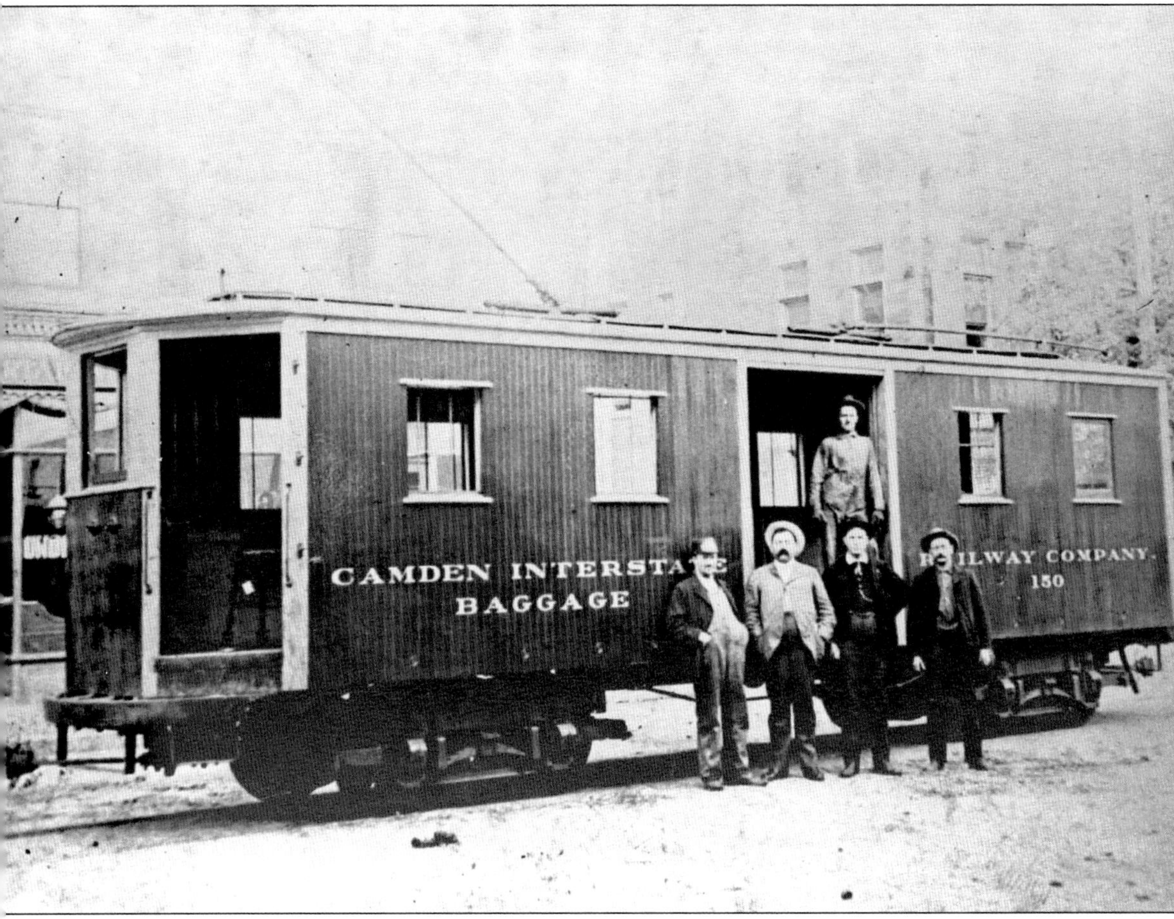

Vinson and Johnson N. Camden purchased bonds for a new company on December 13, 1900, the Camden Interstate Railway Company. The picture above shows, from left to right, John Williams, Harvey Clay, Alpha Cowen, Ed Cole, and Charles Martin (in the car) in 1902.

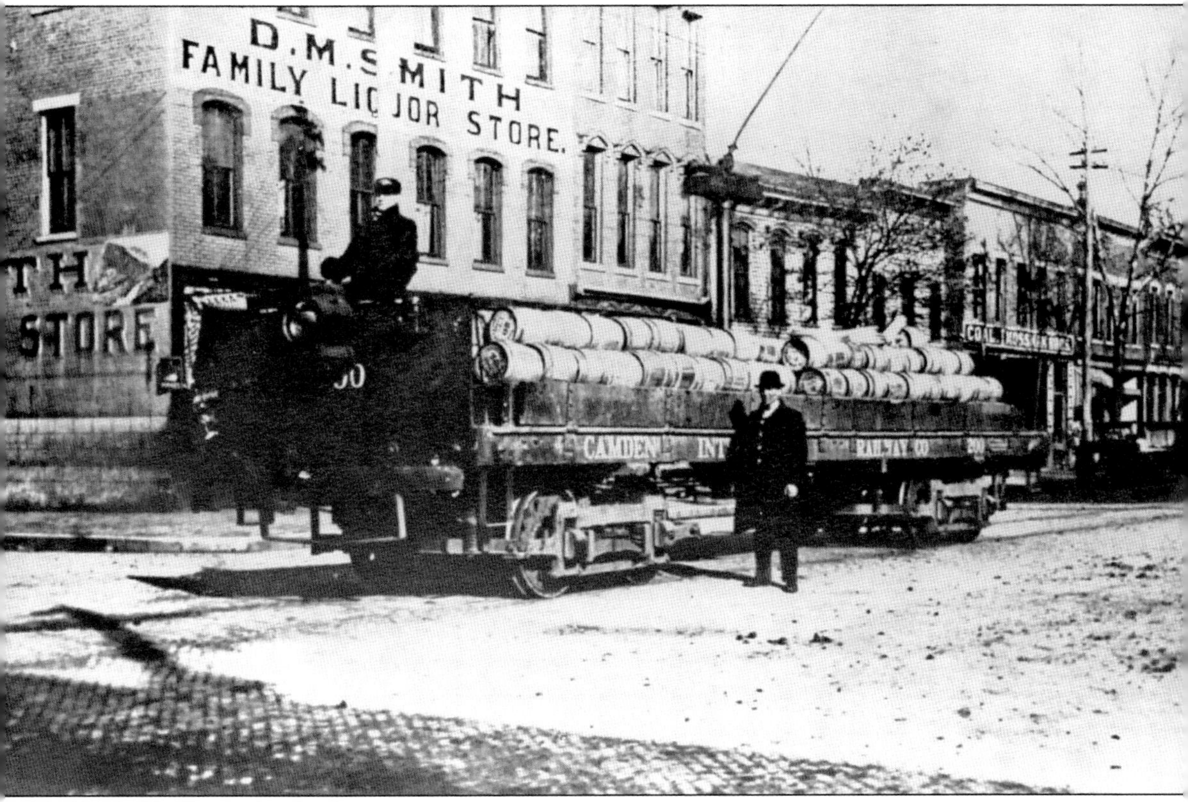

The Camden Interstate Railway carried freight as well as passengers. This car held $300 worth of nail kegs and $200 worth of barbed wire bails. This picture, also taken in 1902, is of motorman Charles Martin (left) and an unidentified gentleman standing in the street.

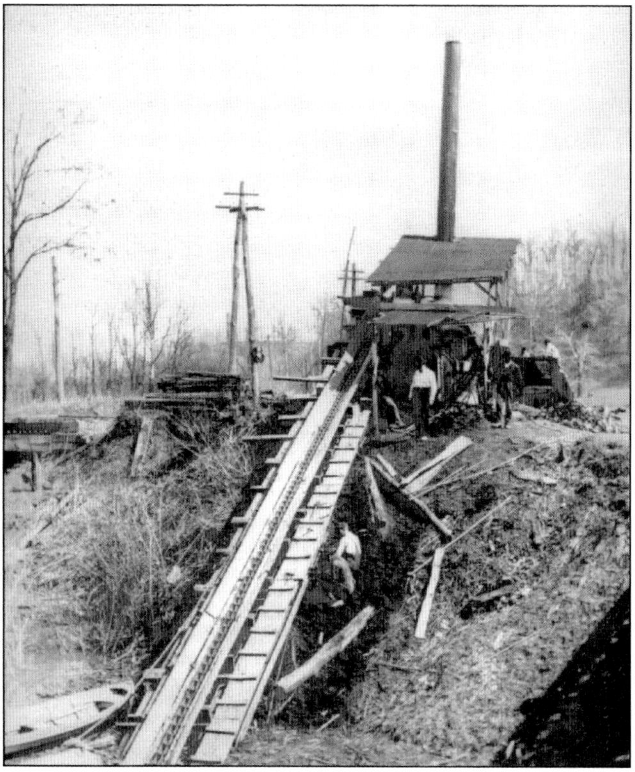

This picture was taken April 2, 1906, at Twelve Pole Creek at a "tie hoist." This hoist pulled rail ties up from the riverboats to be used to lay or repair tracks. The Camden Interstate Railroad is on the left.

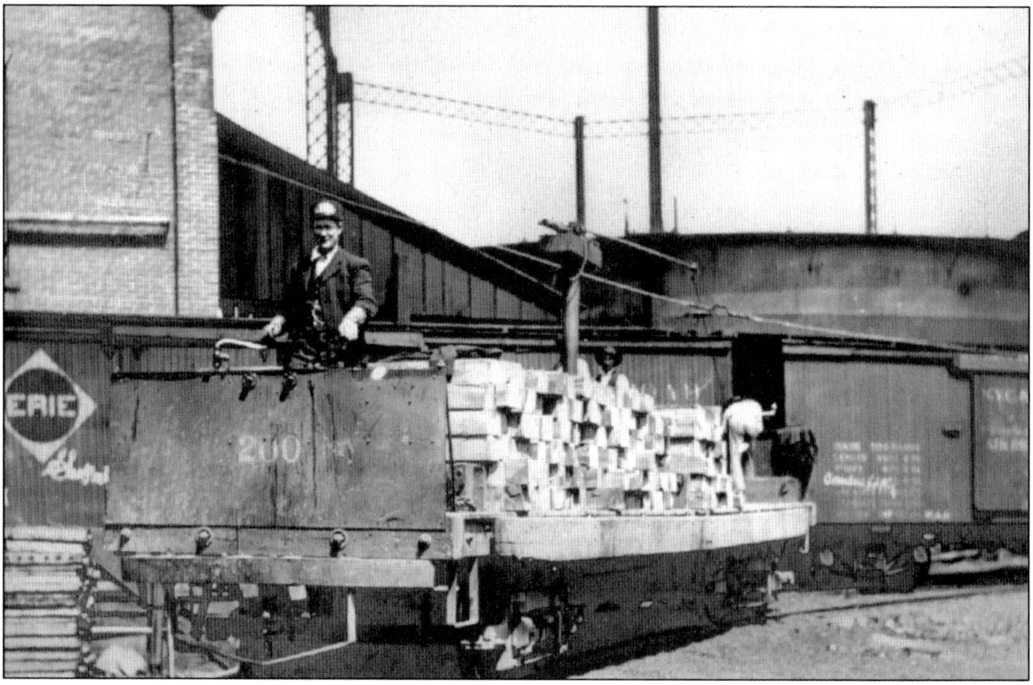

This is Car 200 loading more ties at the rear of the car house at Johnston's Lane or Third Street West in 1906. Loading the ties are motorman "Green Goose" and snatcher "Happy Hooligan." The nicknames of these workers were given but not their real names.

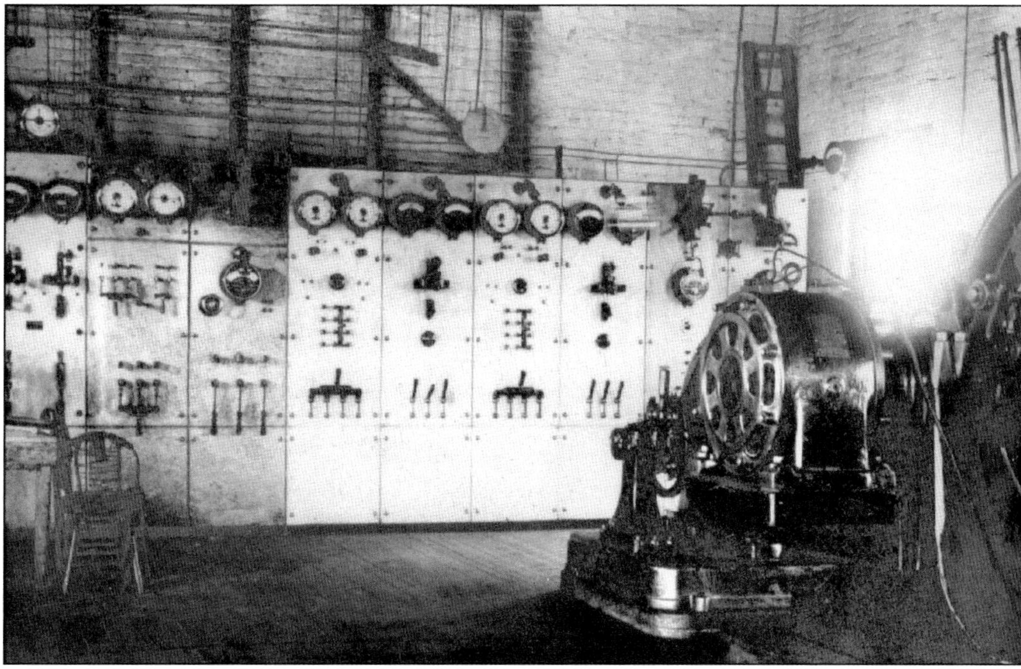

The electric supplied to the electric railway came from Kenova, West Virginia, but a substation was built at Johnston's Lane for the sole purpose of the railway. For a while, this was also the barn until the extension was made to Central City. This was the inside of the station in 1906.

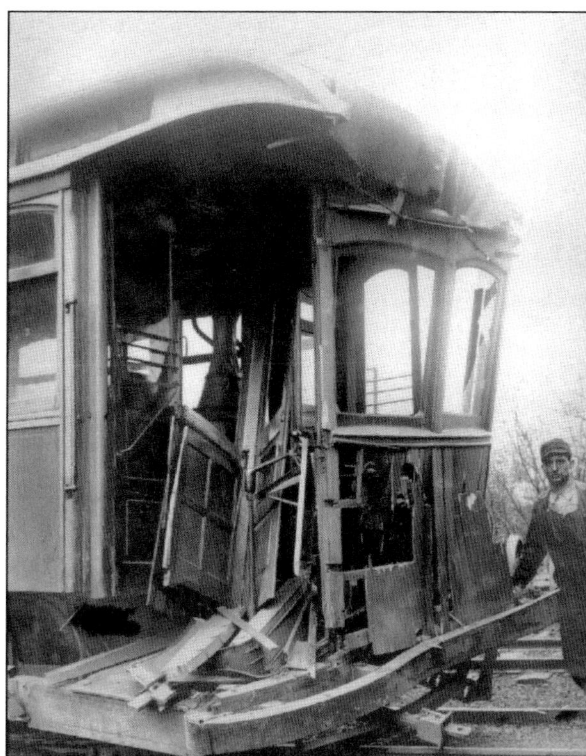

The cause of this car accident is unknown, but it was certainly a pretty good bump. Car 101 was wrecked in April 1906. It was repaired at the Johnston Lane carbarn.

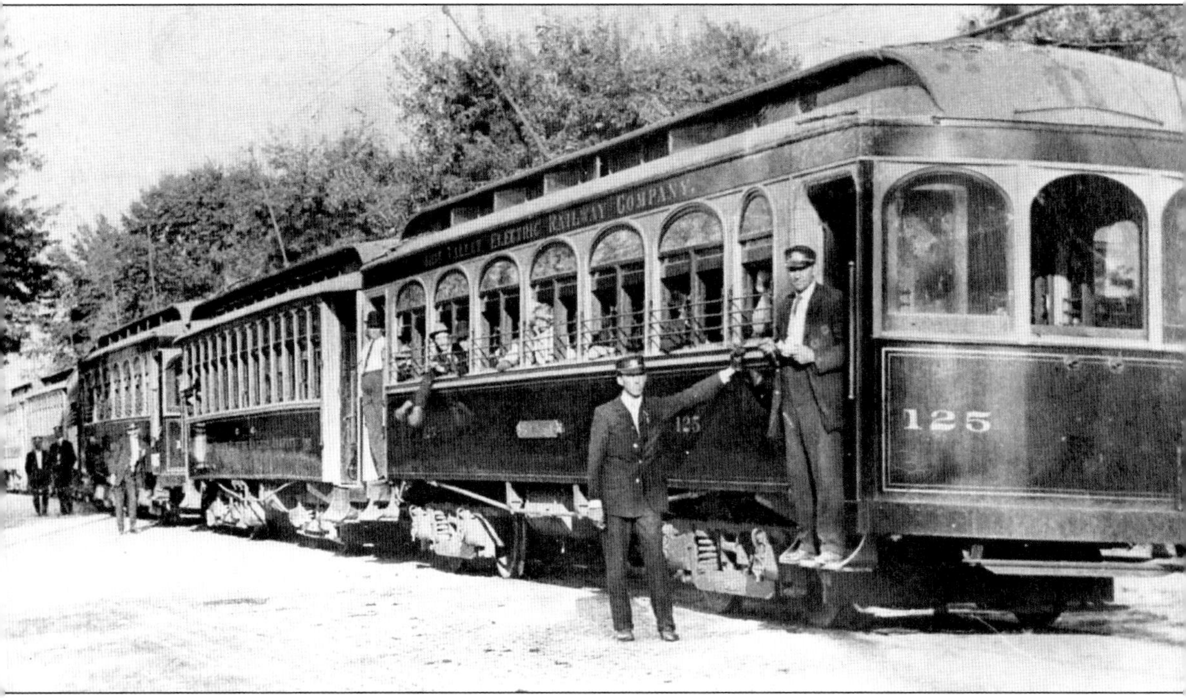

This car of the Ohio Valley Electric Railway Company was a popular run as seen by the number of cars attached. All of these cars had connections to the railway barn on Nineteenth Street West. The Ohio Valley Bus Company name was the new name given by Z. T. Vinson.

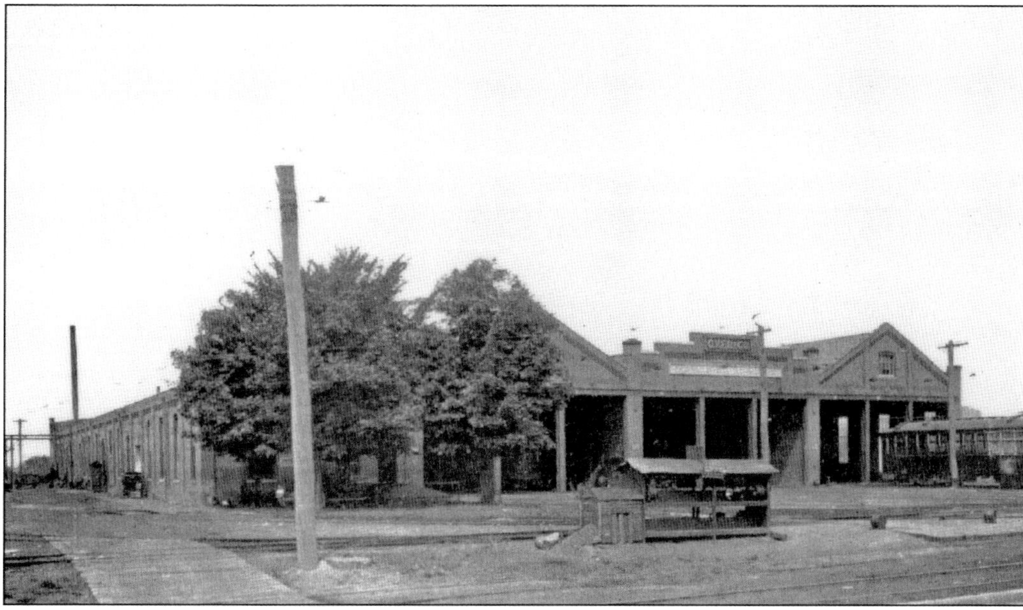

This picture was taken of the Ohio Valley Electric Railway carbarn on Nineteenth Street West. The exact date of this building is not known to the author or Leonard Samworth Jr., but a guess would be around 1909.

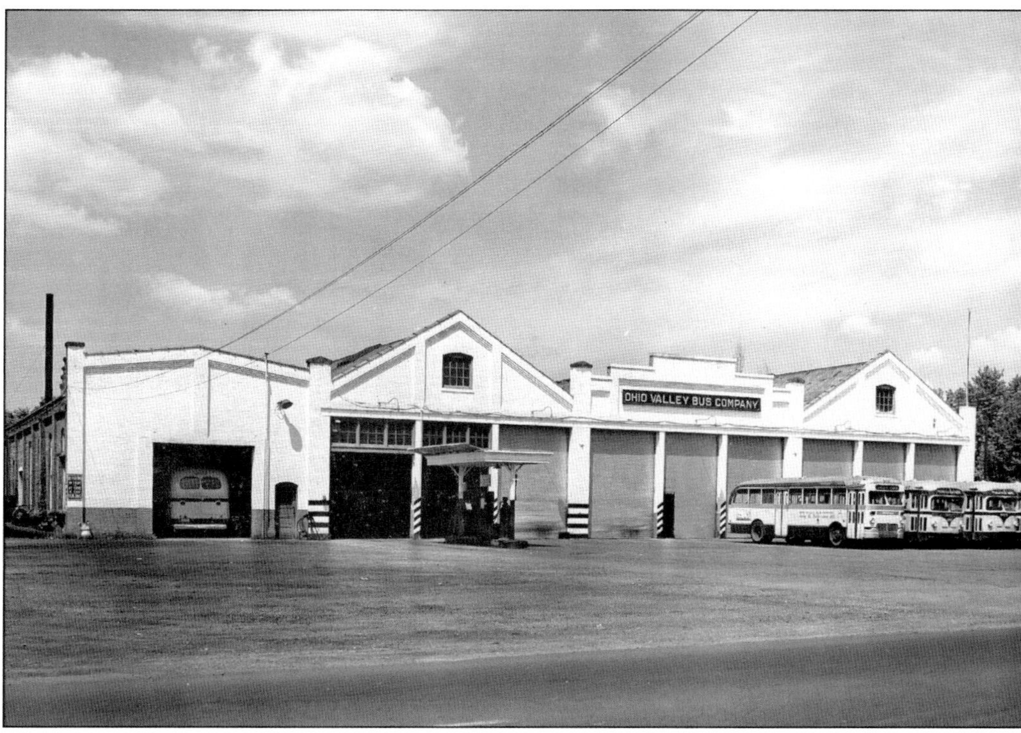

The carbarn has changed very little over the years except for painting and the name. The top picture was taken in 1937 and the bottom one in 1954. When the bus company became the Tri-State Transit Company, the shops were moved to downtown Huntington. The barn is now a free market.

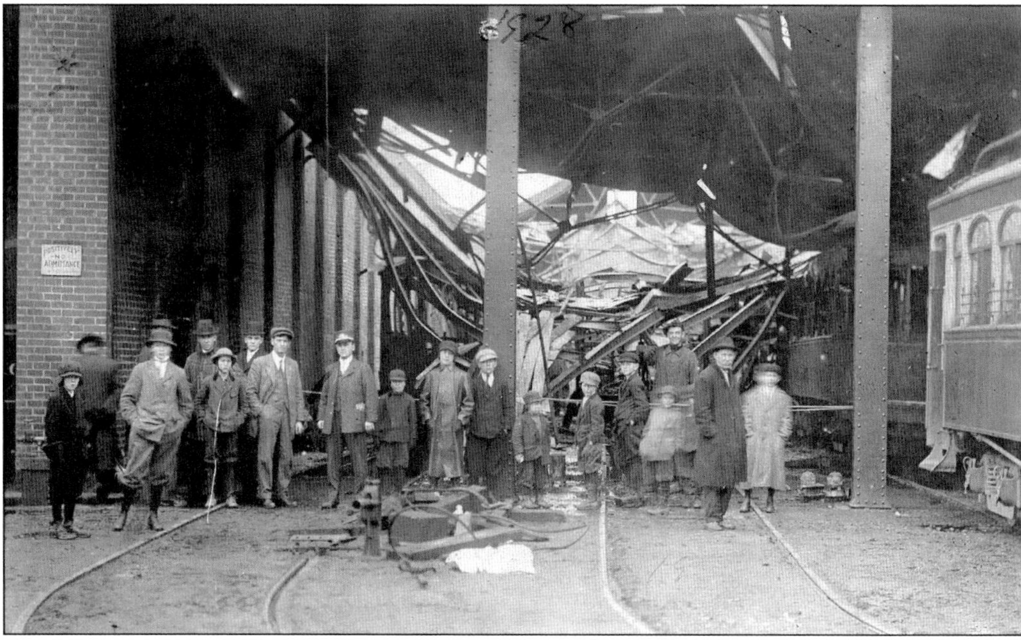

The carbarn had a fire in 1912. The destruction looks to be in one complete section of the barn.

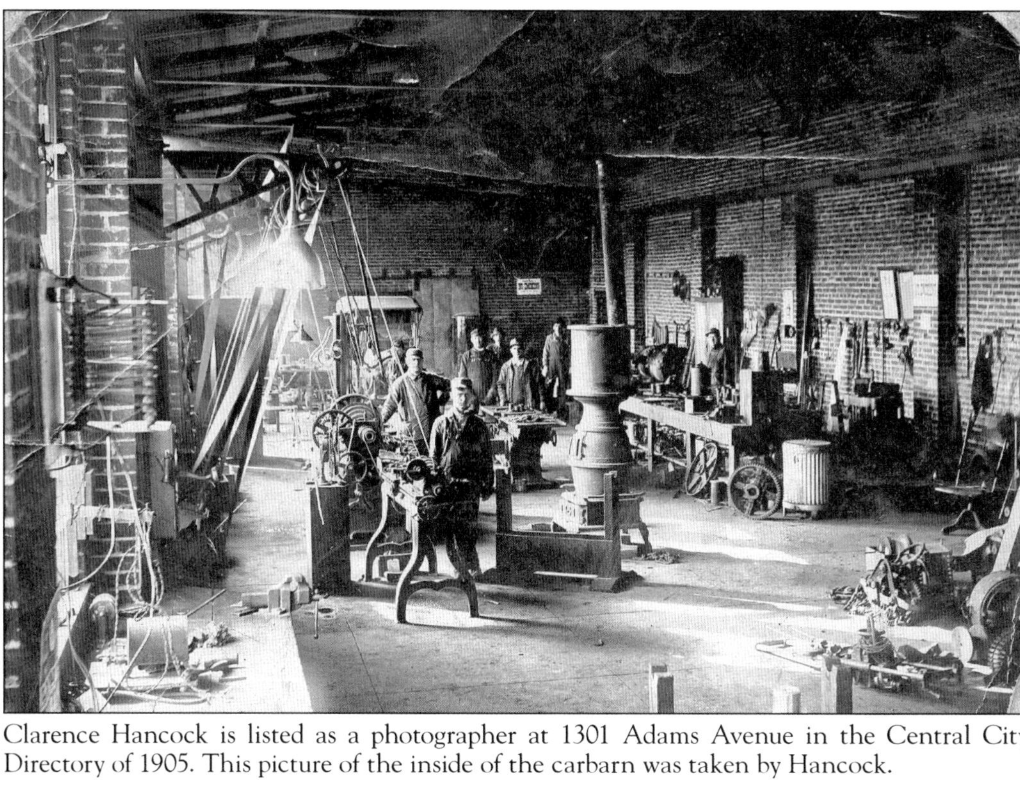

Clarence Hancock is listed as a photographer at 1301 Adams Avenue in the Central City Directory of 1905. This picture of the inside of the carbarn was taken by Hancock.

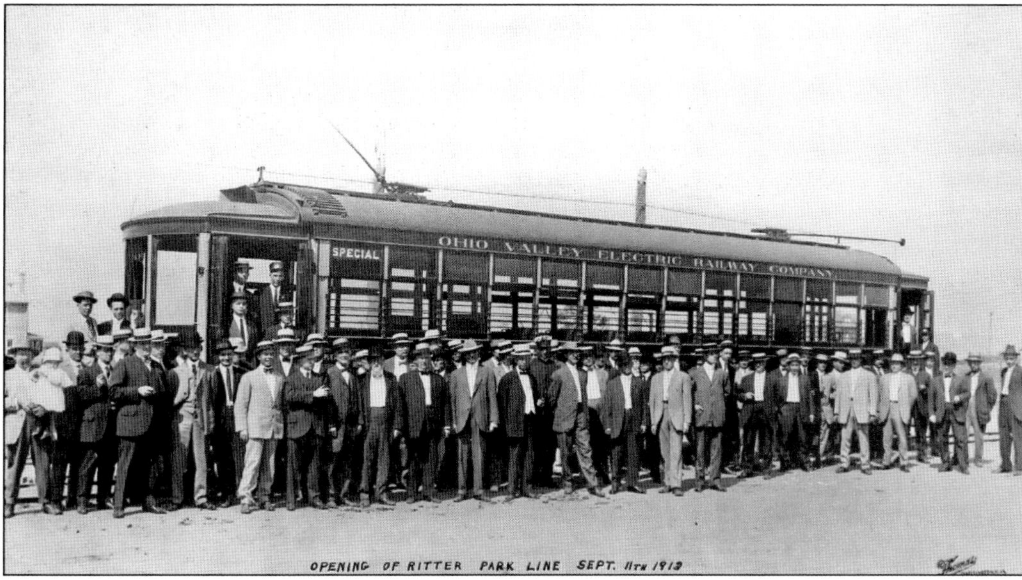

This 1913 car of the Electric Railway Company ran to Ritter Park. Ritter Park is the largest public park in the city of Huntington. Seventy acres was set aside in 1913 as a city park. Part of that park was extended down Four Pole Creek to Central City, which was called West Huntington by then.

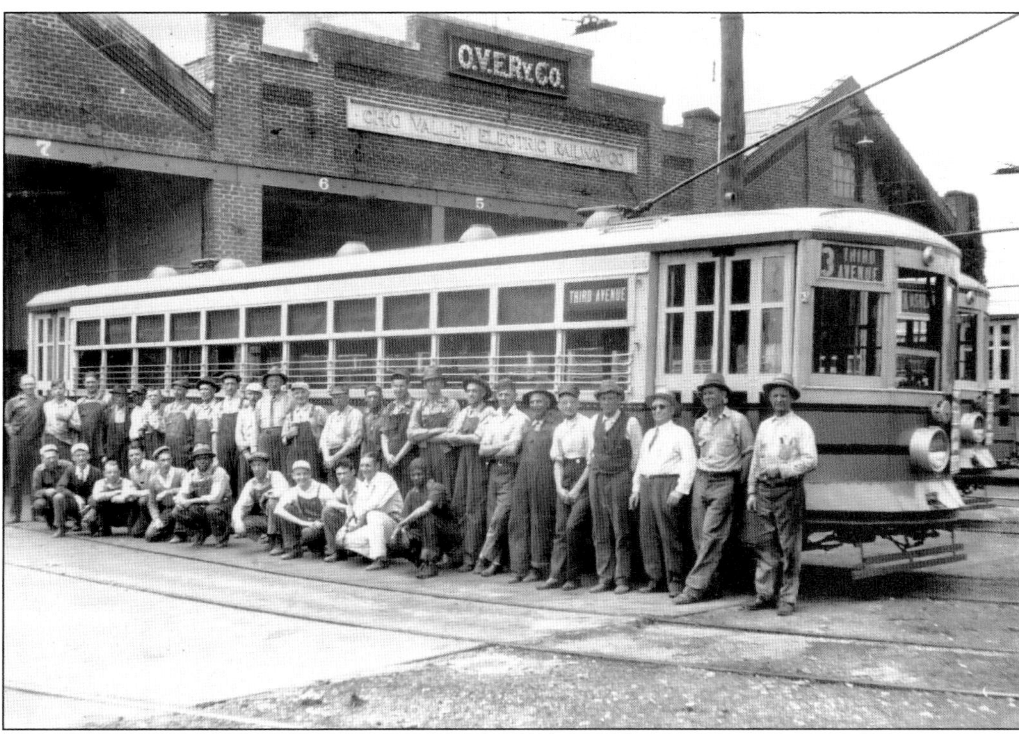

In 1916, the Camden Interstate Railway changed its name to Ohio Valley Electric Railway Company. This was a company picture taken sometime after that. It was owned by the American Gas and Electric Company until 1927.

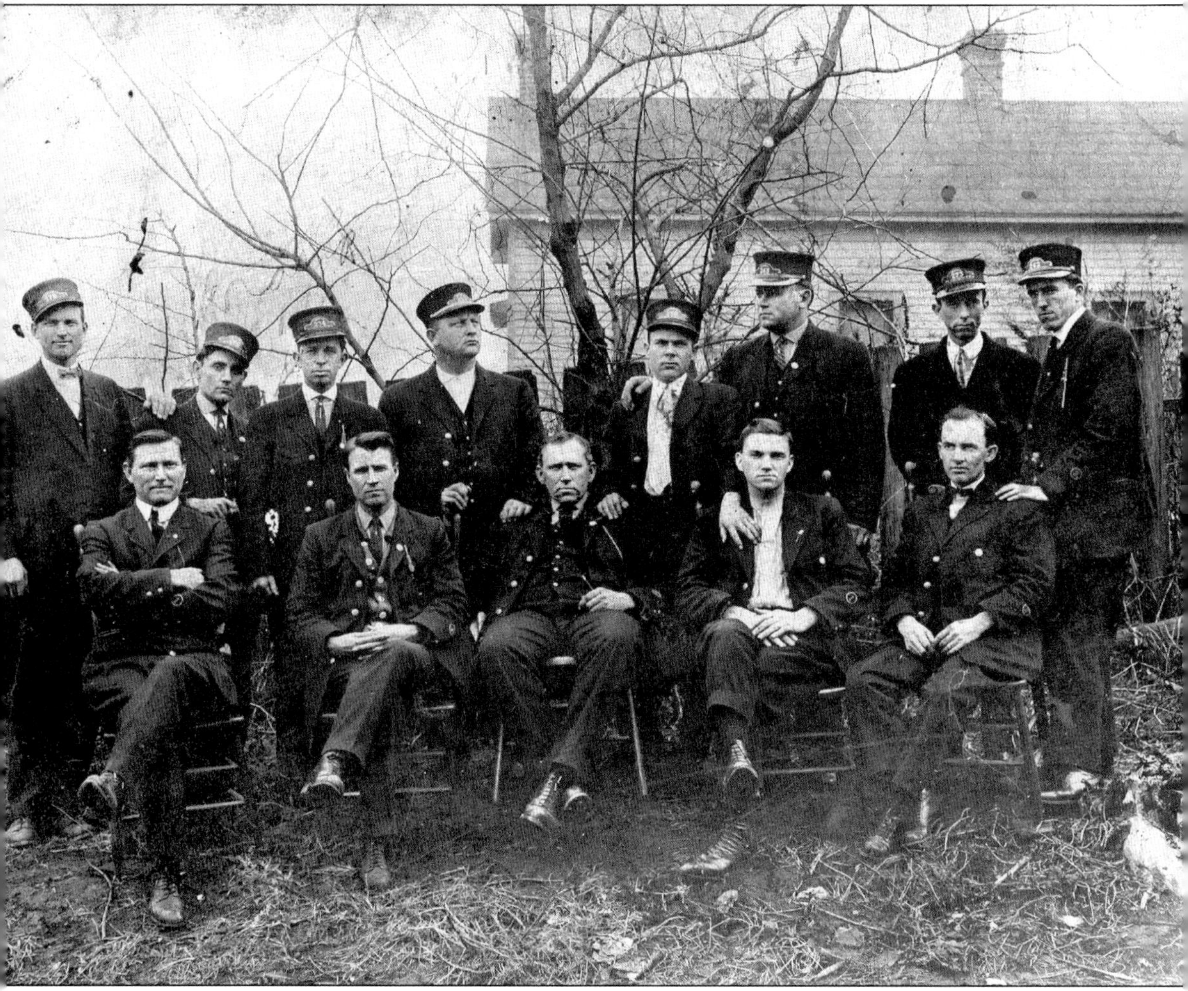

According to a newspaper article, "Many streetcar men stayed overnight at the 'barn' or in their cars as many had no automobile with which to get to or from work in the wee hours. Thus lasting friendships were made." Pictured above from left to right are (first row) A. B. Schaffer, A. J. Baker, Ed Fiser, Carl Phipps, and Alvin Dick; (second row) Oscar Watts, Frank Stephenson, Don Shoemaker, Wesley Lipptrack, Corey Newman, ? Klaunch, ? Farrell, and Walter Honaker.

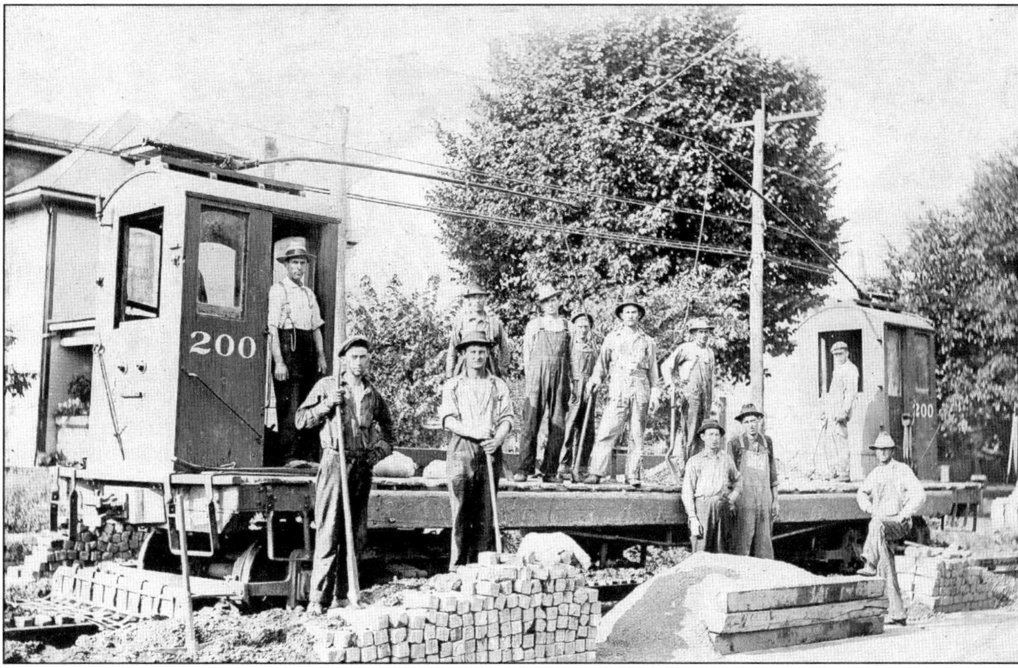

Building and repairs were all a part of the progress. This crew is working from a repair car in 1917. The brick used here is most likely from the Huntington Red Brick Company at Van Buren Avenue near Ninth Street West in Central City.

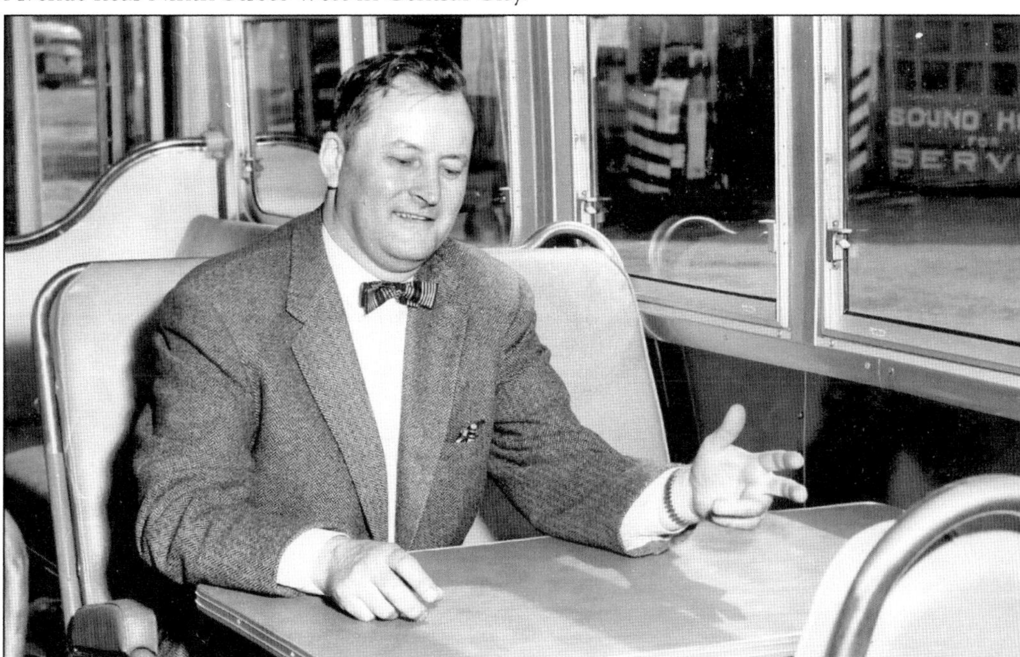

In 1924, a young man from Wilmington, Delaware, came to Huntington to run the Ohio Valley Electric Company. In 1933, this man, Fred Samworth, became president of the company until 1944, when his son, Leonard Samworth Sr., (above) became president of the successor company, the Ohio Valley Bus Company.

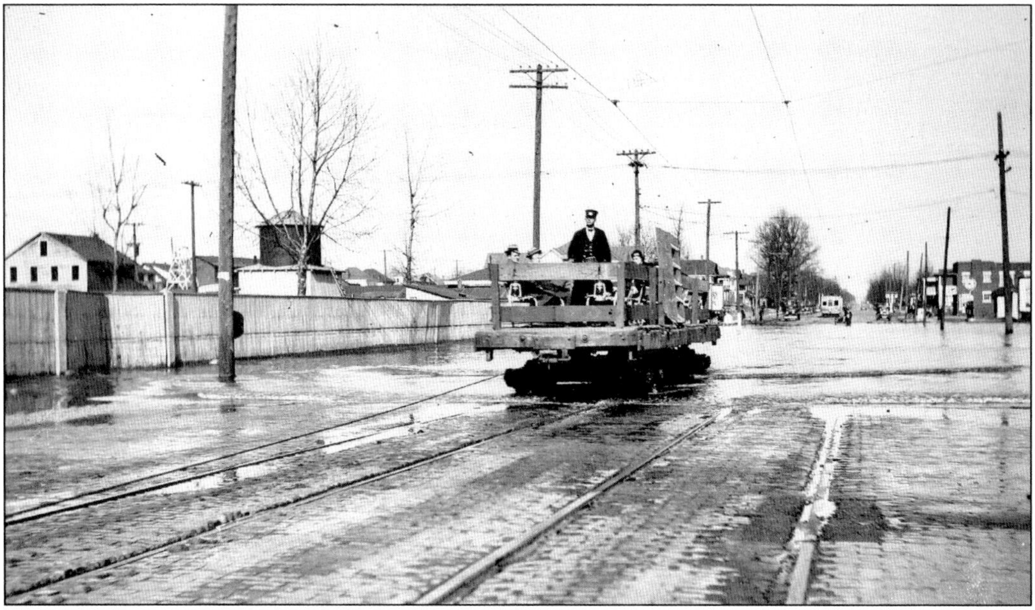

This picture of a maintenance trolley was taken around Third Street West after the 1937 flood. The trolley was actually used to help evacuate people during the flood in January of that year. It was soon after this that Huntington became the first city in West Virginia to be served entirely by buses.

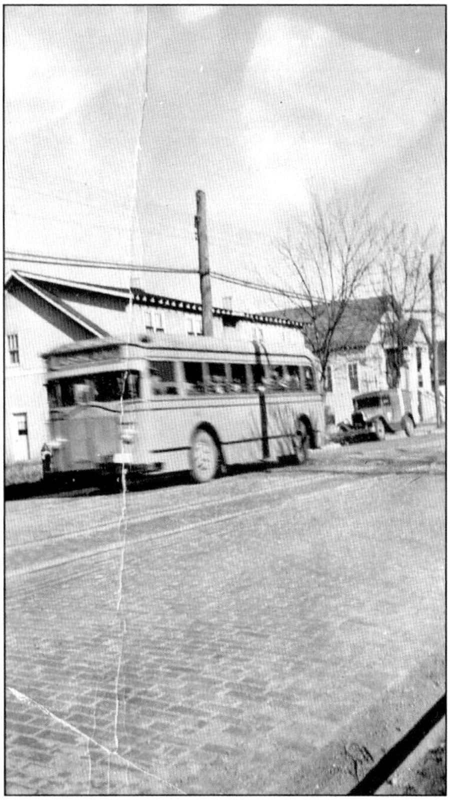

The bus at left is a 1938 model of the Ohio Valley Bus Company and is said to travel at 45 miles per hour. Over the years, many different models were purchased as in any business that wants to serve the public with new and renewed products.

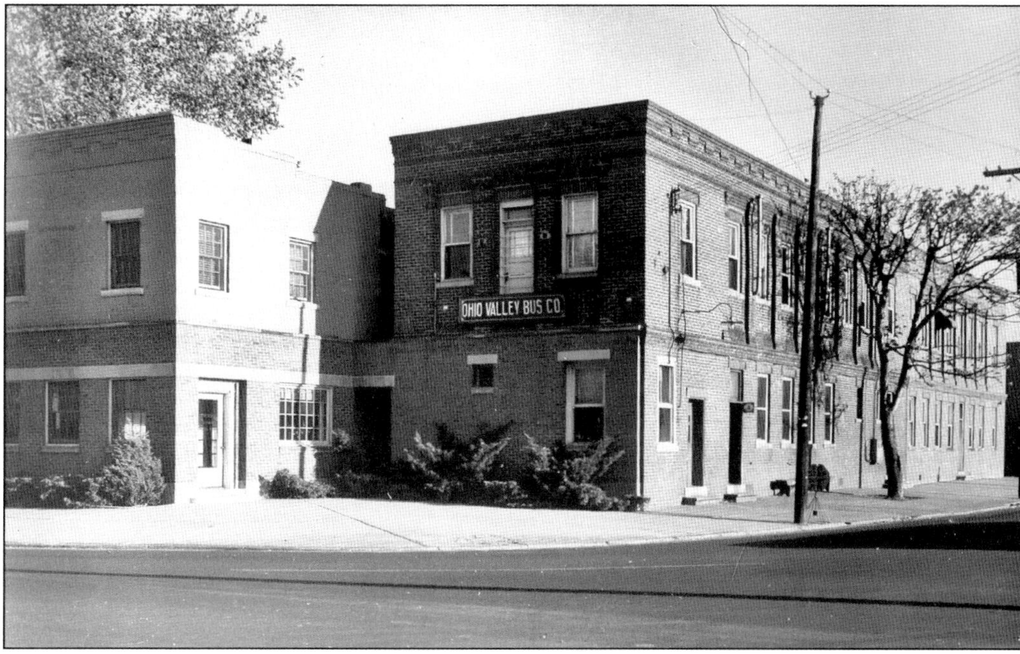

The Ohio Valley Bus Company built an office building across the street from the bus barn at the corner of Washington Avenue and Nineteenth Street West. The office is still used by another business owned by Leonard Samworth Jr., the Ohio Valley Development Company.

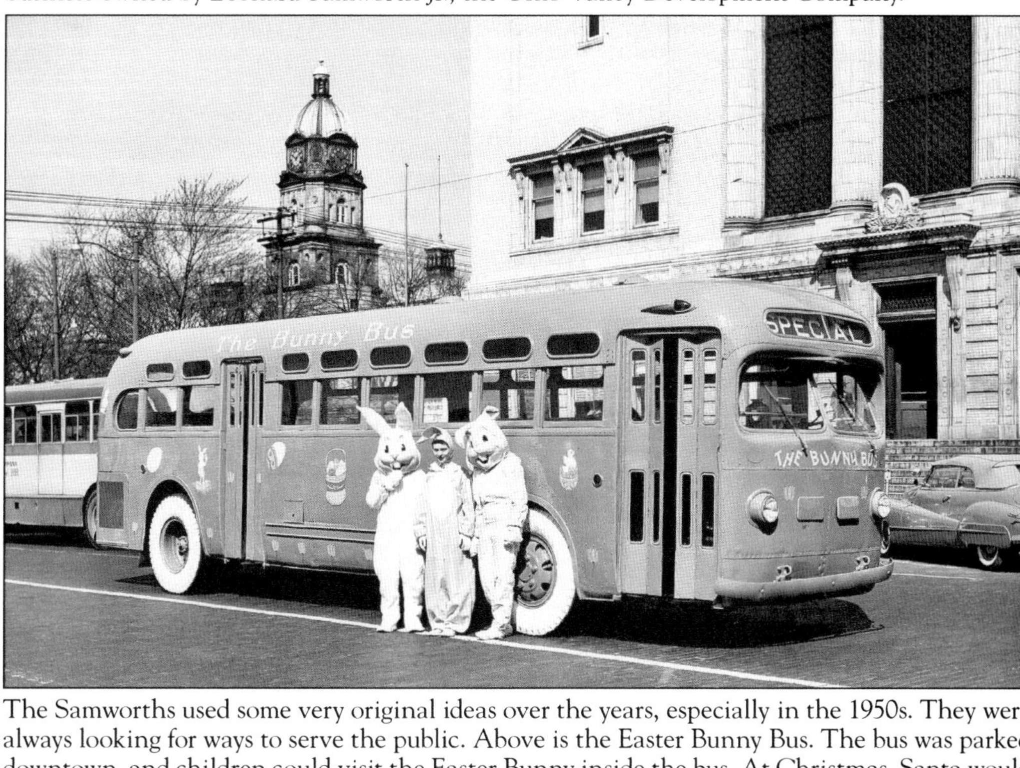

The Samworths used some very original ideas over the years, especially in the 1950s. They were always looking for ways to serve the public. Above is the Easter Bunny Bus. The bus was parked downtown, and children could visit the Easter Bunny inside the bus. At Christmas, Santa would be available on a Santa Bus.

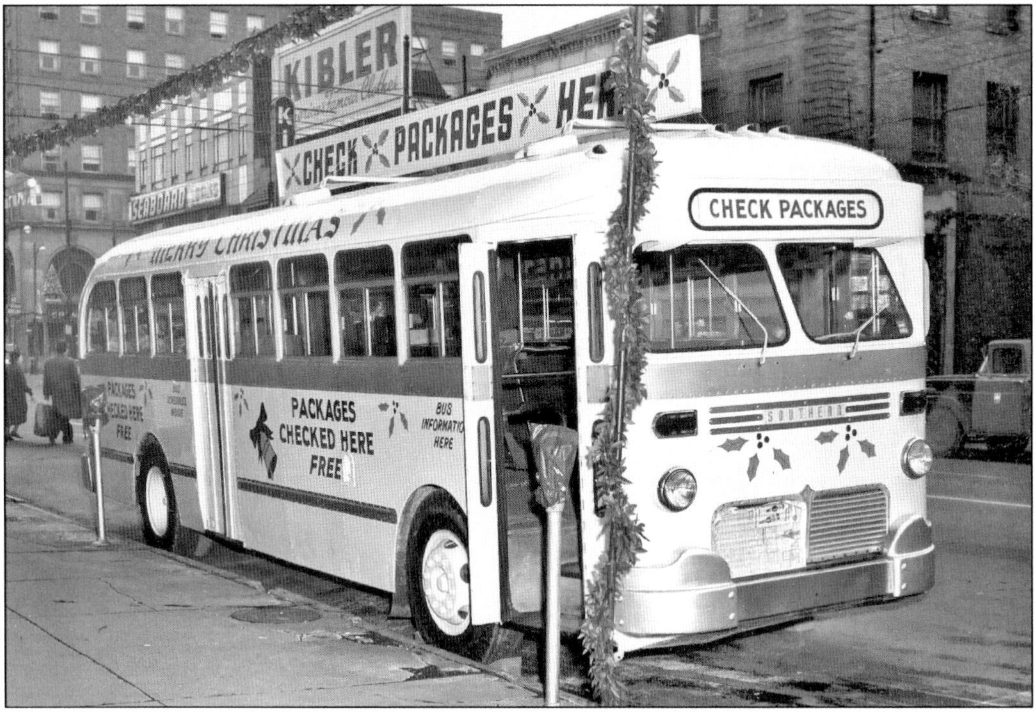

At Christmas, the Samworths were very innovative. Shoppers often did not drive cars downtown. If they did, then cars were parked a few blocks away. A bus was parked downtown around Ninth Street. As shoppers filled their arms with packages, they could check them at the Christmas bus. After finishing the day's shopping, they could pick up all of their packages and head home.

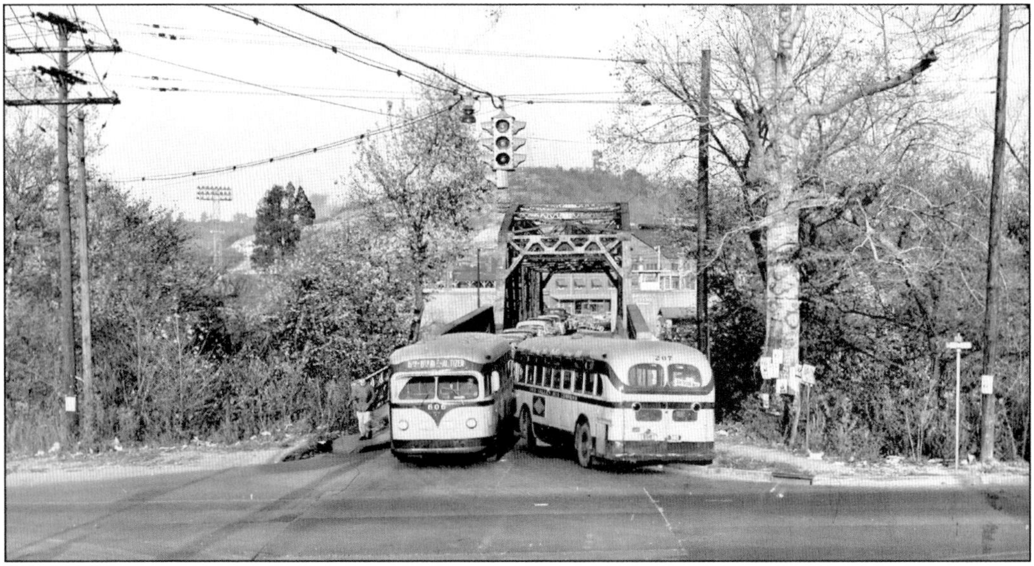
Incoming and outgoing buses passed each other along the routes, but in 1956, these buses look to be a little close at the Nickel Plant bridge in East Huntington. The Ohio Valley Bus Company has become the Tri-State Transit Authority and still serves the Huntington area. The river still transports coal and freight but very few passengers. Trains are phasing out passenger service to Huntington.

Five

Churches, Schools and Recreation

When a variety of people populate an area, interests are as varied as the population. Church was such a vital part of the early family, not only for spiritual and moral beliefs but also for socialization. This was the center of the community. Sundays were not the only days to attend the building. Sometimes the same building was used for the education of the children. We hear of corn huskings, spelling bees, taffy pulling, and other group entertainment that was often held in the church or schools.

Central City had Presbyterian, Baptist, Christian, and Methodist churches. Schools have always been important to families, so education had to be addressed early in the town. Then adults had to find other entertainment. Theaters, parks, and various organizations, such as the Golden Eagles Lodge, were a part of Central City.

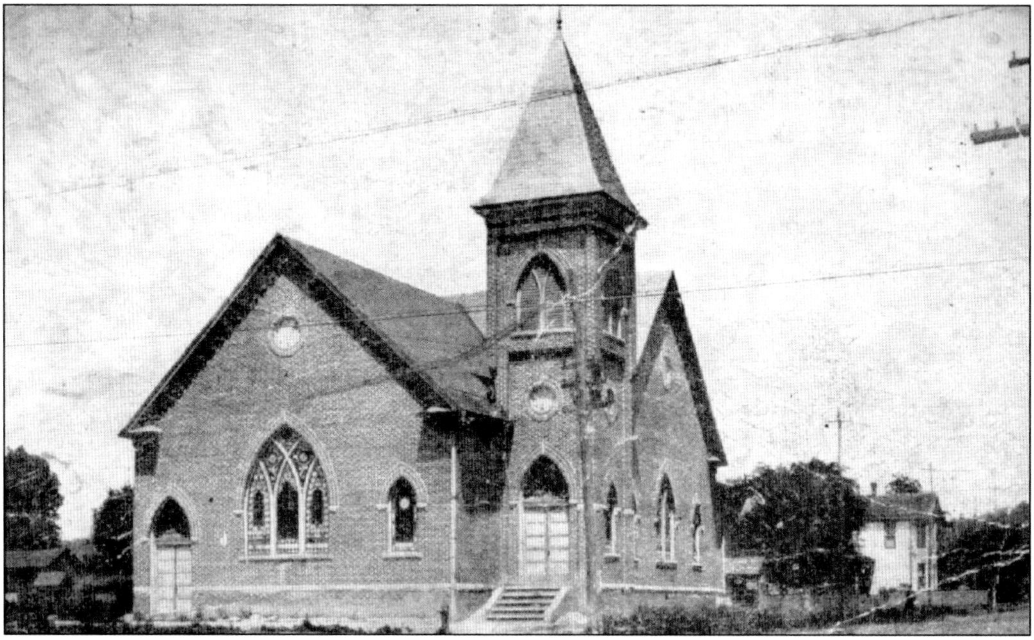

Many of the churches in Central City have celebrated their 100th anniversary because they too were organized during the early days of Central City. Pictured above is one of those churches, the Methodist Episcopal Church. In 1993, this church, now Central Methodist, did celebrate its 100th year.

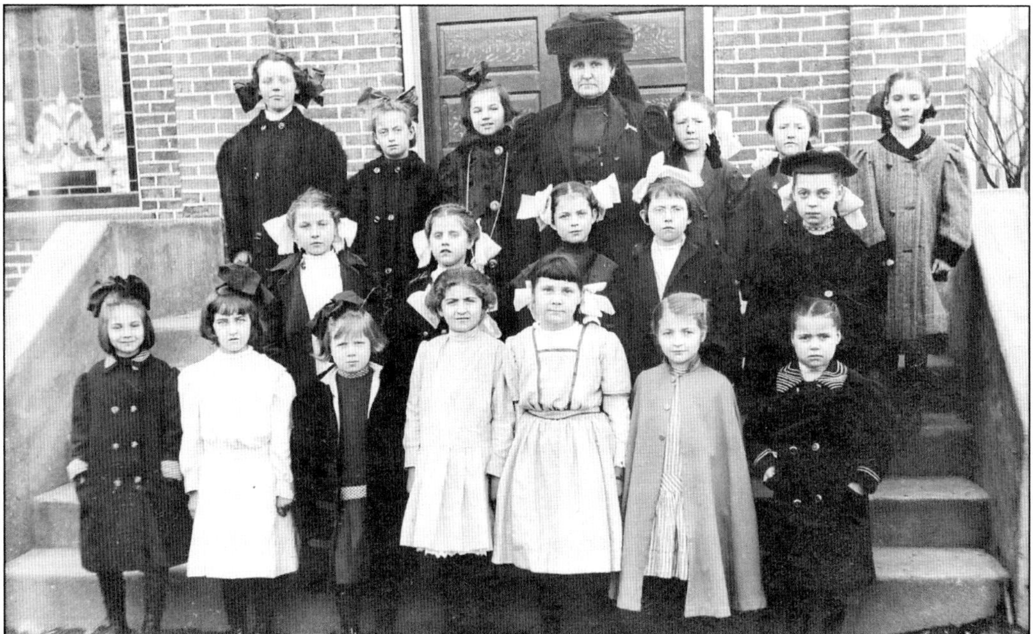

This picture of a girls' class at the Washington Avenue Baptist Church was taken after 1910. When Central City was incorporated into Huntington in 1909, four other churches were listed, First Baptist, Walker Memorial (Baptist), Central Methodist Episcopal South, and Second Presbyterian.

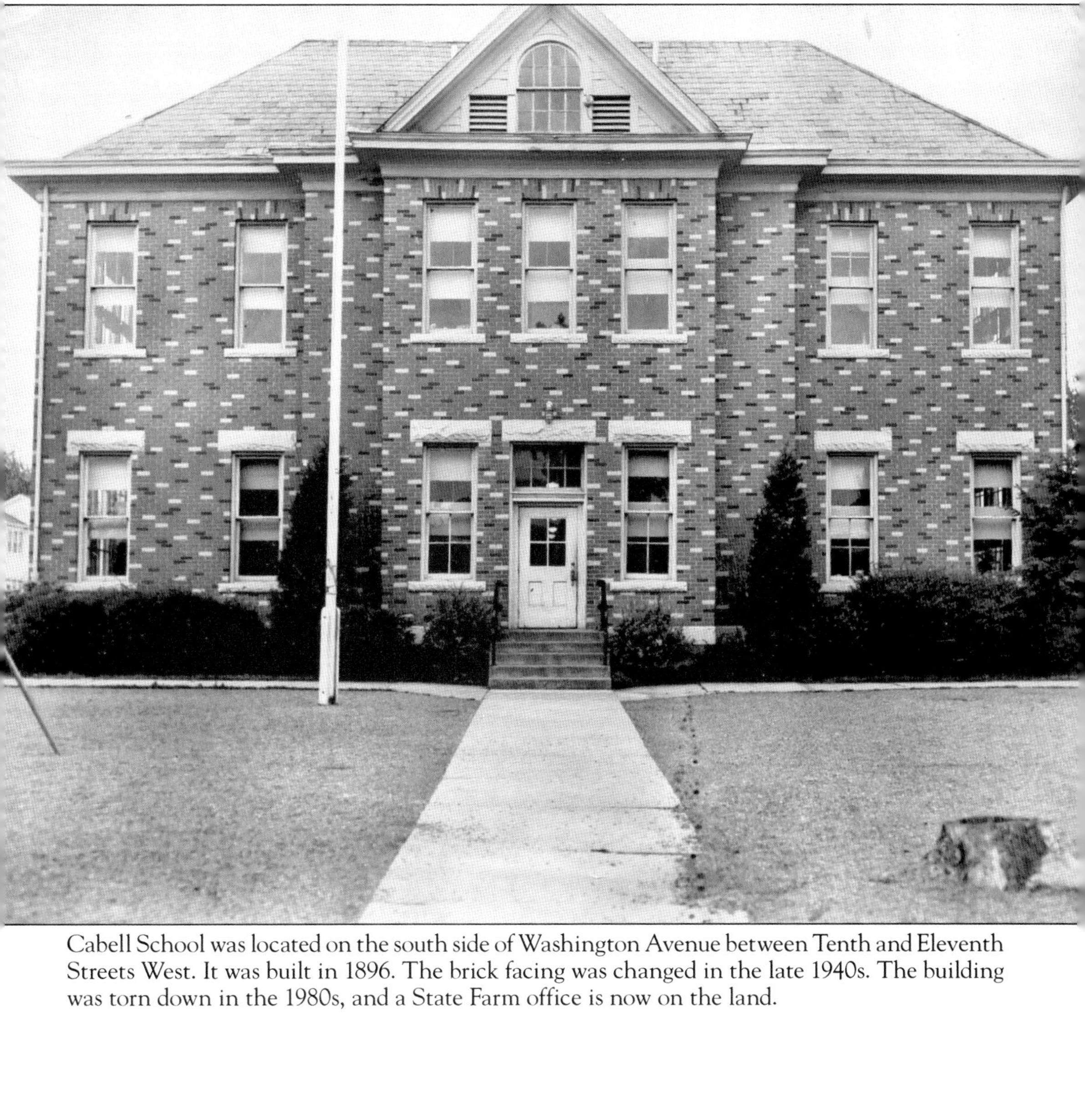

Cabell School was located on the south side of Washington Avenue between Tenth and Eleventh Streets West. It was built in 1896. The brick facing was changed in the late 1940s. The building was torn down in the 1980s, and a State Farm office is now on the land.

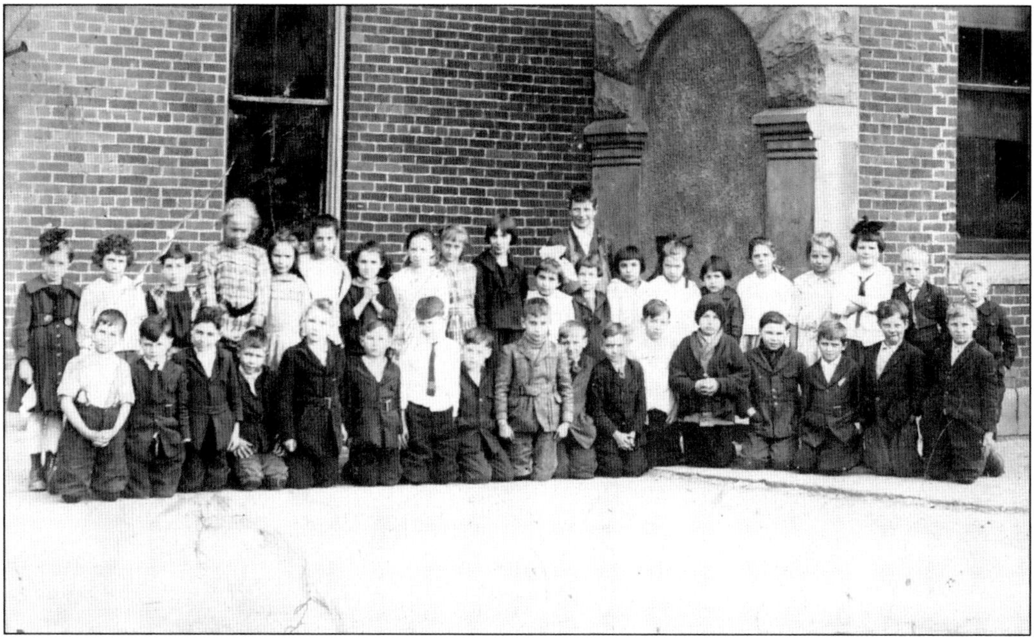

The 1919 second-grade class of Cabell School was certainly dressed up, although children dressed much differently for school in that day. A *Huntington Advertiser* article of August 25, 1895, relates the opening of schools "using the same old buildings" and the possibility "of renting of another building or two." Cabell Elementary School had been greatly anticipated.

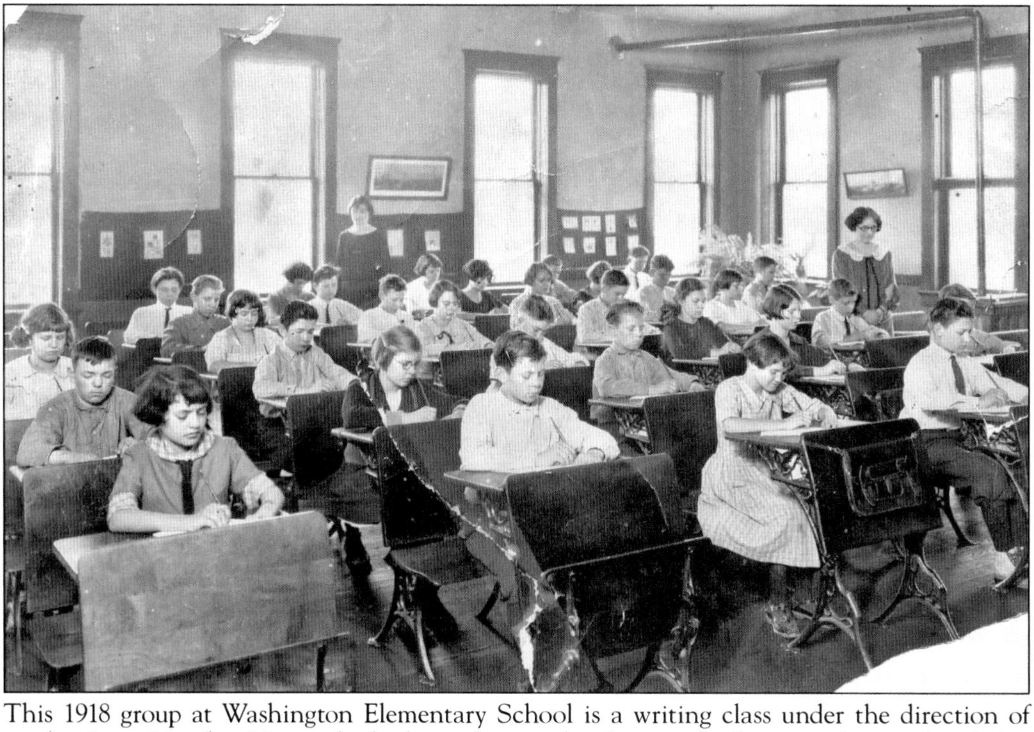

This 1918 group at Washington Elementary School is a writing class under the direction of teacher Irene Hensley. Notice the high windows and ceilings and, of course, the wooden desks. This was a very typical building of the time.

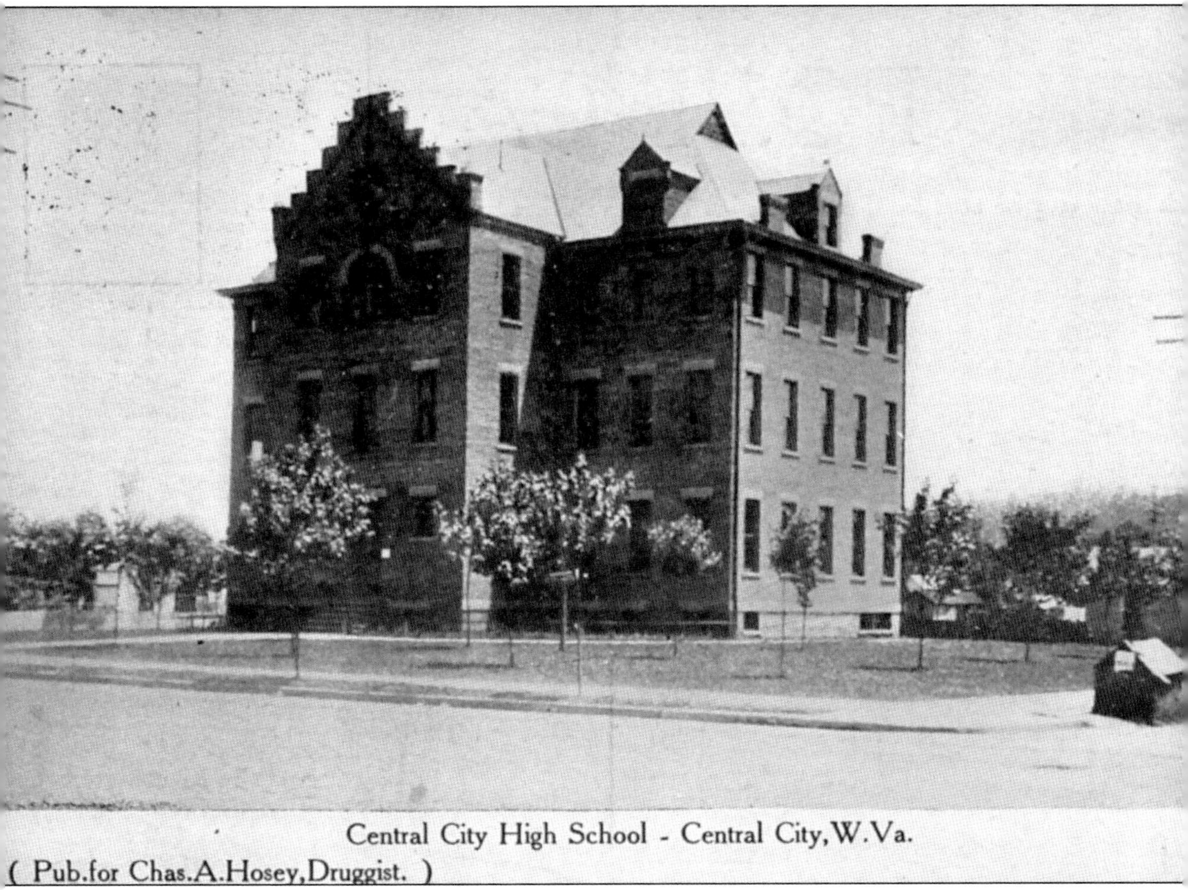

For several years while gathering Central City history, the author was told there was no Central City High School. Earl Bush delivered this picture reproduced from a postcard. According to the 1910 City Directory, it was located at 950 Washington Avenue. Actual years for this school are not known.

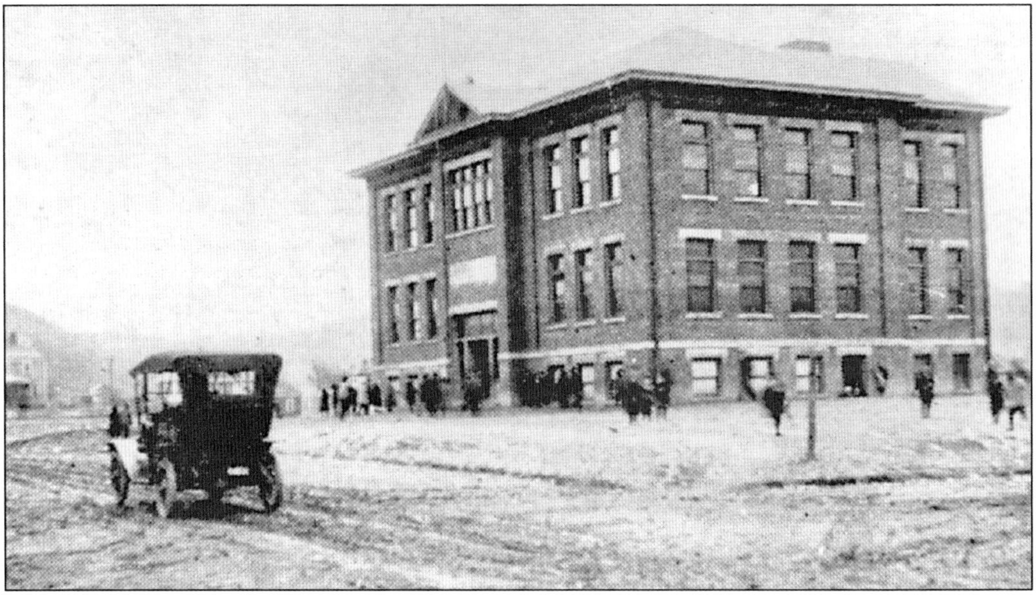

In 1911, Jefferson School (above) was built at Nineteenth Street West and Jefferson Avenue. This school was used until the early 1990s, when a new consolidated school was built and named Central City Elementary on Washington Avenue and Twenty-second Street West. Johnston School was built in 1915 at Seventh Avenue and Third Street West on an opposite corner from the original Samuel Johnston home. This school was also consolidated into the new Central City school.

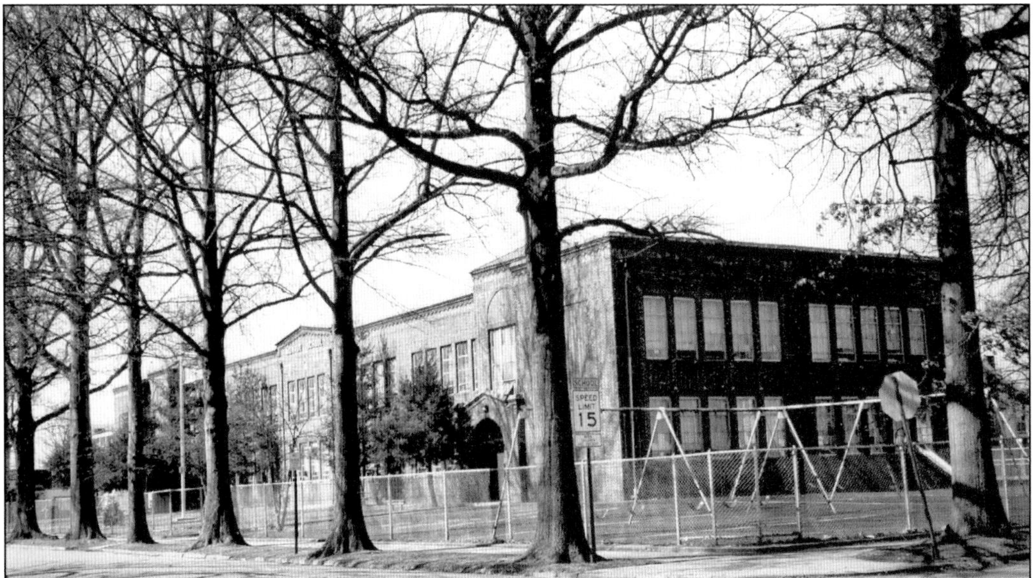

Monroe School was added in 1923. This school was located at Monroe Avenue and Eleventh Street West. The children from this school benefited greatly from the West Huntington Library. It became the Headstart Center for a while after the elementary moved. Monroe was also consolidated into Central City Elementary.

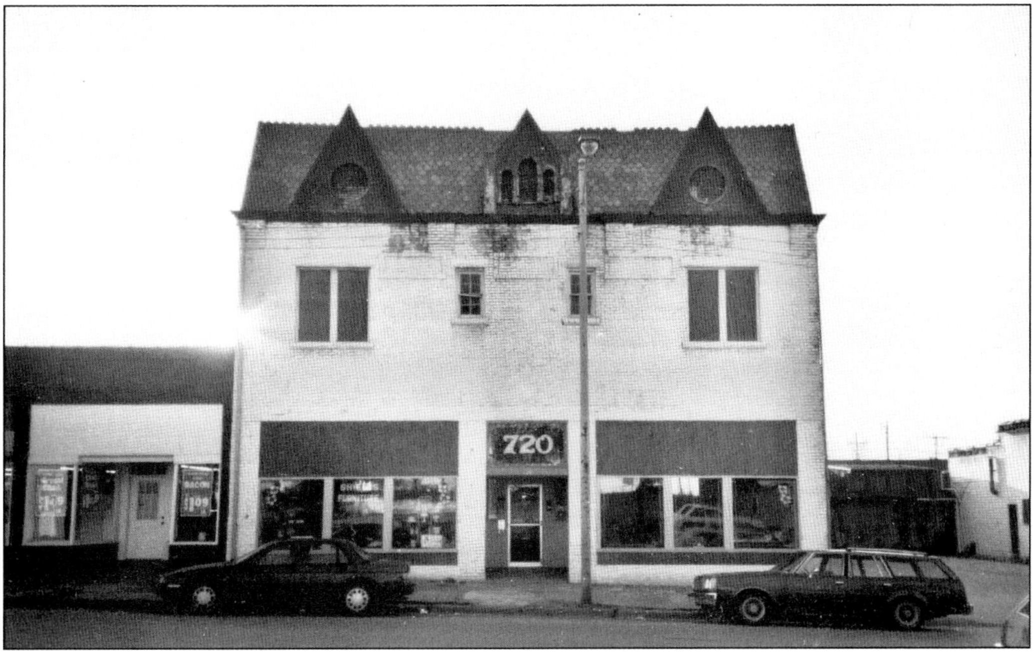

The most-mentioned early theater is the Iola, located in the 700 block of Fourteenth Street West. A story is told of two little brothers who saved a nickel to attend the picture show. They arrived early and found murals on the walls. Thinking this was the picture show, they left disappointedly before the movie started. They were given a second chance later.

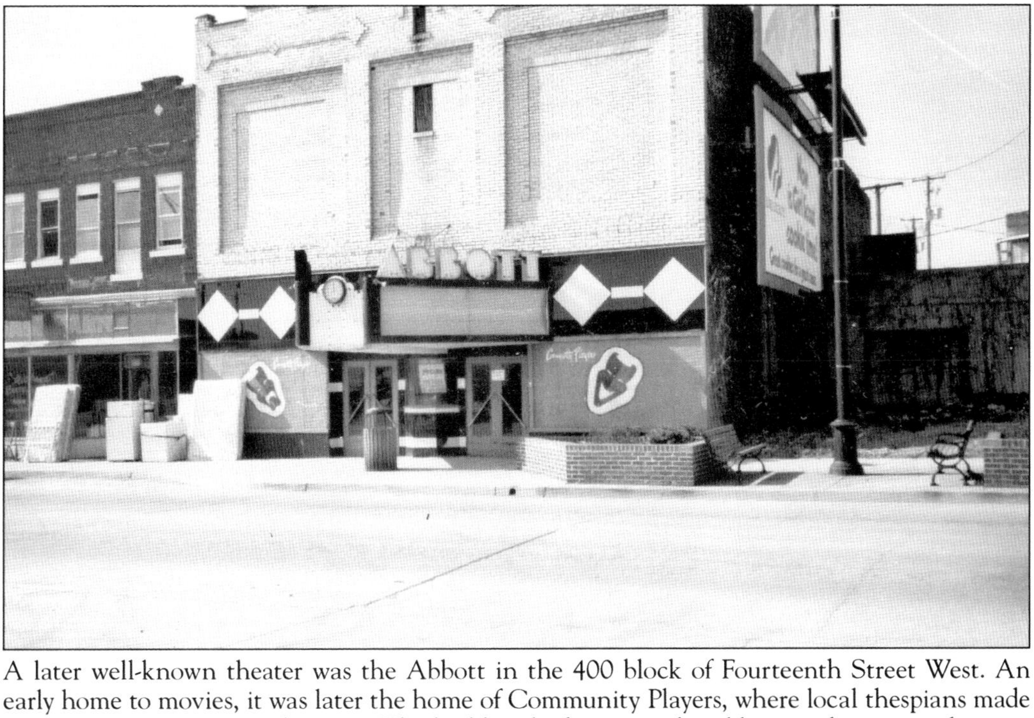

A later well-known theater was the Abbott in the 400 block of Fourteenth Street West. An early home to movies, it was later the home of Community Players, where local thespians made appearances in many productions. The building had structural problems and was torn down in the 1990s. There were a few more movie theaters in the area.

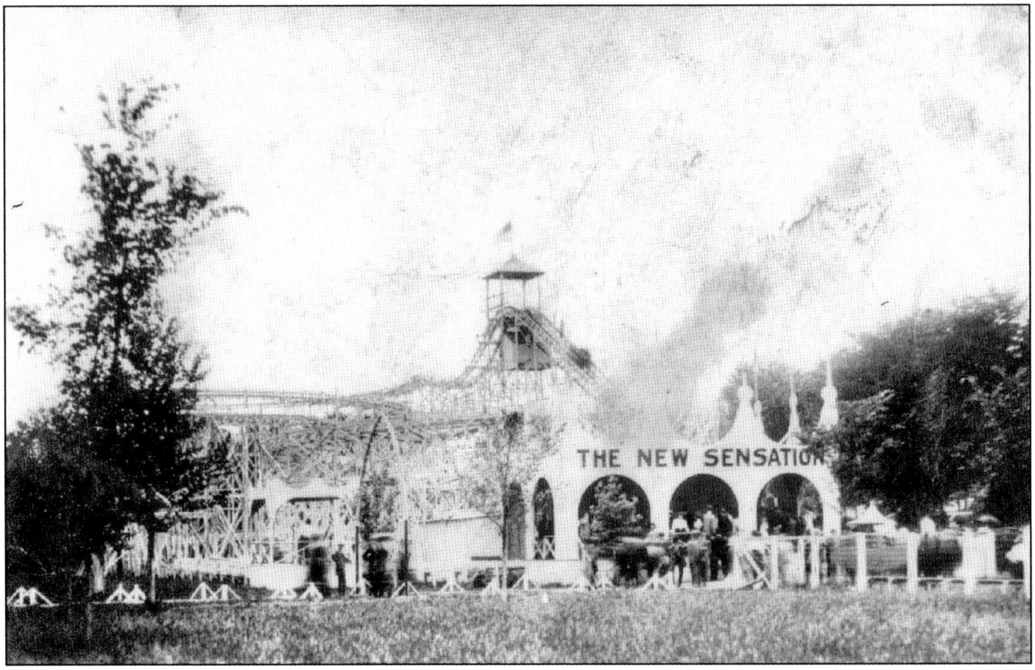

Many railroad companies knew that passengers would have waits between scheduled runs. To keep these people occupied, many companies built parks to accommodate them. Camden Park was one of those facilities made for people to have a place to picnic and be entertained. Since 1903, this park has been the family place to be in the tri-state area. The wooden roller coaster is still operating.

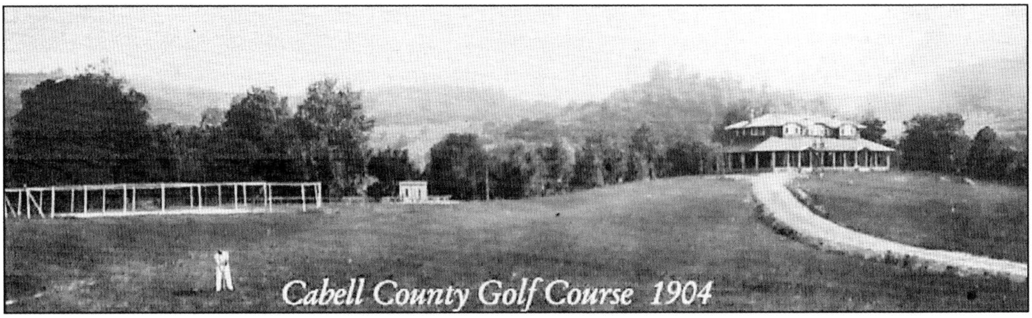

The Cabell Country Club and golf course was constructed at Nineteenth Street West. It was incorporated in 1906 with 145 members. It was later moved to East Huntington, and the original grounds became St. Cloud Commons, the current site of baseball fields and a community lodge.

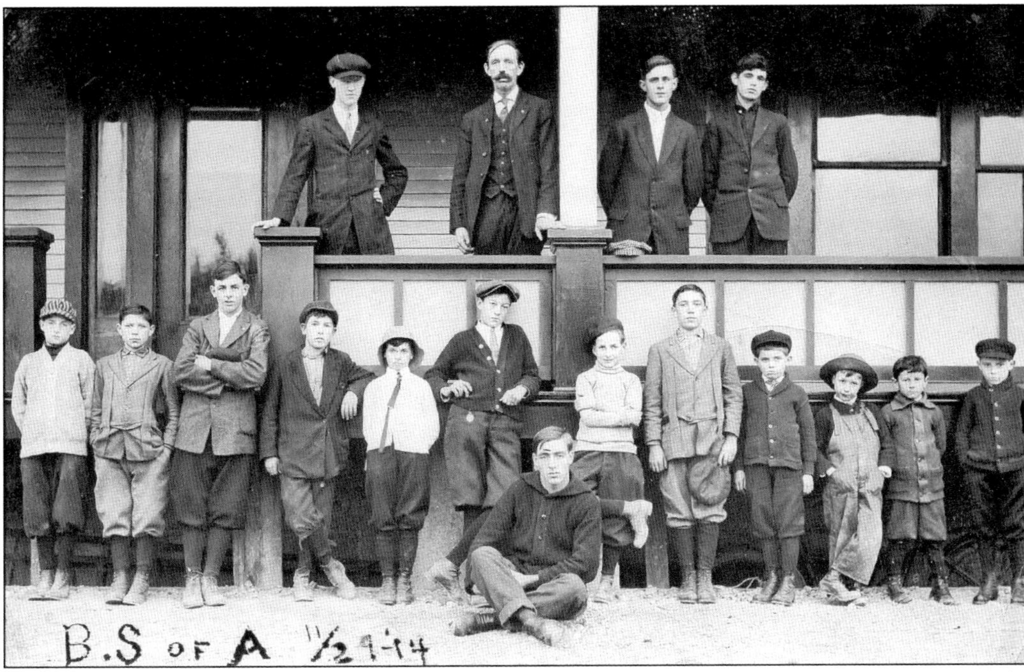

The Boy Scouts of America were incorporated in 1910. Central City evidently has one of the earliest American troops. Although we have no identity of the boys and leaders in the picture, we do have the date as November 29, 1914.

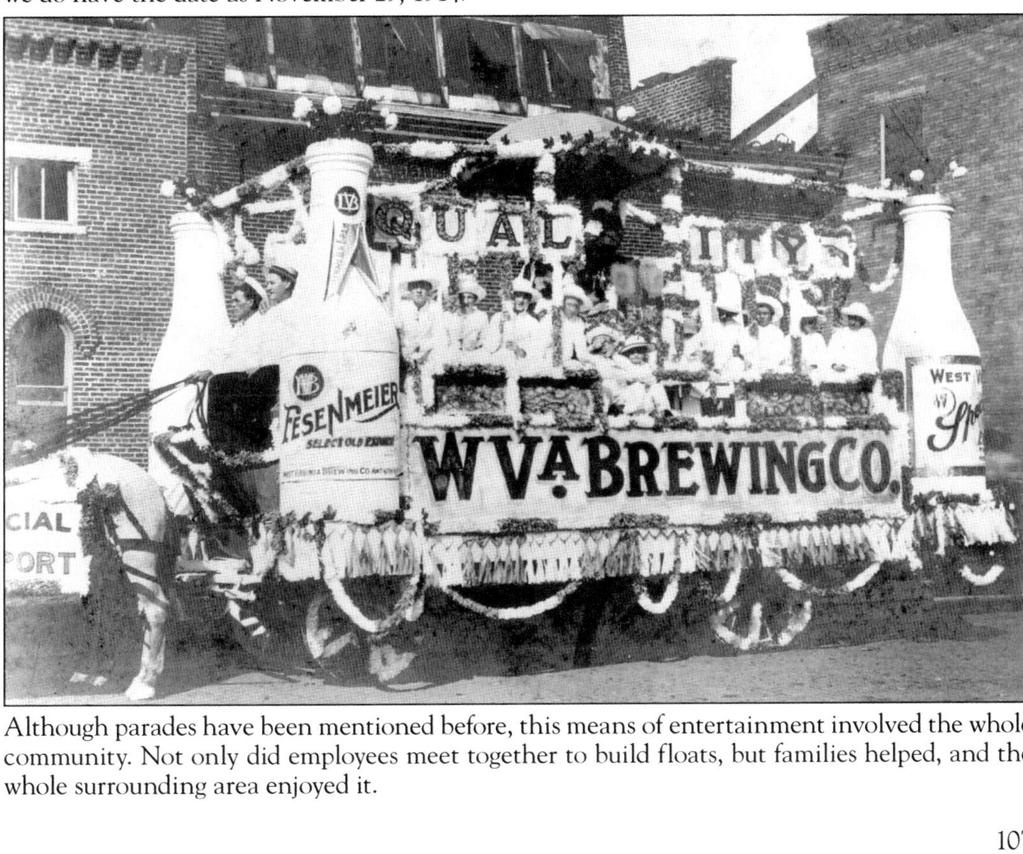

Although parades have been mentioned before, this means of entertainment involved the whole community. Not only did employees meet together to build floats, but families helped, and the whole surrounding area enjoyed it.

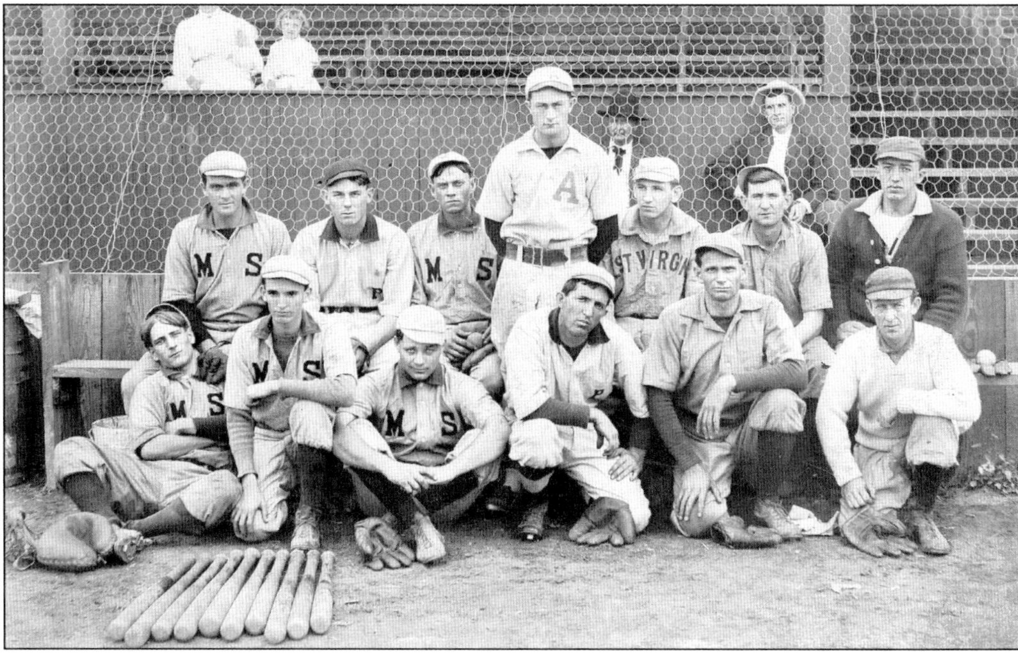

League Field on Virginia Avenue in Central City was a very popular summer gathering place for families. Many of the local factories and businesses sponsored teams such as Heiner's and Fesenmeier's Brewery. This picture is of the "West End Ball Boys" of Camden Park.

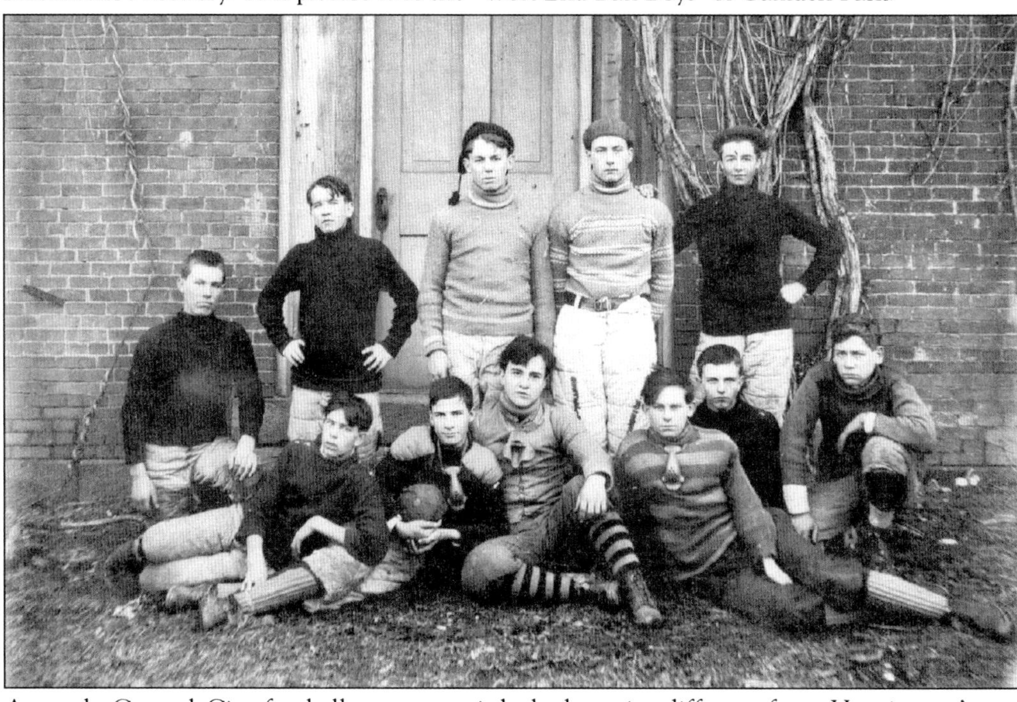

An early Central City football team certainly looks quite different from Huntington's own Thundering Herd of Marshall University. Sponsors for some teams were by lodges and other clubs from Central City. Sports, especially baseball, were a very important part of family fun during the years of Central City.

Six

Central City Today

Central City was no more as of 1909. Residents soon had new addresses, mostly just converting Central City to Huntington, West Virginia. Businesses that had the name Central City kept that name, but as they disappeared so did the name. The only people familiar with the town were older people whose families had lived in that early time. As businesses failed or left the area, buildings stood empty, beer halls flourished, and the area became a place to be avoided.

Today the area is alive and well. The introduction of the Huntington Tumbler exhibit at the library in 1988 along with the Central City reunions led by Winnie Arthur were the motivation for the development of the new Central City area. Her constant hard work with community, city, and state officials brought the cause to the forefront. The Old Central City Association that was formed by people interested in preserving and promoting Central City has made the name prominent again. Antique dealers chose the area and have banded together to publicize the area as "The Antique Capital of West Virginia." The yearly celebration of Old Central City Days is a locally well-known festival.

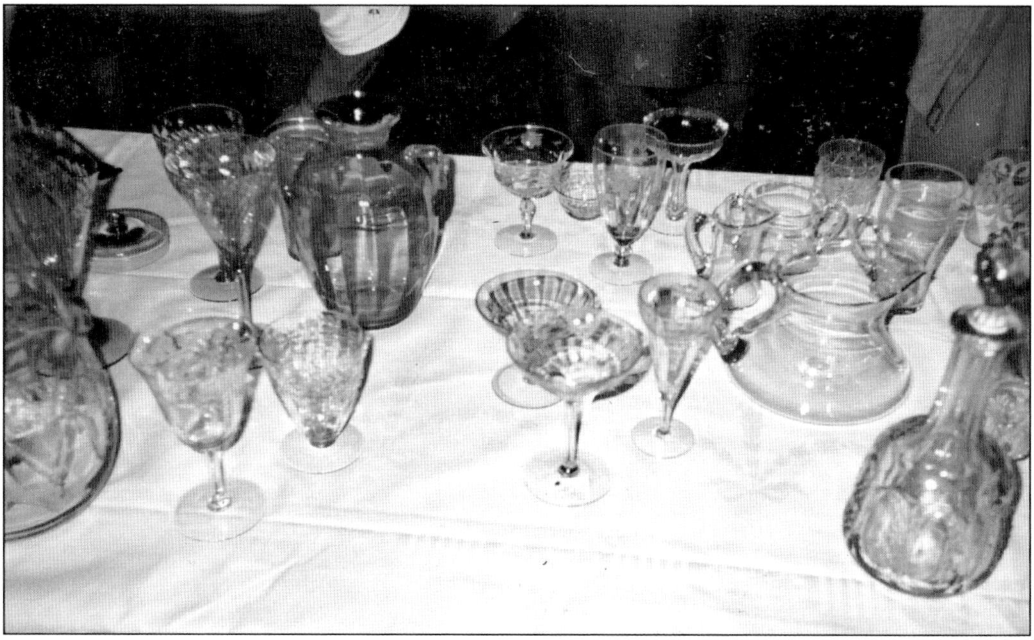

The Huntington Tumbler Glass, above, was the first clue in finding "Old Central City." This display was part of the original glassware exhibited by the Westland Homemakers in 1988. The colors and designs are comparable to much of the finest glassware.

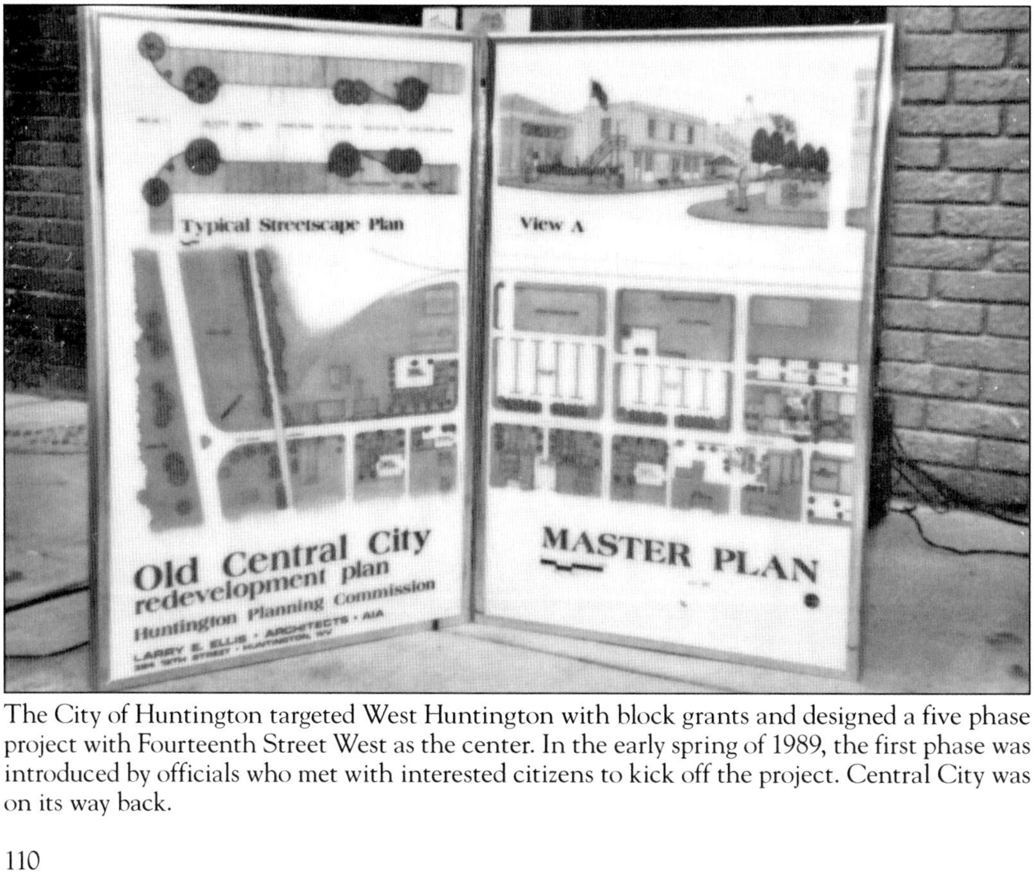

The City of Huntington targeted West Huntington with block grants and designed a five phase project with Fourteenth Street West as the center. In the early spring of 1989, the first phase was introduced by officials who met with interested citizens to kick off the project. Central City was on its way back.

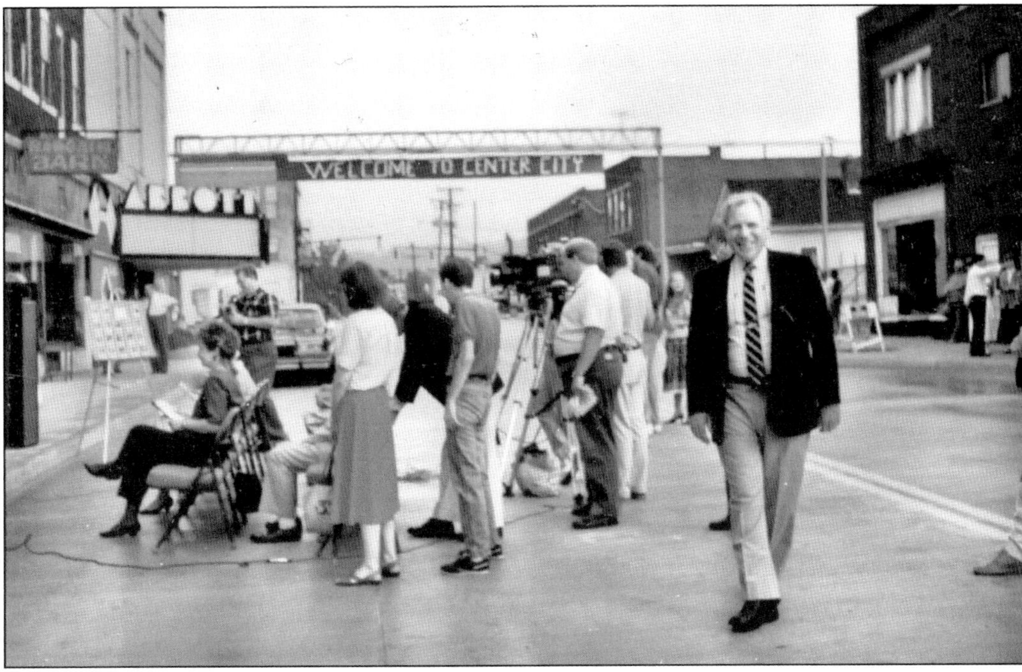

The first block to be improved was the 400 block. This block contained the old West Huntington Public Library and part of Heiner's Bakery. On the far right is Earl Heiner Jr., who attended the kick off. If you notice the banner over the street, even city workers didn't recognize the name "Central City" and thought the celebration to be for "Center City." The banner was hung on the overhead pipeline of Heiner's Bakery.

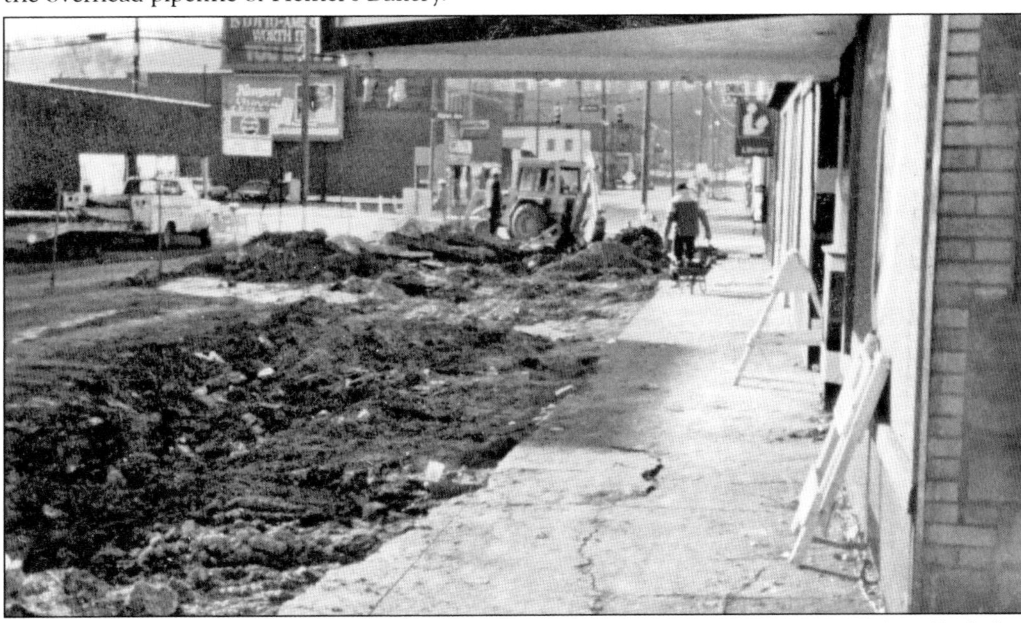

The first phase included a new street, sidewalks, curbs, and lighting, both street and traffic lights. This phase took eight months. The construction workers found blue clay under the brick, and more substantial filler was needed to complete the project. The library and businesses struggled with the loss of sidewalks as well as the street being closed to traffic.

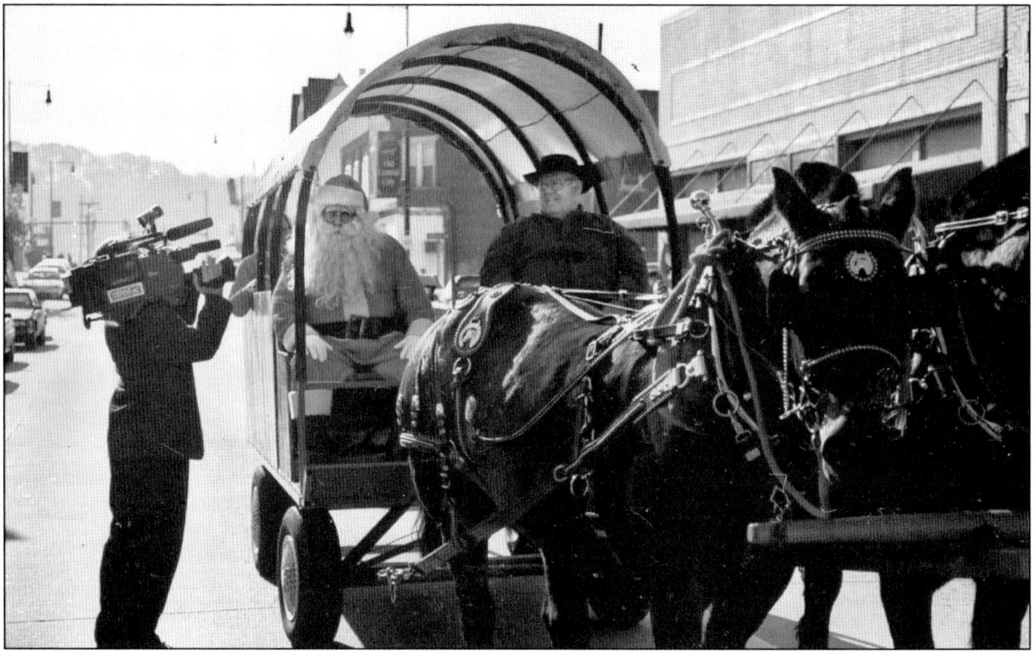

The Old Central City Association sprung into action and took advantage of the publicity the area was getting with the improvements. The first activity was a successful "Christmas in Central City" in 1990. Area elementary schools were asked to sing, some area merchants gave door prizes, Santa arrived, and in spite of the cold, everyone had a great time. The picture above was a later Christmas as Santa arrived.

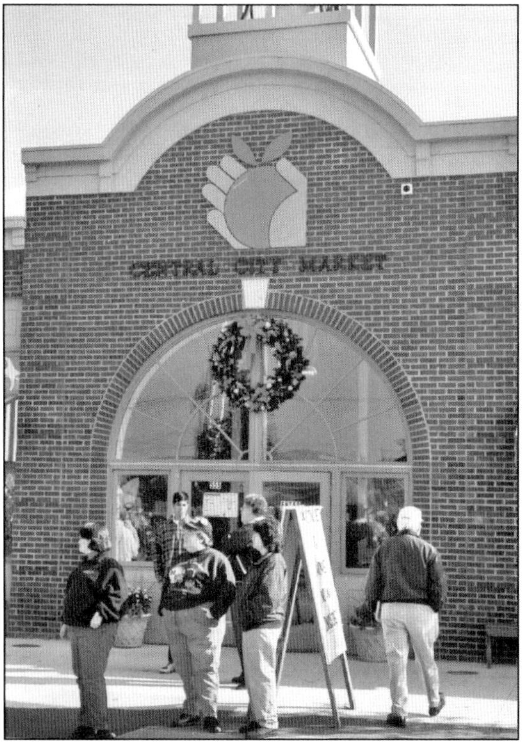

After the building of the farmer's market and the park, decorating for Christmas became a more festive occasion. A Christmas tree is decorated in the park; the gazebo is decorated and lighted. For a couple years, a small parade signaled the arrival of Santa. In this picture, some shoppers are awaiting Santa.

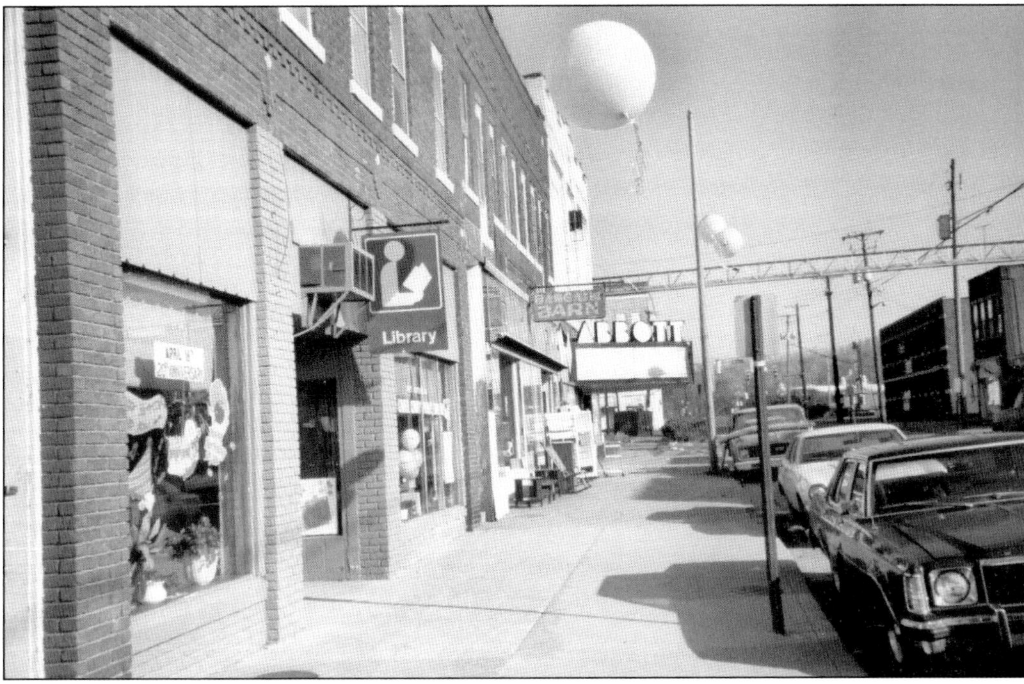

The Cabell County Library Board also saw the growth potential in West Huntington. The West Huntington Branch had been in a storefront building in the 400 block since 1968. It was a pleasant library, but the old building presented many problems. The board decided it was time to move on. This old building burned in the 1990s and was torn down.

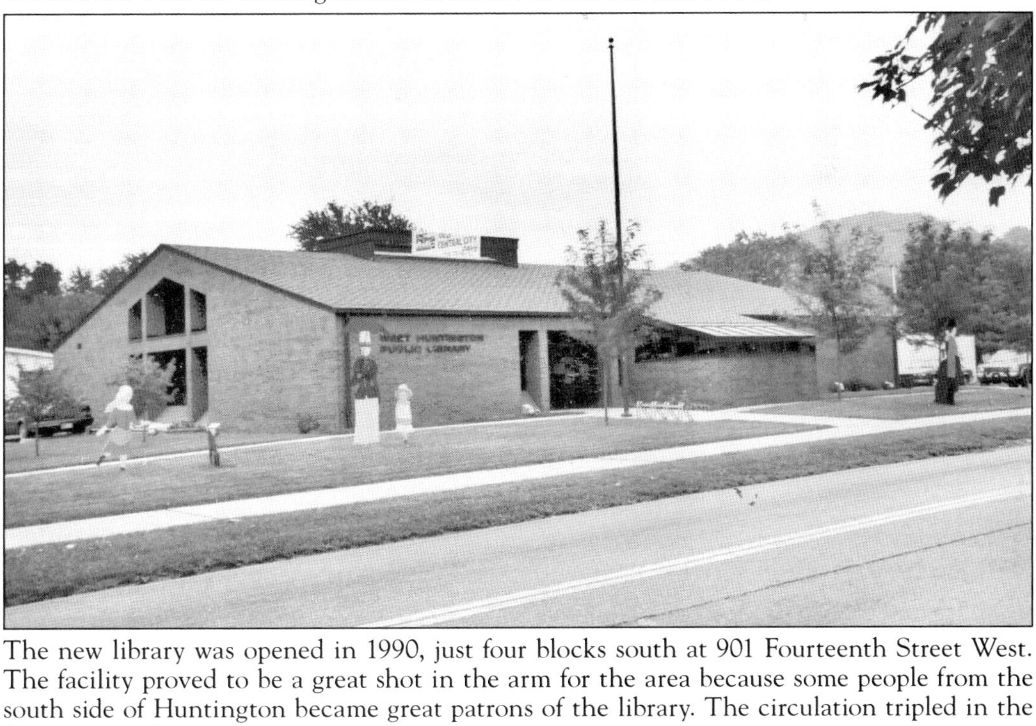

The new library was opened in 1990, just four blocks south at 901 Fourteenth Street West. The facility proved to be a great shot in the arm for the area because some people from the south side of Huntington became great patrons of the library. The circulation tripled in the first six months.

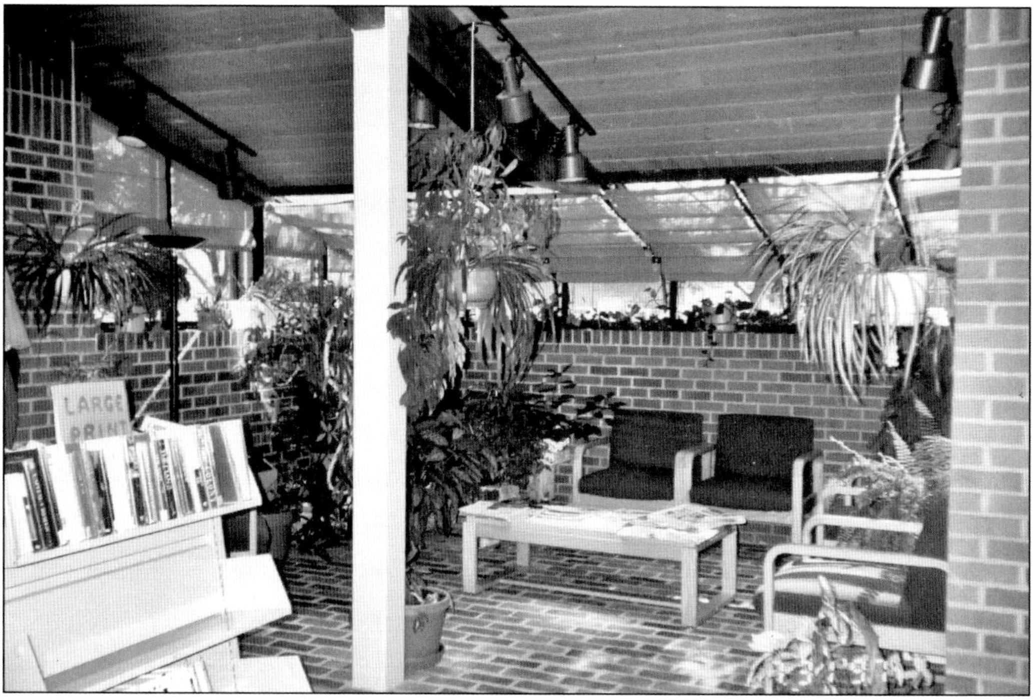

When the library was being built, the contractor cooperated with the library, and bricks were taken from the street construction in front of the old library and used as the floor of the solarium in the new library. One of the bricks is dated 1908.

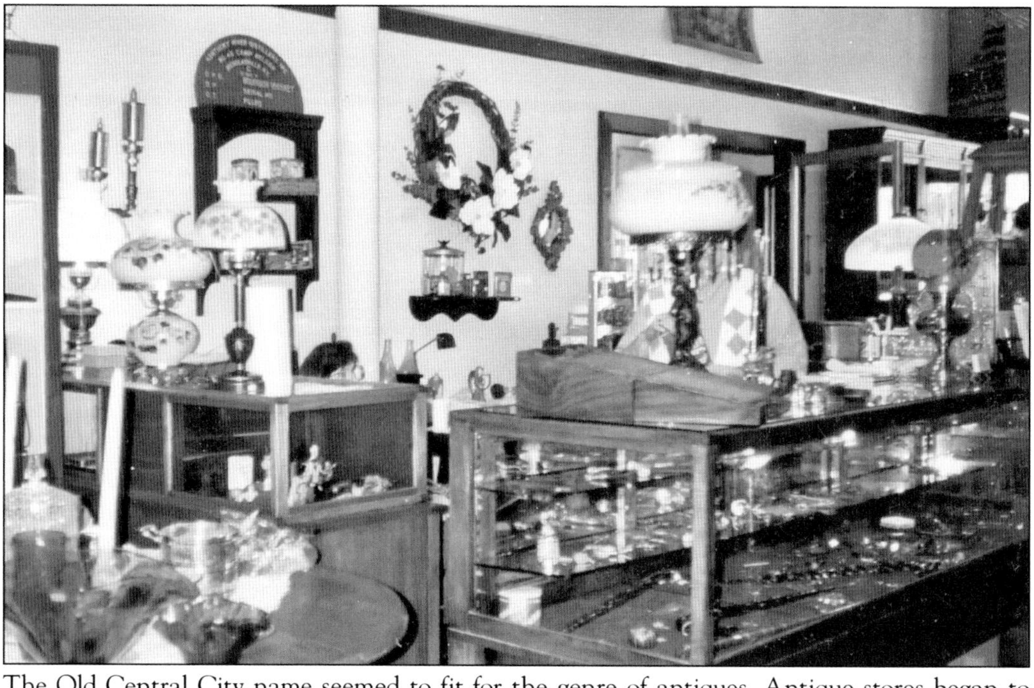

The Old Central City name seemed to fit for the genre of antiques. Antique stores began to open in every block. The membership of the association began to grow. Brochures were printed listing all of the area businesses that became members, and Central City was on the move.

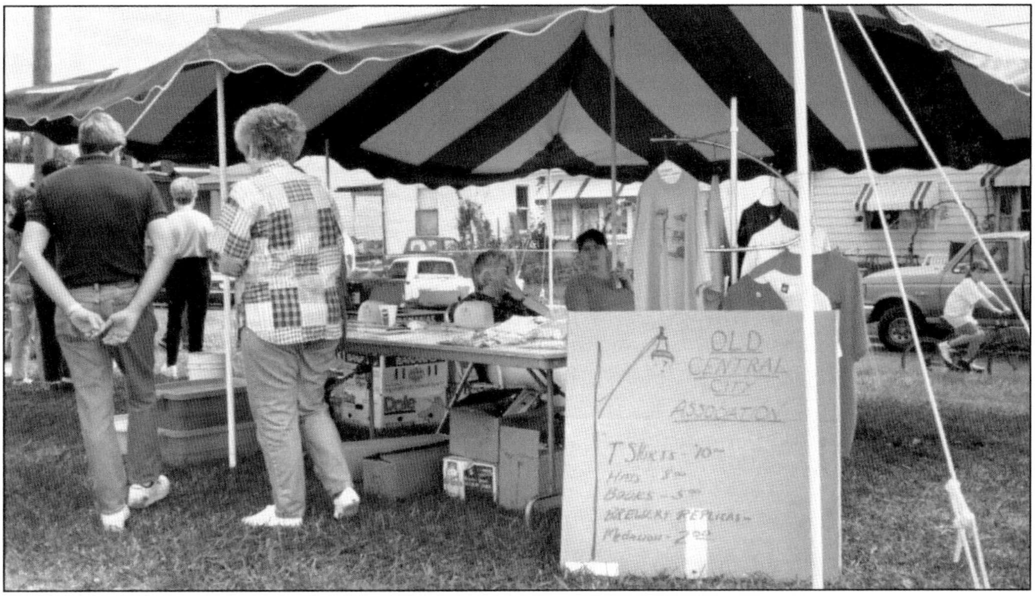

In 1992, the Old Central City Association (OCCA) decided to try a festival, Old Central City (OCC) Days, as a dry run for the 100-year celebration in 1993. With a shoestring budget, they planned a two-day celebration centered on Fourteenth Street West. The first two were scheduled on the last weekend in July because that was the anniversary of the incorporation of Central City. However, in future years, because of the heat and the opening of a continuous farmer's market, the activity was moved to the third weekend in June as it is today. The author, Lola Miller, is seated at the center of this picture.

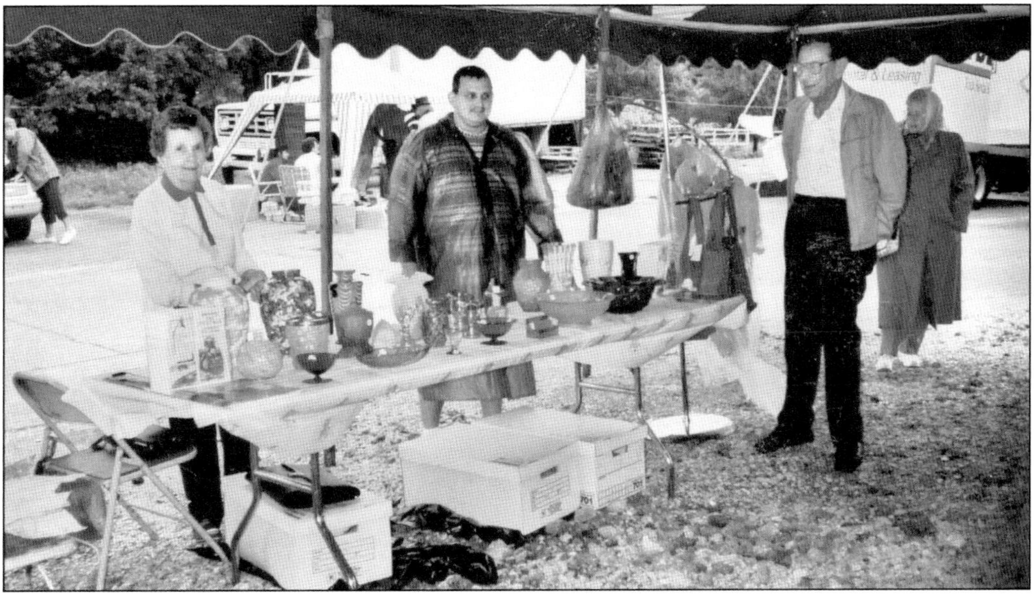

The first OCC Days featured a flea market on the old B&O right-of-way, which became the future site of the gazebo and farmer's market. Here on an old gravel strip used mostly for parking was a wonderful sight—many people helping celebrate a renewal of Central City. The first was such a success that the festival has continued every year. This picture shows Winnie Arthur (left), Ken Bolen (center), and Charles Arthur.

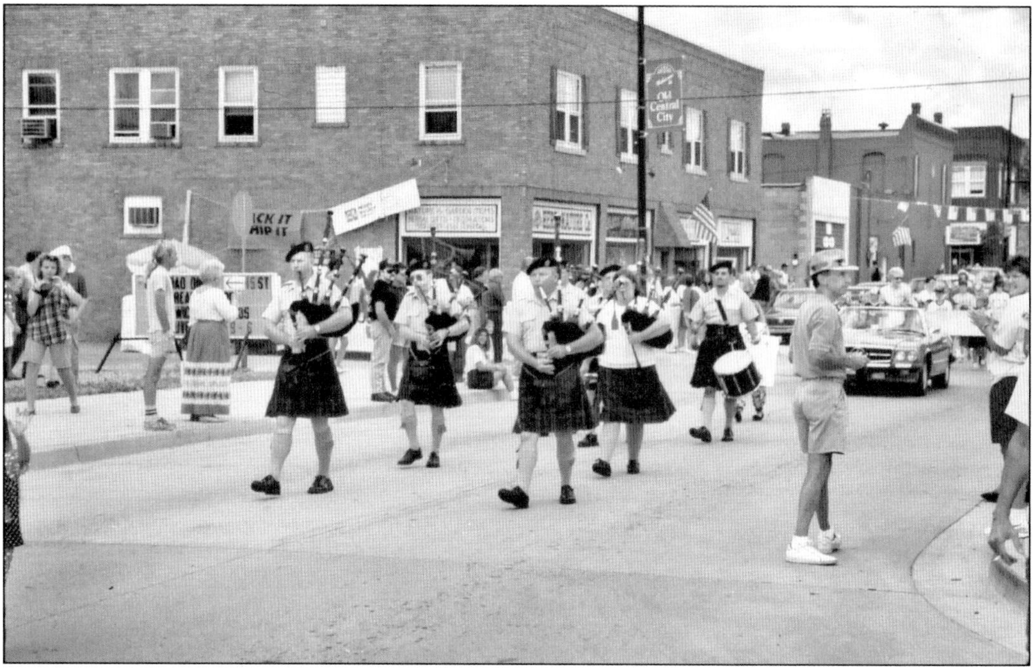

What is a festival without a parade! The Kanawha Valley Pipes and Drums participated in the parade for about four years. The parade was small but enjoyed by all. This picture was taken c. 1995.

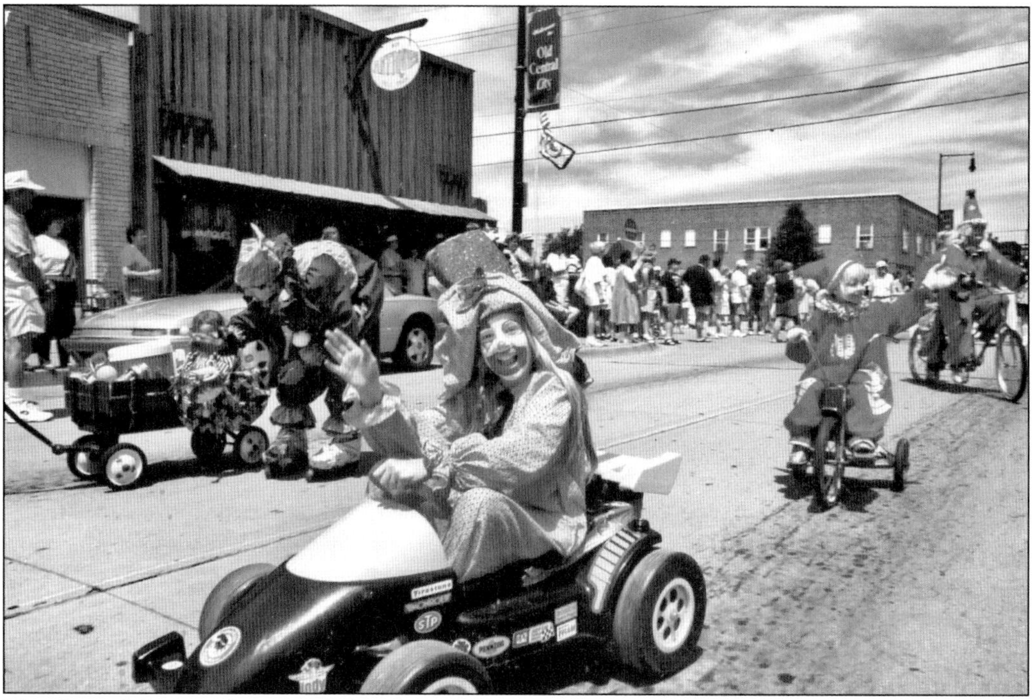

The date of the parade coincided with a clown college graduation sponsored locally. Part of the graduation activity was participation in the Central City parade. The clowns ranged in age from 5 to 50.

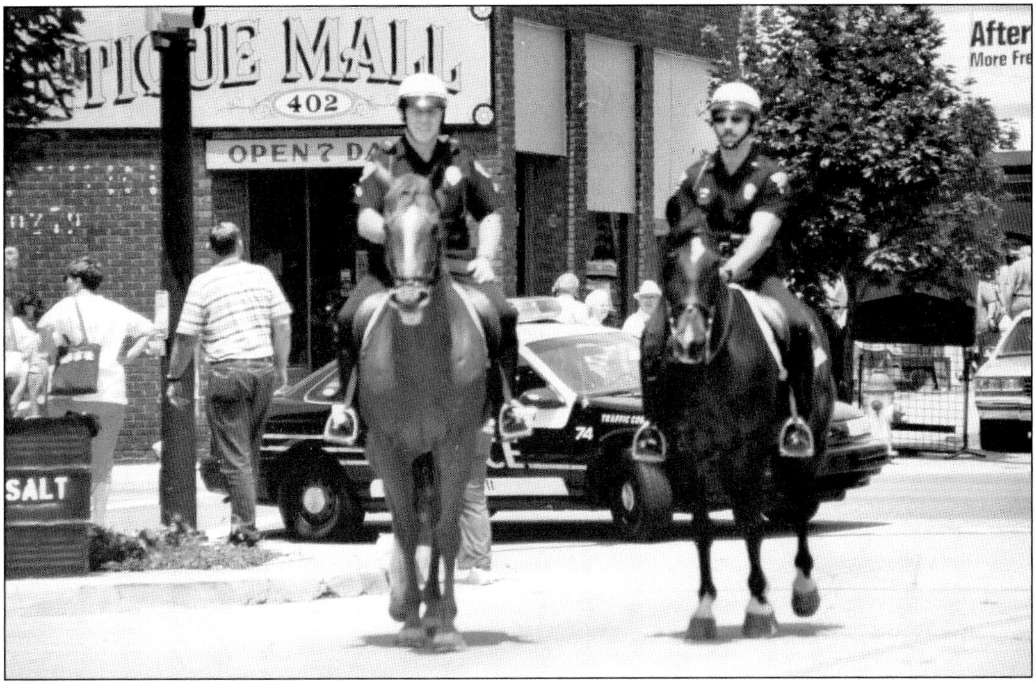

Central City's police protection has also changed. This unit of the Huntington Police Department participated in the parades and also made their presence known during the festivals.

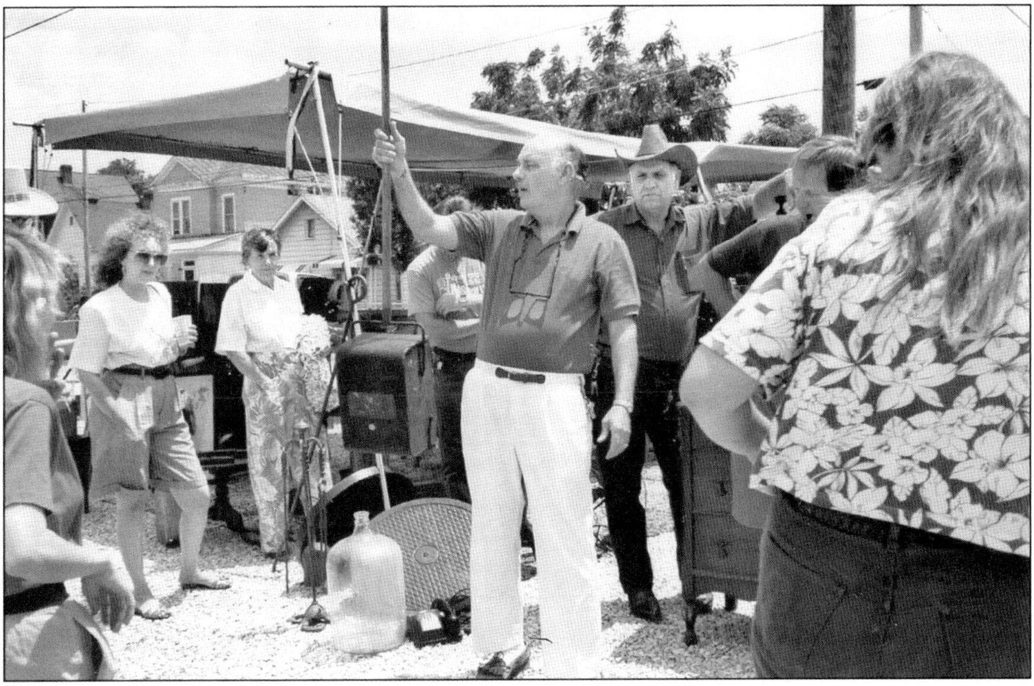

Jim Hardiman, one of the first antique dealers on the street and an avid supporter of OCCA, is explaining the use of an unknown item. The area where he is standing was also the site of a farmer's market on Saturdays before the new facility. Farmers brought their produce and sold from the back of their trucks.

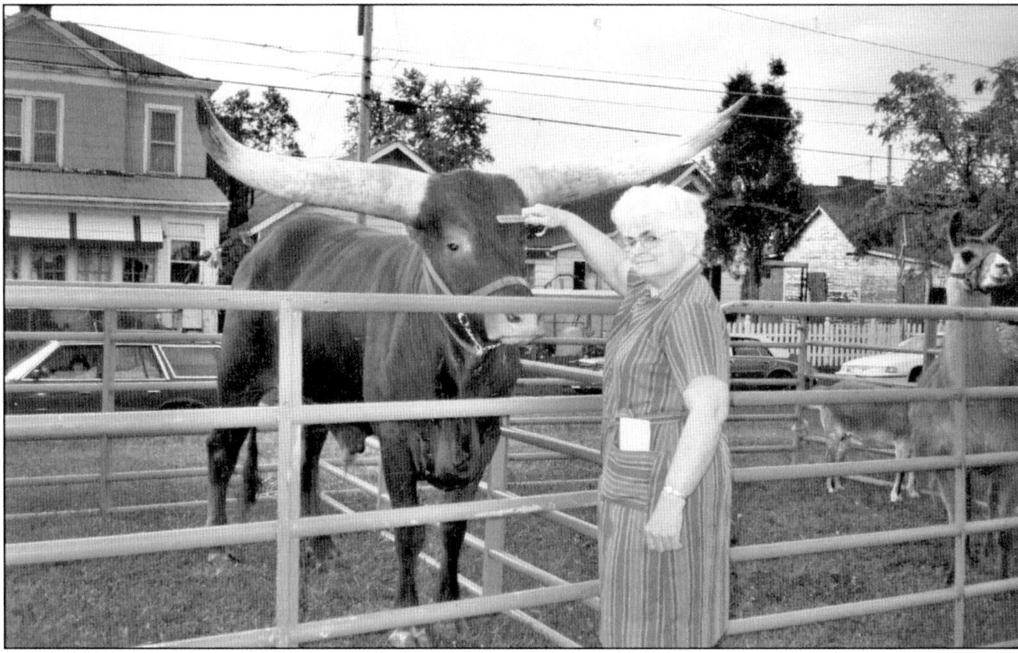

One of the early guests of the festival was this Texas longhorn joined by the first OCCA president, Sally O. Cyrus. Sally was manager of her parents' store, Cavendish-Cyrus Hardware. She was the organizational guru for the early growth of the Central City group and was an absolute go-getter.

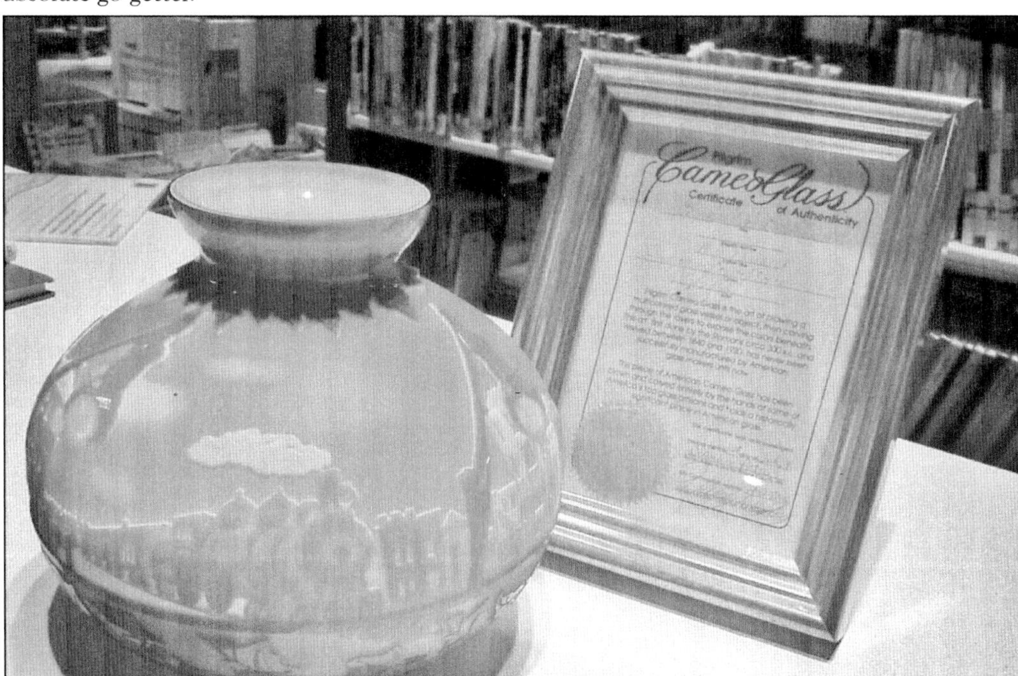

Pilgrim Glass Factory had one of their resident artists, known only as Kelsey, design a Cameo Glass vase for the 100th anniversary. Only six were made. The vase has scenes in a circle around the outside that shows historical aspects of Central City.

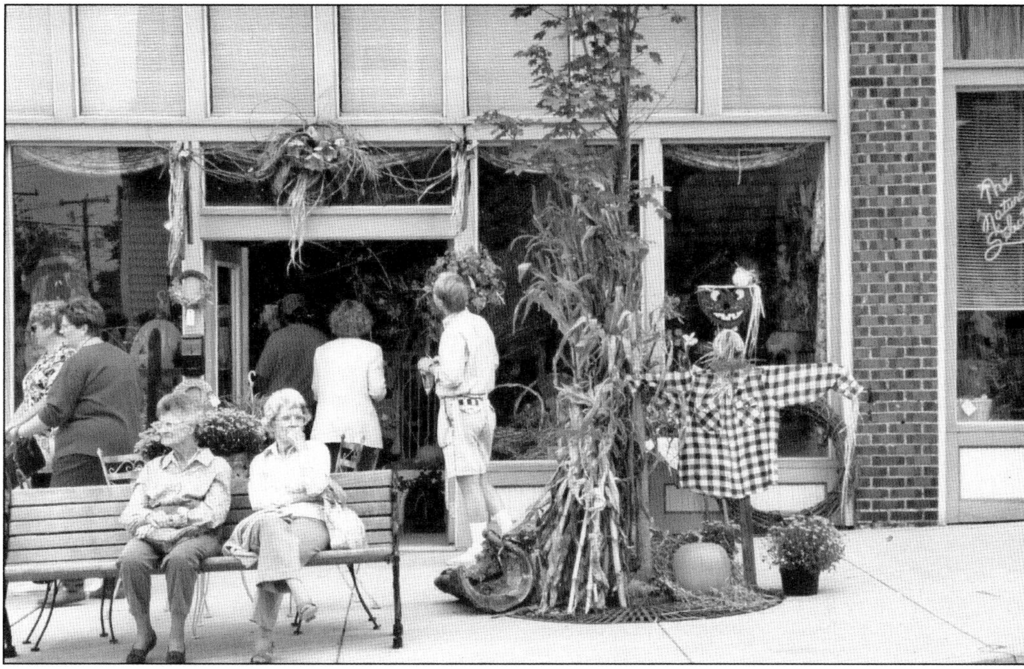

In 1993, a Harvest Fest was added to the celebrations of Central City. It rained horribly and although participants had to stand on wooden flats over puddles but under a tent, pieces from an advertised "largest pumpkin pie" were served, and a square dance was held on straw in the mud. The picture above was taken in 1994 during much better weather.

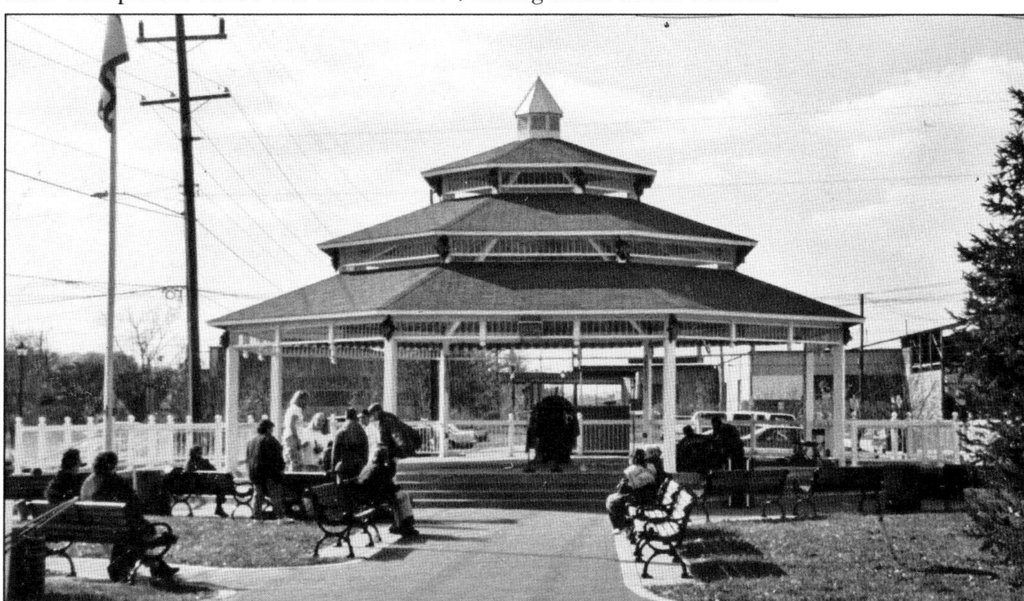

Three city blocks were completed and the fourth phase of restoration was begun. This was the Central City Park with a very large gazebo. West Virginia senator Jay Rockefeller attended the dedication and commented, "Now this is a gazebo." A large flagpole was dedicated later in memory of Bob Chapman by his wife, Mayme, and their family. Bob and Mayme were early supporters of the Central City reunions.

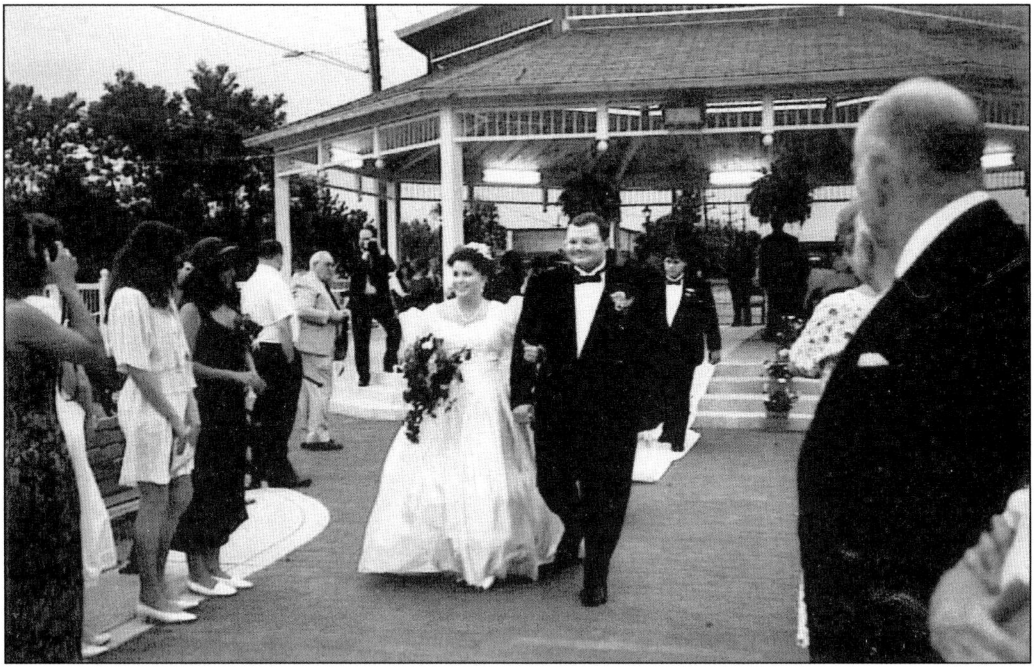

The gazebo is utilized for many activities such as gospel sings, band concerts, square dances, art exhibits, and many other things. One of the first reservations for the gazebo was the wedding of Lynn Hudson and John Gallaher on May 28, 1996.

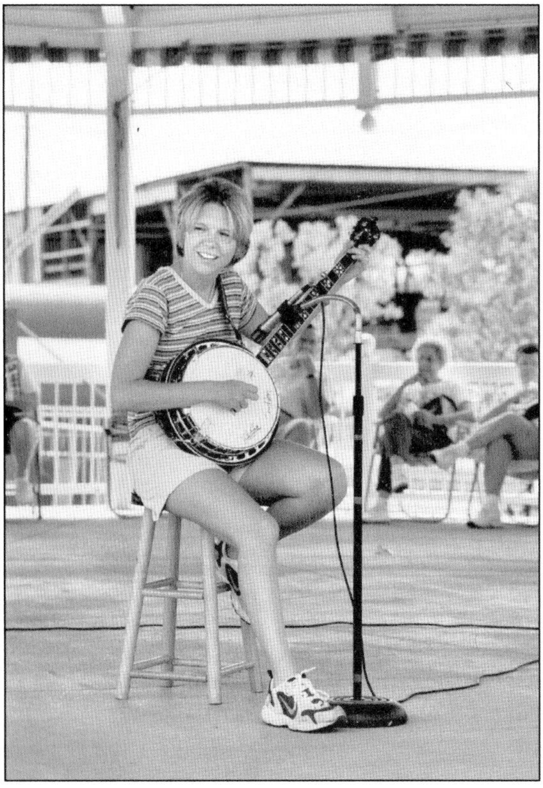

One of the activities needed for a festival is entertainment. Because of the lack of funds, local talent was sought. We found a very talented neighborhood teenager who played the banjo. For several years, Jessica Bills was a featured act, and everyone enjoyed watching her grow into a wonderful young lady. She is now married and a musical therapist.

An attraction added to the festivities in 2000 was a marble tournament. A local marble artisan, Thomas Thornburgh, brought the tournament to Old Central City Days. On Friday afternoon and evening, youngsters come from all over the area. The early hours are dedicated to practice for anyone who wants to enter the contest. The winners go on to state contests.

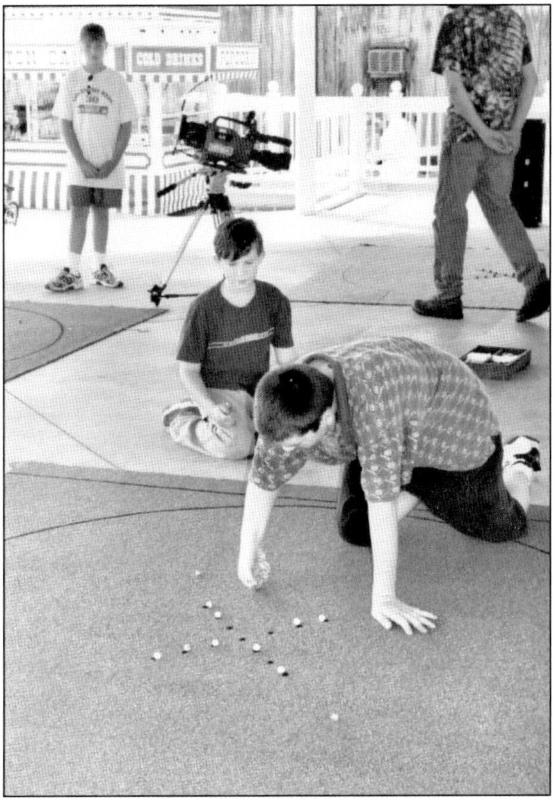

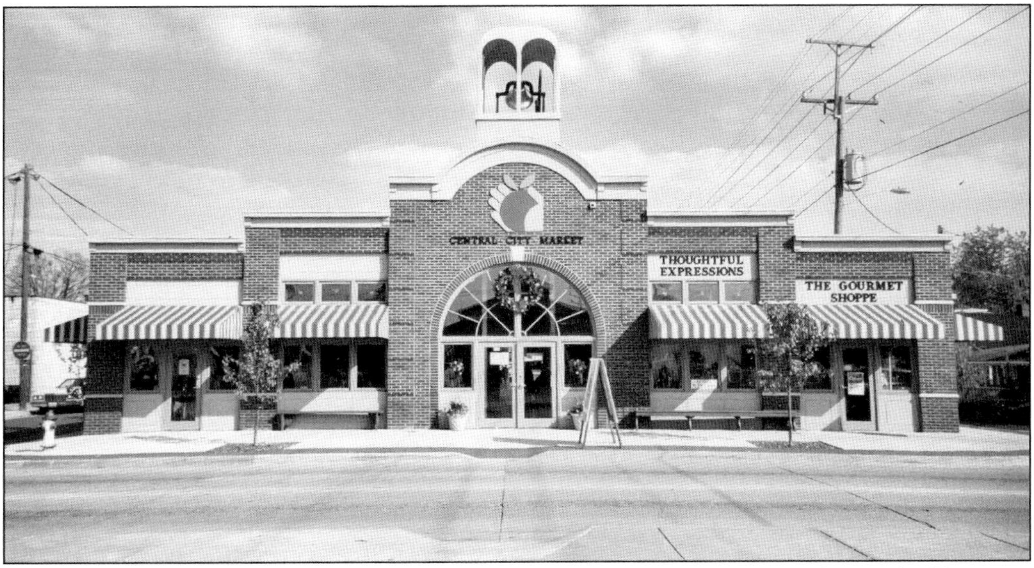

The last phase of the block grant project was the addition of a farmer's market. A building was built to house year-round products. The bell tower contains a bell donated by the Perry family of Heritage Farm, longtime supporters of Central City. Activities are scheduled often at the market, ranging from the sale of fresh produce, pumpkins, and Christmas trees, to antique and flea markets during Old Central City Days. Today the inside market handles bulk foods as well as West Virginia products.

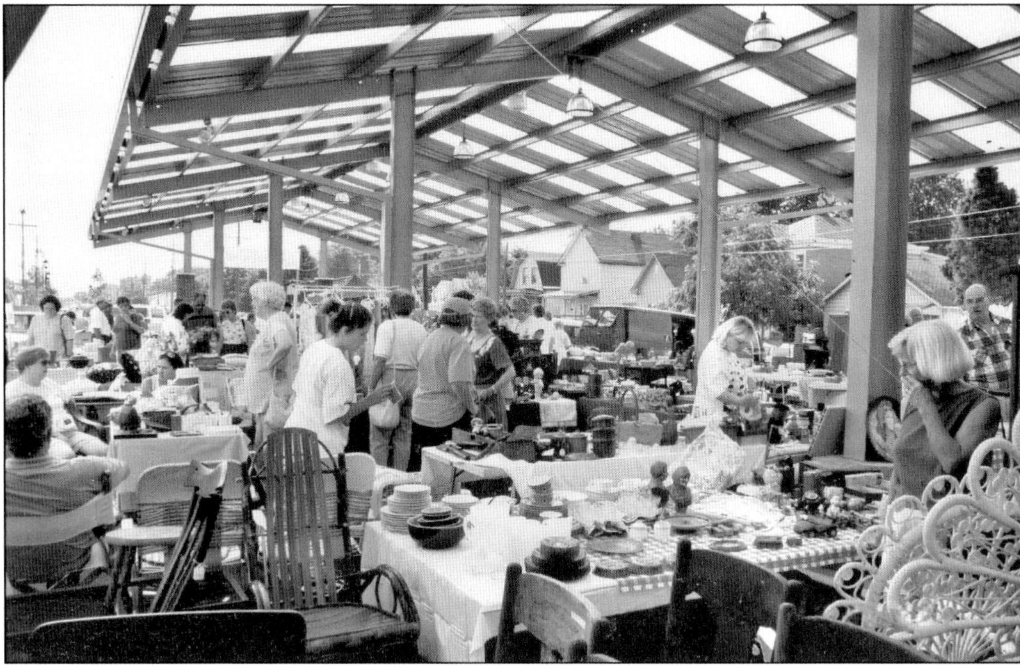

The back area of the market was paved and a canopy built over it. This provides protection for an open-air market almost year-round. This picture is the antique/flea market during Old Central City Days. This is a far cry from the gravel lot with no protection from the sun and rain.

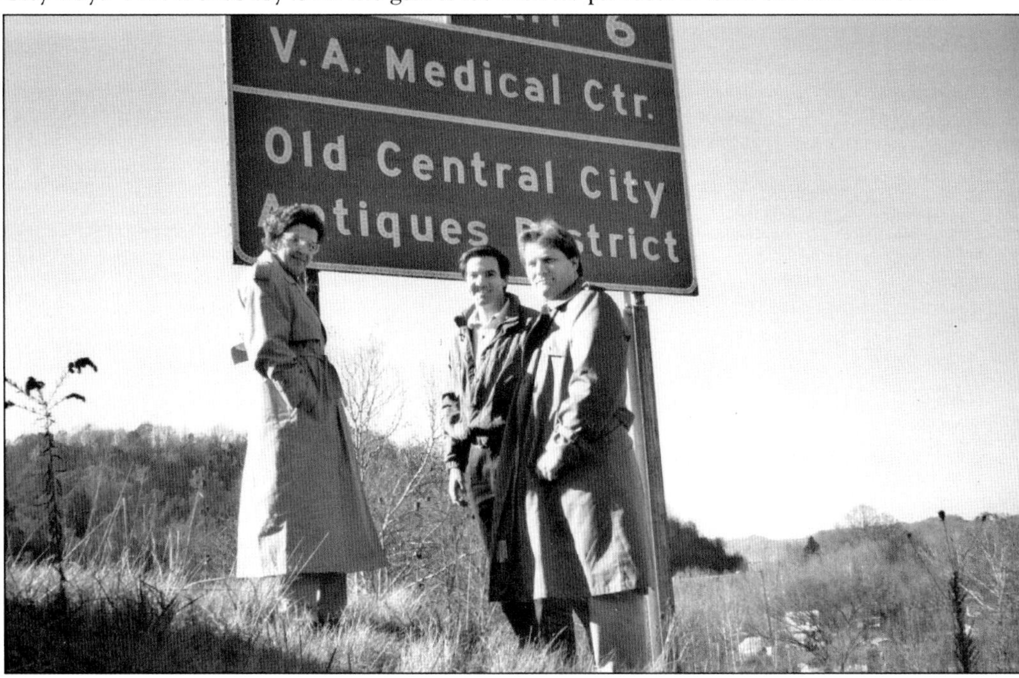

In 1994, Winnie Arthur, Sally Cyrus, Loretta Baker, and Ken Bolen linked with our state delegate, Evan Jenkins, to have a marker on Interstate 64 to direct people to our antique district. This was realized in the spring of 1995. Pictured are antique dealers Loretta Baker (left) and Mark Hall (right) with Delegate Jenkins in the middle.

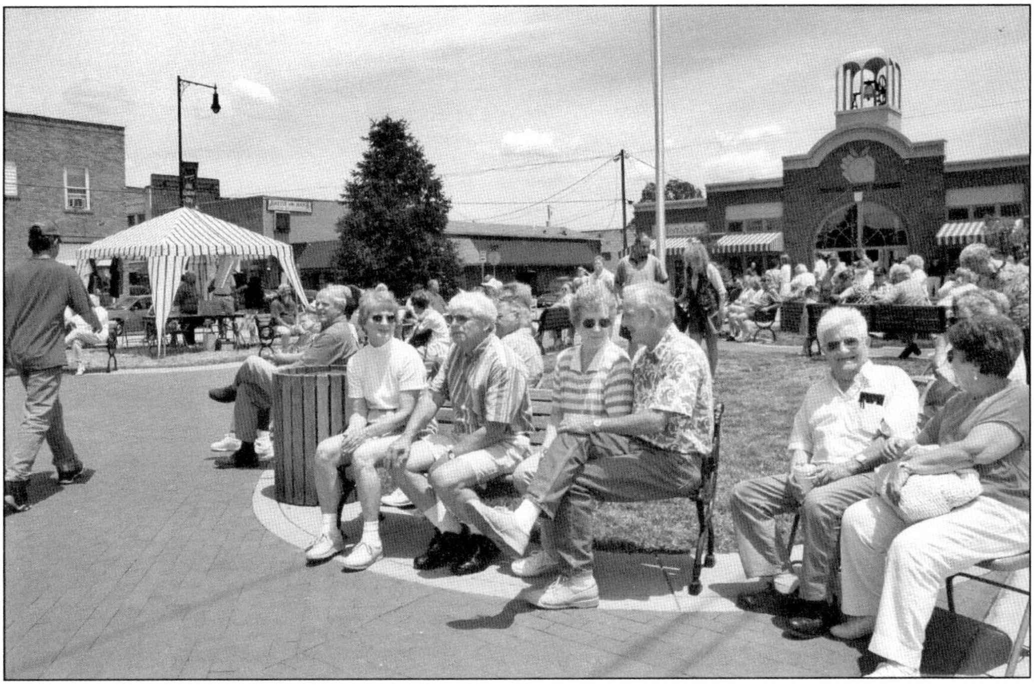

Now instead of people avoiding the area of Fourteenth Street West, the facilities open to the public are very inviting. This gathering, at the Central City Park in front of the gazebo, is waiting for some entertainment to begin at one of the Old Central City Days.

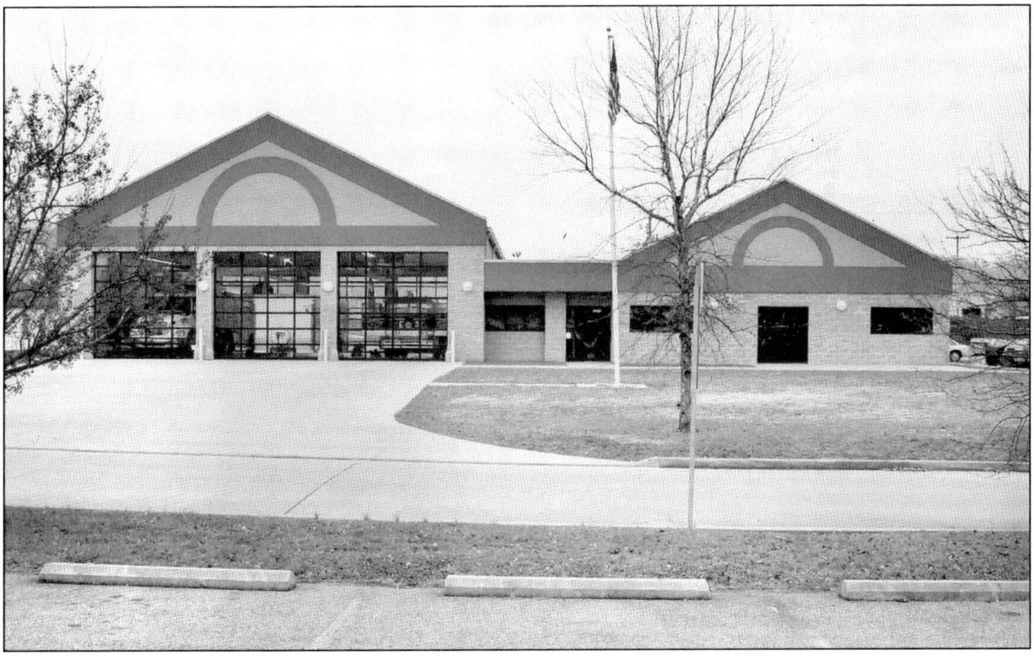

The newest addition to the revitalized Central City is the new fire station. This station, located just one block from the first one, is the newest in the city of Huntington. It is just across the street from the gazebo and a welcome improvement to the area. It is hoped that the old station could become a Central City museum.

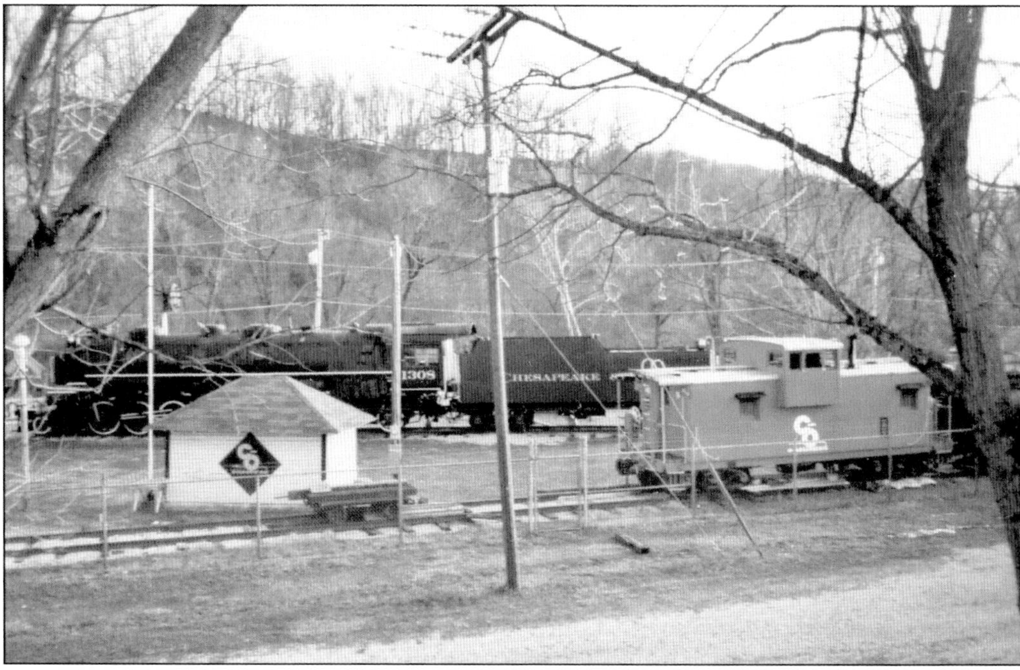

Three other attractions have made the Central City area a great tourist attraction. Above is one, the Collis P. Huntington Railroad Historical Society Park, which stands a block away from the original C&O passenger station. This engine is visited by schoolchildren who also come to the city "safety town" next door, sponsored by the Huntington City Police Department.

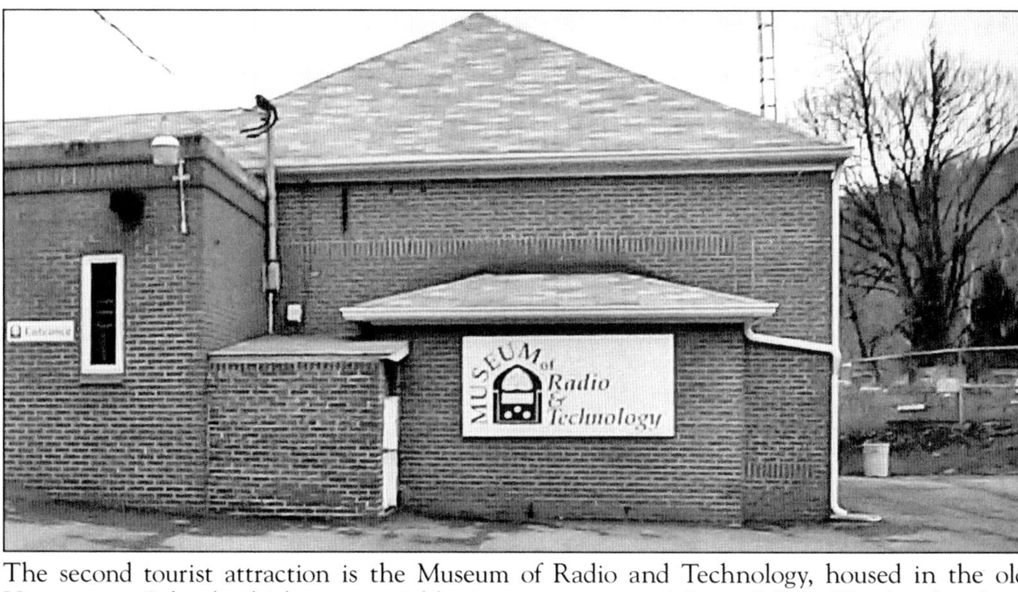

The second tourist attraction is the Museum of Radio and Technology, housed in the old Harveytown School, which was a neighboring community of Central City. The families from this area are very much a part of the memories of Central City. The museum is an attraction for radio enthusiasts from all over the eastern part of the United States.

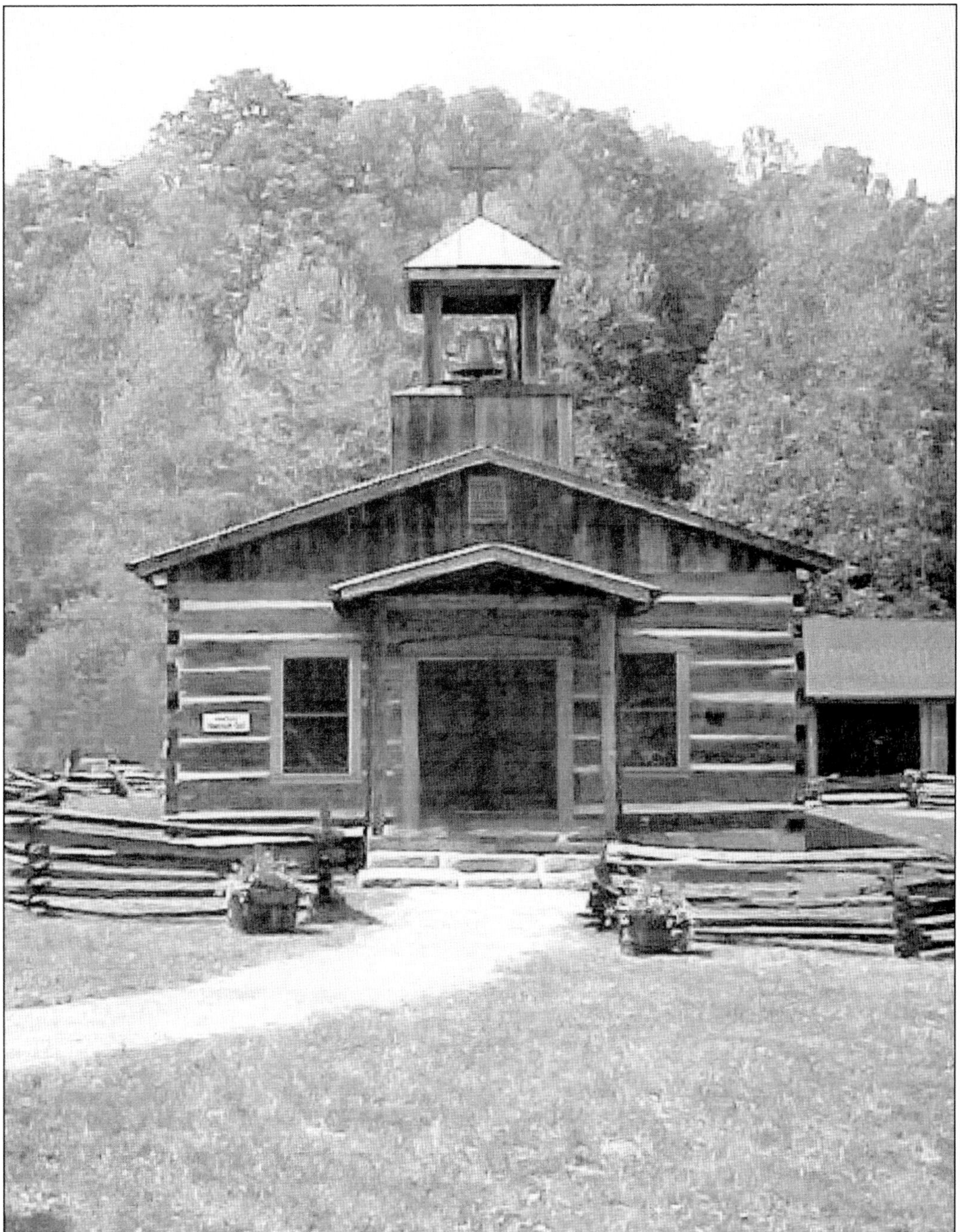

The third attraction, Heritage Farm, has been a labor of love of the Perry family. A. Michael and Henriella Perry began collecting pioneer memorabilia when their three children were small. This collection has grown into a very large farm museum with school, country store, chapel, barns full of exhibits, and now several bed and breakfast inns. Many of the log buildings on the grounds have been imported here and rebuilt log by log. The first funding for the Old Central City Association was made possible from a gala held at the Perry farm in 1991.

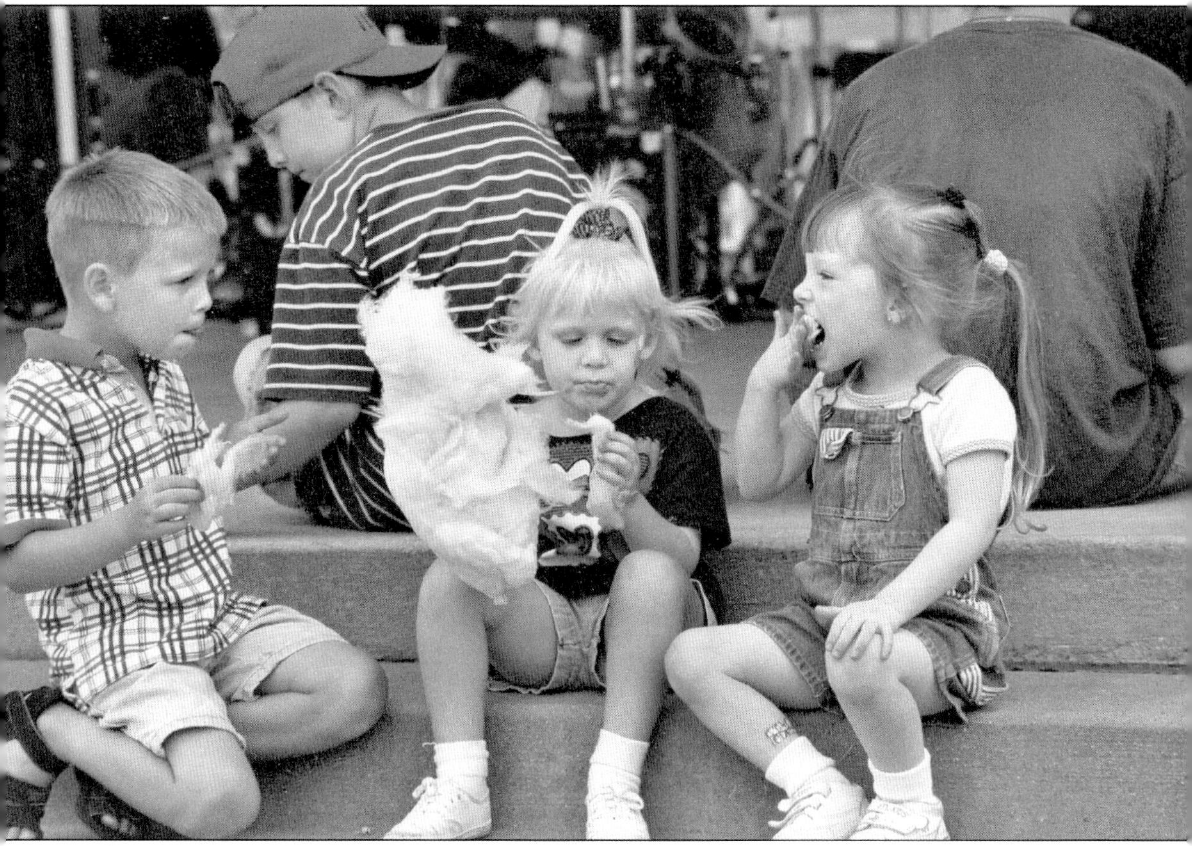

This image of children enjoying their cotton candy on the gazebo epitomizes the atmosphere that Old Central City desires for the new and improved area. What a wonderful sight! It reminds one of what the days must have been like 100 years ago, when people enjoyed the simple things of life.

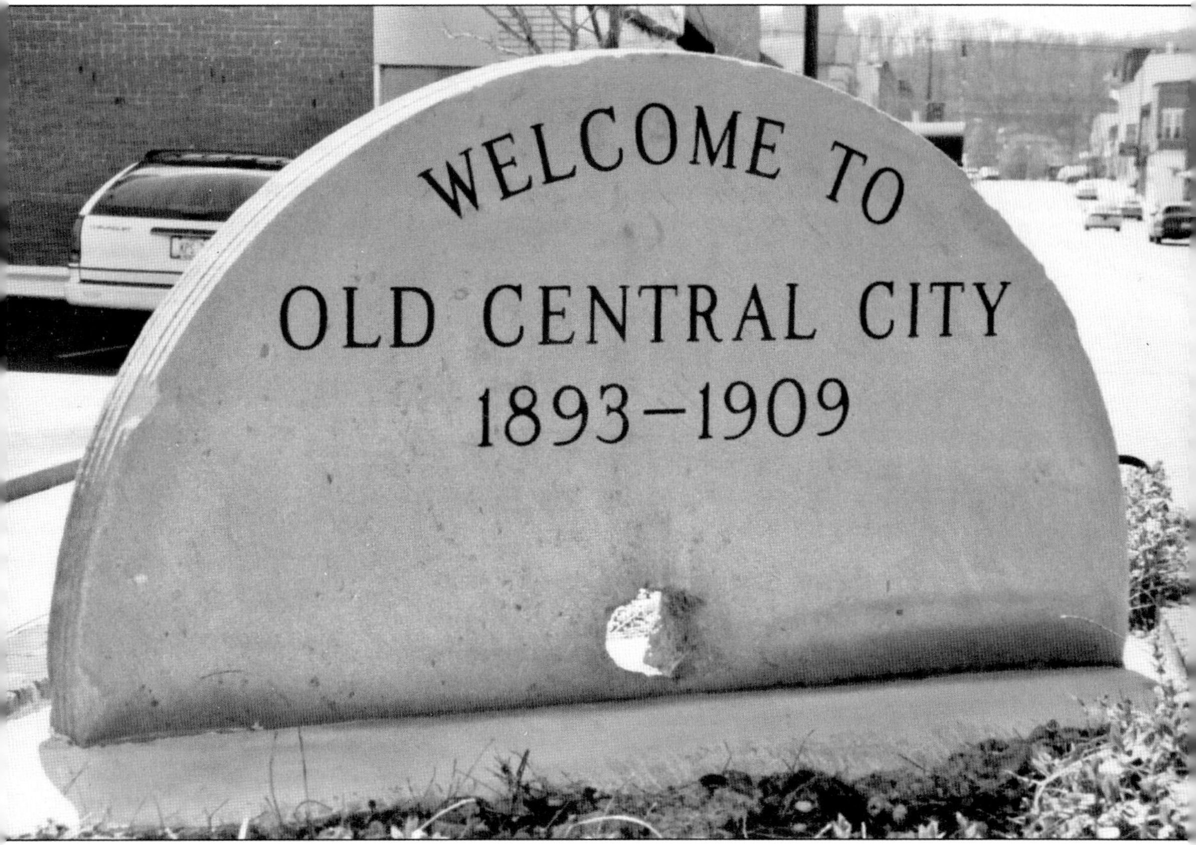

This millstone was found and engraved for the corner of Fourteenth Street West and Adams Avenue. Led by Winnie Arthur, several Central City friends saw to its installation. After 100 years, Central City is a name recognized again in the tri-state area and beyond.

Mayors of Central City

1893—M. V. Chapman
1894—George McKendree
1895—Alex Hazelett
1896—W. T. Hall
1897—Jefferson Champion
1898—M. M. Spitler
1899–1900—J. E. Matthews
1901—William Seiber
1902—W. H. Gooding
1903–1908—William Seiber

City Clerk Recorders

1893—George McDermit
1894–1895—D. P. Jones
1896—Floyd S. Chapman
1897—J. W. Huffman
1898—E. O. Pannell
1899–1900—Floyd S. Chapman
1901–1902—C. V. Cottle
1903–1904—J. K. Crowley
1906–1908—D. W. Frampton